Spiritual Manifestations

Spiritual Manifestations

By

Charles Beecher

GYAN

Published by

Gyan Publishing House
5, Ansari Road
Daryaganj, New Delhi-110002
Phone: 011-47034999, 9811692060
E-mail: books@gyanbooks.com

Distribution Network
gyanbooks.com
India, USA, Canada, UK, Australia, France

ISBN : 978-81-212-6300-9 (PB)
First Published, 1879

2nd Impression 2022

Printed at: Gyan Press, Delhi.

SPIRITUAL MANIFESTATIONS
Author: Charles Beecher

SPIRITUAL MANIFESTATIONS.

BY

CHARLES BEECHER.

ἡ γὰρ ἀποκαραδοκία τῆς κτίσεως τὴν ἀποκάλυψιν τῶν υἱῶν τοῦ Θεοῦ ἀπεκδέχεται.

For the earnest expectation of the creature waiteth for the MANIFESTATION of the sons of God.—ROM. viii. 19.

1879.

CONTENTS.

SPIRITUAL MANIFESTATIONS.

CHAPTER I.

THE MOVEMENT.

THIS work is dedicated to all sincere Spiritualists of every name. It is not intended to be controversial. If passages of a polemic spirit occur, it will be through inadvertence, and they are apologized for in advance.

In every soul there is an invisible realm, a heavens and earth of thought, a universe within. The author describes his own. The right ascension and declination of his readers' inner constellations are not given in any tables; but these rise above his own mental horizon. This, if one can see it, is his home, his inner world. It is not a world without a sun. "Lord, thou hast been our dwelling-place in all generations!" The one thing which he feels that he knows by direct and certain knowledge is God, filling his inner sky with light, life, and love.

It is sometimes said we know nothing of matter or mind but their properties. But to taste the sweetness of honey is to taste honey; tasting is knowing. So the soul knows the goodness of God by absolute contact. "I in thee, and thou in me," said Jesus. It is sometimes said that one ought to reason coldly on such topics, as on the problems of algebra. But can a child, hearing vague reports of his father's death, discuss the probabilities dispassionately? Vague rumors have gone abroad that God is dead; can the soul coldly discuss the possibilities of such spiritual orphanage? No person can be coldly intellectual on questions where his affections are vitally interested. The most liberal minds are sensitive when their profoundest beliefs on such topics are rudely assailed. Belief is next of kin to love. Thrust a magnet into the debris of a machine-shop, it will come out tufted with iron-filings. The magnet loves those iron-filings. So magnetic minds are tufted with ideas; and there are minds in every age that feel a sweet, loving attraction for thoughts of God. "How precious are thy thoughts unto me, O God!" It is a simple fact of soul-history. "O God, thou art my God; my soul thirsteth for thee, my flesh longeth for thee!"

Now the difficulty lies in comparing the inner thought-world of one mind with that of another. When the rumor comes in under the bright arching sky of the inner thought-realm, full of sunshine, that other souls are saying, God is dead, one knows not what to think of it. Rumors are unreliable. Words are ambiguous. What is it that is actually taking place in those inner thought-worlds out yonder? And can they see or know what is taking place in this thought-world in here? The task is to embody one's conceptions in words which will be mutually intelligible in his own thought-sphere, and in other thought-spheres. Imprisoned in his castle, words are but carrier-pigeons, with messages tied under their wings. What if the message come untied in mid-air? What if some fairy substitute another? What does the word *red* mean to persons affected with color-blindness, or *yellow*, or *green?* What is the seeming length of a second, or a minute, to minds of different make? What inward differences in the conceptions of melody, and harmony, of fragrance, taste, and touch, of number, size, and relation, may there be in minds with different perceptive faculties? And what different ideas, and associations, may the word GOD call up in minds of different original configuration, and educational development? May not a large portion of the controversy agitating the world even on the highest of all themes arise from this source?

The author would be presumptuous indeed should he attempt to give laws to the inner thought-realm of other people. He meditates a humbler but more useful task, to invite them to inspect his own. He who sets forth a theory of the universe, exhibits necessarily a picture or study of his own interior skies, his thought-world. And it is valuable in proportion to the distinctness and correctness of the transfer, on the same principle that the dissection of the living body is useful in the study of physiology.

There will doubtless be much in this little treatise that may seem improbable to most readers, whether viewed from the standpoint of science, or of the conventional belief. The author speaks only for himself. No person is responsible for his sentiments. He does not speak as the representative of the Church visible or invisible, nor of his professional brethren, nor of his kindred. He wishes first to be able to think out a system, which shall seem consistent, and which shall include all facts, so far, as known to him; and secondly, to find words which shall be unambiguous, with which to show the same to others.

The negations of other minds may be either their non-seeings of what he sees, or their seeings of his non-seeings or mis-seeings. Of course, he will earnestly consider them. The positive affirmations of other minds, either their more distinct seeings, or additional seeings, will be joyfully welcomed.

It is, in one sense, of little importance what one soul, shut up in its watch-tower, thinks. And yet as the shore of ocean is composed of insignificant grains of sand, the ocean itself of insignificant drops of water, so the sum of human attainment consists in the combined workings of multitudinous insignificant minds. Every successful effort to clothe in words that will not be generally misunderstood, the emotions, experiences, and beholdings of an earnest spirit imprisoned in its fortress of flesh, cannot but be of value.

No theme can be better adapted to call forth such an expression of one's inner self, than that indicated by the title of this work. Modern spiritualism, as it is called, raises about every question that has ever interested and agitated the human breast. Is there a spirit-world, or are we, like John Olden Barneveld, to shut up our view "within the flaming walls of this life?" If there be a spirit-world, what are its laws, its history, and its relations to our present mode of existence? What is this material system, and what are its laws, and what is matter itself, and the difference, if any, between the ultimate cause of the phenomena of matter, and that of the phenomena of mind? Is there an all-comprehending plan underlying the history of the mental and physical universe, or is all resolvable into mere blind force or law? All these and kindred questions come up naturally. Whatever else may be true of spiritualistic literature, it possesses the merit of a certain sort of comprehensiveness. The movement is remarkable, as that of a large class of the common people, taking hold of and discussing with apparent relish, almost every topic in philosophy, science, and theology, ever mooted in the history of the world.

If the movement be prompted by spirits, it is remarkable; if it be not, it is certainly none the less remarkable. If matter thinks, which is the same as to say, if thought is simply molecular change, — if matter thinks, it is remarkable that it thinks persistently and obstinately that there is a spirit-world.

The movement is a remarkable one also, if not the result of spiritual agency, from the persistency with which such agency is affirmed, through what are regarded as merely subjective phenomena. The author has never heard of a case in which these subjective laws or influences, whatever they are, have obtained a response stating the non-spiritual origin of the movement. If the phenomena are subjective, one would think circles might be formed among those who accept this explanation, in which some such response might be obtained as this, "There are no spirits; the so-called spiritual manifestations are all of material origin." The author has never heard of any such response being received.

The movement is also remarkable, because it is a religion — a household religion, which is rapidly extending throughout Christendom. It is not in its published literature, its periodicals, its lectures, and its public mediums, that the greatest strength of the movement lies. It is in its private, or family circles. Directions are given for forming such circles, and in one out of every four families, it is said, a medium will be found. The family circle is to the spiritualist household what "family prayers" are to Christian households generally.

The movement is also remarkable from the extremes of thought and character represented in it. The majority of spiritualists may be uneducated, illiterate, unrefined, but not all. There is a respectable minority of high culture, and eminent literary and even scientific attainment. The majority may seem to occupy a position hostile to Christianity, at least in any of its existing visible embodiments, but there is a respectable minority who breathe a Christian spirit, avow many sentiments in common with the evangelical communions, and wish to be known as Christian Spiritualists.

And above all, it is remarkable because that portion of the body calling themselves Christian Spiritualists, antagonizing certain obnoxious features of the movement, proclaim the movement itself, minus those features, to be a revival of primitive Christianity, a restoration of apostolic gifts; nay, some go so far as to claim, the actual resurrection of the dead, the second advent of Christ, and the inauguration of the millennium. In the writings of such, the Bible is constantly appealed to and copiously quoted, with apparent earnestness of conviction. Sermons are preached, revival hymns are sung, and arguments and appeals made, which, upon a common audience, are adapted to produce a great effect. Many sincere Christians, especially those who have lost friends, are identified with the movement. Such a development, notwithstanding all its admixtures of incongruous elements, is worthy of serious attention. In the midst of so many conflicting opinions it would be folly to dogmatize; the utmost any individual can hope for is, to contribute something to aid those who are endeavoring to turn the movement in right directions. Among the points held in common by spiritualists may be mentioned the following:

1. The real objective existence of spiritual beings, in great numbers, with diversities of physical, intellectual, and moral character.

2. Spirits can and do communicate with us in various ways.

3. There are different spheres, or grades, or ranks, in the spirit-world.

4. The communications or revelations we receive are reliable and good in proportion as they emanate from spirits of a higher sphere, and commend themselves to our reason and conscience. To obtain manifestations of truly good spirits, we must be in sympathy with them.

5. The prophets and apostles were mediums, and their communications are to be judged on the same principles as all other spirit manifestations, by their accordance with our best reason and conscience.

6. Many, perhaps most spiritualists would be willing to add, that the Bible is substantially true as a history, and contains the best religion yet known, and a code of morals that cannot be shown to have any defects.

7. Death effects no change in character, but such as a man is here he finds himself in the next life; and his situation will be decided by the law of elective affinity.

8. While there are many spheres, all spirits may be classified dynamically in three classes — celestial, above matter; terrestrial, in matter; subterrestrial, beneath matter, that is, unable to sway it except through the organism of the living. These three most general classes are conventionally named Heaven, Earth, and Hades.

CHAPTER II.

MYSTERIOUS PHENOMENA.

IN the present chapter it is proposed to give a few specimens of the evidence of the reality of spiritual manifestations. It may not appear conclusive to other minds. The writer speaks only for himself. He would premise, however, that there never has been in his mind any sense of improbability of the existence and agency of spirits. All the great religions of the world may be wrong in things where they differ, but it seems improbable they are wrong in things where they agree. This world is crowded with so many different forms of life, it has never seemed improbable that other worlds or spheres should be, and that among them there should be those possessed of organisms inappreciable by our present senses; and that they should be able to communicate with us by natural laws to us unknown.

This seems no more incredible than the hypothesis of the existence of ultimate particles of matter. Able minds, such as Leibnitz, Boscovitch, Priestley, Faraday, and others, have maintained that all material phenomena can be accounted for on the theory that particles are mathematical points of force. Hickock calls dead atoms "deadheads." Huxley characterizes them "as pure assumptions, as the spirits of the spiritualist." Herbert Spencer says, "The hypothesis of molecules and atoms enables the chemist to work out multitudinous interpretations that are verified by experiment; but the ultimate unit of matter admits of no consistent conception." *

In vain we increase the power of the microscope. No eye has ever seen an ultimate particle. Yet science accepts them as a probable hypothesis. One can draw convenient diagrams, with colored cubes and other forms, and show the binary, ternary, and other compounds so deftly. The chemist is like "the man under authority who saith to one go, and he goeth, to another come, and he cometh, and to his servant do this, and he doeth it."

The spiritualist does the same in respect to the hypothesis of spirit agency, with this advantage, that whereas no one has ever claimed to have seen an ultimate particle, men have in every age claimed to have seen spirits. The abstract probability of the existence and agency of spirits is therefore equal to, if not greater than that of the existence of ultimate particles of dead matter.

This being premised, the following are offered as specimen facts, occurring mostly within the range of the author's observation, or that of intimate friends. As a pastor, the author has found in different communities where he has resided more or less of latent belief on this subject; a sort of hidden folk-lore; so that he has received the impression that there are few families which have not in their possession incidents of second-sight, ghosts, apparitions, or other mysterious phenomena, which yet, for various reasons, they shrink from making public.

The first class includes cases occurring in open daylight (as well as in the night), involving a variety of physical phenomena, where the spirits producing them appear to be, and in some cases confess themselves to be,

* Studies of Sociology, p. 311.

of a low grade, and to act from no quite intelligible motives.

The following narrative was recently made to the author by Prof. Austin Phelps, D. D., of Andover, and is given as nearly as possible in his own language:

"The circumstances to which you refer took place when I was just commencing at Andover, and at a time when I was much pressed with official duties; some time I think in 1850 or 1851. They covered a period of about seven months. My father was residing in Stratford, Connecticut, with his second wife, who also had several children by a former husband. She was at that time in ill-health from the first approaches of the malady (which we did not understand at the time) by which she was subsequently bereft of reason.

"My father had paid little attention to such matters previous to his coming to Stratford, except that he had tried to mesmerize my brother, who suffered from heart-disease, and had afforded him some relief. The phenomena of spirit-rapping he had only noticed as items of news in the papers of the day. The greater part of the strange occurrences did not come under my own observation, but were narrated to me by him, in whose testimony I confide as much as in my own. I cannot pretend to give dates, or the precise order of events, but some of the main facts as they occur to my recollection.

"The first thing that took place of an unusual nature, was on a certain Sunday. The family, including the servants, according to custom, had been to church, leaving the house locked up. On returning, they found the front door wide open. The first thought was that robbers had been there. No signs, however, of their presence appeared, on searching the rooms, until they came to my father's room, and there they found three full suits of his clothes stuffed out with old clothes, &c., and laid out side by side upon the floor, with boots, hat, &c., like a row of corpses, somewhat as I have seen them after a railroad collision. This seemed very strange; but the general impression was that it might be a roguish trick of the boys, or of some one unknown. In the course of the day, as my father was walking across the parlor, no other person being in the room, a key was thrown from behind over his head, and fell on the floor at his feet. He picked it up and put it in his pocket. Soon after a nail was thrown in the same way. In the evening, as the family were sitting together, suddenly a turnip fell from the ceiling in their midst. Then they began to hear little raps in various directions. They tried to trace them, but could not.

"Things went on for some time. Noises were heard in different parts of the house. At the dinner-table, the spoons would fly up out of the vessel and fall upon the table. The forks would do the same. Once my father took the spoons, and the servant put them in the closet and locked the door, and brought him the key. In the space of ten minutes, the spoons were back on the table again, without visible agency. Father then took them himself and put them in the closet and locked the door, and in ten minutes, without any one seeing them come, they were on the table again. He unlocked the door; they were not there.

"Meanwhile the knockings, &c., continued day and night, and many of the neighbors hearing what was going on, began to come in to see and hear. As a specimen, a thing like this took place: One day at dinner, a package of six or eight silver spoons were all at once taken and doubled up—bent double by no visible agency. My father had them placed in the closet, locked the door, and kept the key himself. A sister of his was there at the time on a visit, and a neighbor came in inquiring about what she had heard. The sister got the key, went to get the spoons, unlocked the door, and there lay the spoons as straight as before, with no dent or crease, or sign of having been bent. This is only a specimen. There were dozens of such events.

"Of course, there was much excitement and talk, and all sorts of opinions were expressed. Many most unjustly attributed it to my father's wife and her children. It was known that she did not like Stratford, and was desirous of removing to Philadelphia. It was also noticed that the phenomena were in some way connected with her and her children, rather than with my father and his children. In modern parlance, they were the mediums. She was a Christian woman, member of the Episcopal church, and much grieved at the charge, and denied it in the most solemn manner. Indeed, the whole visitation was made a subject of daily prayer in the family. And all cognizant with the facts are perfectly certain that neither she nor her children were consciously implicated. If they were mediums it was by no will or wish of their own. It was more like a case of possession.

"For example, one of the most startling occurrences was this: One day my father heard one of the children crying, out in the yard, (it was the boy whose presence had been most followed by the knockings, &c.) The boy was found up in an apple-tree, tied fast with a rope, in a situation where it seemed impossible he could have gotten by himself, or by any human agency.

"For some time after these things commenced, even after the idea of communicating by the alphabet had occurred to him, my father resolved to have nothing to do with it. But at length he became weary, and resolved to try. Pursuing the usual course, as he had seen described in the papers, he met with a ready affirmative response, (three raps,) and wrote down intelligent sentences.

"The first question of course was, 'Who are you?' To this various answers were given, sometimes one name, sometimes another, all of parties deceased, but most frequently came the name of a brother of Mrs. Phelps. The next inquiry was as to his object, or what was the matter with him. His answer was in substance: 1. That he was in hell. 2. That Mrs. Phelps had been cheated in the settlement of an estate by a person named D'S——. My father not recognizing the name, which was French, asked his wife if she knew such a person. She said no, and asked how the name was spelled. He spelled it, and she said, 'Oh, you pronounced it wrong: it was D'S——;' giving the correct pronunciation; and she remembered there was such a person — a head clerk in a firm that had been in some way concerned in the settlement. My father went to Philadelphia and made an investigation of the facts. He found evidence sufficient to confirm the suspicion of fraud excited by the communications, but nothing sufficient to convict in a court of justice; nothing, in short, resulting in rectifying the settlement.

"On one occasion my father was sitting in a small ante-room, about five feet square, at a little desk where he kept his accounts. He was alone. An incessant rapping being kept up, he at length said, 'What do you want?,' and on using the alphabet, the answer was spelled out, 'Put your hand under the table.' He did so, and his hand was grasped by a human hand, warm and soft like mine.

"At my father's request I went to Stratford to see and examine into the case. I went with strong prepossessions, having heard what was said about my mother-in-law,—that it was probably in some way contrived by her and her children. I was soon entirely undeceived, and convinced that I had been unjust to her, and that she and her children were wholly innocent of any complicity. The phenomena that I witnessed were not so striking as some that my father told me of. I was accompanied by a brother of my father, Dr. Phelps, who was far from being credulous or visionary—in fact, tending rather to materialism than to belief in the supernatural.

"We occupied the same room, and slept soundly till midnight, when we were awakened by what seemed like a deep sigh breathed through the key-hole, and repeated several times quite loudly. Then there was a tremendous hammering, outside our door, in the hall. We got up, struck a light, went into the next room where father slept, and asked him what that noise was. He answered, 'You know as well as I do; judge for yourselves.' We went and examined, and found on the banister marks and dents, as if it had been beaten with a hard substance. We went up-stairs and found the servants' doors locked, the children all asleep, and no evidence whatever to connect the noise with any of them. The noises continued at intervals till morning. The next day we searched the house thoroughly, but found nothing, except in the attic there was a suit of father's clothes stuffed as before described, and stretched out on the floor.

"The next night the noises were still more abundant. 'Let us follow the noise,' I said. 'I will go inside the door, you outside.' We followed till we came to the apartment of the oldest daughter. It was in the evening, about nine o'clock. With her permission I stepped inside the room, and the doctor staid outside. The knocking came on the door between us. Said I,

'Doctor, the knocking is on the outside of the door.' 'No,' said he, 'it is on the inside.' The young lady was in bed, covered up, and out of reach of the door. We examined the panel, and found dents where it had been struck. Just then, as I stepped back into the room, a hair-brush was thrown, apparently from the door, and fell at my feet. It was a most inexplicable thing.

"I omitted to say that a serious feature of the business was the burning of my father's barn, in broad daylight, when no person was in the building, or near it, so far as known.

"One thing I saw, bearing on that matter, in the course of our investigations: One of the children slept in a cot-bed in my father's room, and one evening we saw a smoke rising from that bed. We turned up the bedclothes, lifted up the mattress, and found underneath a newspaper ignited, which blazed up.

"The general character of the responses was rather low. Many of them were simply ridiculous. For instance: When the alleged spirit seemed to be in an unhappy state, we asked, 'Can we do anything for you?' Answer, 'No.' 'What do you want? What would you like?' Answer, 'A piece of pumpkin-pie.' Many communications came just so ridiculous. Throughout the whole there was nothing of any importance — no religious truth. He said, indeed, he was in hell, but the idea seemed to be, he would get out hereafter; there was a general notion of progress, and all would come out right some time. There was a good deal of truth in the Bible, but a good deal of nonsense, too, and he seemed, to use a common expression, to be specially *down on* St. Paul. A good deal of what came reminded one of Swedenborg's ideas. The idea of the Atonement seemed to be specially distasteful, even repulsive. Christ, they seemed to think, was much the same as other men. There were, however, some that professed to be good spirits, who said they were there to keep the bad ones in order. But, on the whole, the development of thought was characterized by a consummate pettiness. There was no object worthy of revelation.

"In the retrospect, my father subsequently said, his religious convictions were not at all affected; he still held to the faith of his childhood, with the exception that his views of scriptural demonology were more distinct; and his belief strengthened that spirits, good and bad, do have access to us, and that they are in conflict.

"For my own part," concluded Professor Phelps, "I could not account for what I saw and heard from reliable witnesses, on any other theory but that of spirits, though I have never gone quite so far as to admit that any of those concerned were good spirits. That deceitful spirits can assume to be good is plain. And the most probable hypothesis, until science can prove something else, is that such was the fact here."

CHAPTER III.

PLANCHETTE.

THE following communications have been placed at the author's disposal by his sister, Mrs. Stowe. They are inserted as specimens of the better class of communications received by means of planchette. The inquiries were quite private, and prosecuted solely for the sake of investigation. The lady who acted as a writing medium was not a public operator, and has discontinued the exercise of her peculiar gifts. She was believed to be ignorant of the history of the persons professing to communicate through her. The spirit communicating purports to be that of Charlotte Bronté.

"Do you know the Duchess of Sutherland?"

"Yes. I know her now. She is happy; life even for her had its trials, but they are over. Be satisfied that she has found rest."

"Did you know her while on earth?"

"No."

"Are those who are beautiful in this world, beautiful there?"

"Yes; but the degree of spiritual beauty here makes the truest beauty with us."

Some one then remarked that she must be a beautiful angel, because she had beauty of character as well as of person.

"Are all good persons alike beautiful?"

"Yes; but one's face retains its characteristics, although, as you say, it is glorified. The best are the most beautiful: mere physical beauty would pass for naught here."

"If I could communicate with the Duchess of Sutherland, I would like to ask her if she remembers a conversation I had with her as to whether our departed friends retain their interest in us."

"Yes; friends here, as during the earth-life, do know and love each other."

"She said in that conversation, that she feared that if the blessed dead could see us in this world, it would grieve them, because we live so far below what we should." Immediately after this was said, the following communication came, very rapidly:

"Mrs. Stowe, the blessed dead know that you of the earth are but human; you cannot be perfect. Speaking from my present knowledge, I can say that it is everything if you try and continue in well-doing. Be patient. I think of you ever, you and all the dear ones, and I am, my dear, as in the sweet days so long ago, your true and affectionate friend and earnest well-wisher."

"Is the Duke here present?" Immediately in a large hand was written:

"God bless you all. S."

Some one said, "That must be the Duke." It wrote: "I was very tired — heartily sick of the pomps and vanities of life. I wished to be better myself, and to do more good. But how could I? Circumstances were all against one in my station living a true, manly life. The joys of this life were saddened by the knowledge that I could do so little, when I would do so much for the good of those dependent on me."

"And have you found a wider sphere of usefulness?"

"Yes, thank God; no more boundaries to confine my efforts for good."

"When I dreamed, the other night, of the Duchess of Sutherland coming to me, I wonder if there was any reality in it?"

"Yes, yes. You had a dream which was not all a dream. Yes, my dear, I am with you oftener than you think."

"You must have met many, many friends in the other life?" Here we enumerated the names of all those who had died since we were at Dunrobin.

"Very many; it is so sweet to once more clasp in one's longing arms those so long absent — mother, father, husband, and children."

"You love dear old England yet?"

"Yes." After a pause: "We fear sorrow will come upon dear old England before many more years."

"What sorrow?"

"Our Queen will come to us, and you know in what hands the government will then be. Edward Albert is not all that he should be; he has not the strength of character necessary for a ruler; but, poor boy! let us be charitable — he is young and has a noble wife; he may still be redeemed."

Mrs. Stowe said, "Is the Queen unwell now?"

"She is not strong. If E. A. could, or would, be more like his blessed father, she would abdicate in his favor."

"How strange that he should be such a character, when he was so carefully educated by his father and mother!"

"Certainly; but too many children are born. He, as well as many others, should never have lived."

"I do not understand that."

"I mean that the sins of the father are visited upon the children, even unto the third and fourth generation; and constitutional passion, and the disposition of the parents, are oftentimes aggravated in the children. Do I make it clear to you? I'm afraid not."

"How does God judge children, who thus inherit constitutional tendencies to evil?"

"Does He not tell you in His Word that charity is the greatest of all virtues? He speaks what He does know, and because He has so much."

"But Prince Albert was a perfect saint."

"Yes; but his grandfather? Parents, you see, cannot be too careful. The Prince was not immediately responsible for E. A.'s sins; but he should have looked into the past, and contemplated the future, before bringing his son into the world."

At another time the following answers were given. Reference was had to an aunt of Mrs. Stowe, whose history * the medium had never known.

"Did you know Mary Hubbard?"

"Died 1813."

"Where?"

"Litchfield."

"What of?"

"Consumption."

"What caused her disease?"

"Poor Mary! her marriage was her curse."

"Where is she now?"

"Safe at home, with her best-beloved sister."

"Who was that sister?"

"Roxanna." Then, without any question:

"After a life of worldly strife,
After a life of carking care,
After a life with terrors rife
And ghastly sorrows which do wear

* Outlined in Autobiography and Correspondence of Lyman Beecher, D. D., Vol. I. p. 136.

Into the shuddering soul of man,
  There cometh peace, that perfect peace,
  And lasting rest, where the wicked cease
From troubling — and our lives are made complete."

"Is there any time in that world?"

"No; a thousand years are but as a moment."

"Do they influence us?"

"You are always surrounded by spirits."

"What kind, — good or bad?"

"By both."

"Can we feel their presence?"

"Sometimes."

"Can we communicate with them?"

"No; God wills it otherwise; there is an unconscious influence."

"Are those who loved each other in this world together there?"

"Yes; together in the Lord."

"Do the elder take care of the younger?"

"Each one is capable of taking care of himself; but the sweet relation of parents and children is recognized."

"Do they know things that happen on earth?"

"Yes; they know when human beings are happy, but are spared the knowledge of sin."

Some one said then that a planchette had assisted a man in his business.

"Would it be a good plan to consult you, Planchette, upon business?"

"Not always; for we are not always allowed to tell the truth; you would have implicit faith in us if we did; and you should only believe in the 'True Word.' Humanity strives for too much light."

"Do you enjoy this kind of communication?"

"Yes; because this is the only way we can communicate with human beings; and we like to open unto you as many mysteries as possible."

"Well, then, who are you, and what is your name?"

"A. C. Bronté."

"When were you born?"

"April, 1816."

"When did you leave this world?"

"March, 1855."

"Do you retain the same traits of character in the other life which distinguished you here?"

"Not altogether. My principal characteristic was a constitutional absence of hope. Now I am at peace, inasmuch as there is no call for hope where I am."

"Is your sister Emily happy now?"

"Thank God, yes."

"Is your brother there?"

"Poor boy! Let the grave cover his sins, — more *her* sins than his."

"Is he happy now?"

"Alas! alas! Death prevents repentance."

"Is not God's mercy the same there as here?"

"My knowledge of Bramwell is limited; he may be, not in hell, but in Hades, mistranslated *hell*."

"Were you happy when you first left this world?"

"Yes."

"Where did you awaken?"

"Not in Heaven, but in the place of departed spirits; but I knew that this place was merely the presence-room of Heaven."

"Do you suffer from the separation from those you loved on earth?"

"Not as you suffer. The memory of friends remains with us, and we wait and watch for them."

"How do you know each other in that world?"

"Faces are not changed, only glorified."

I said to Planchette, one time when we were writing, "You are the nicest, prettiest planchette I ever saw."

It immediately answered, —

"Thank you, ma'am."

Mr. F., who was reading the "Nation," tried putting his hand on the planchette in company with Mrs. K——: it immediately drew a rough picture of a newspaper, and wrote over it, "Read your 'Nation.'"

The following conversation occurred at another time.

"Good morning, Charlotte!"

"Good morning." (Written in a fine, small hand.)

"Do you enjoy this bright sunshine?"

"Yes; but it is dull and dreary by the light I feel and see. It is all light with us."

"Has the great mystery of life, then, been made clear to you?"

"Yes; all is clear as noonday now; but my heart aches for those who are still in the dark."

"Have you power to do them any good?"

"Yes; that is one reason why I watch over S. T. R."

"And do you now understand why you suffered so much in this life?"

"Yes; all things worked together for good; but it was so hard — so hard there."

"Has the character of your sister Emily developed, as you thought it would, under happiness?"

"Yes, fully."

Here I stopped and said to Mrs. K——, "Charlotte wrote the work 'Shirley,' to give her ideal of her sister Emily's character, as she would have been under a happier development of circumstances." I then said to Planchette:

"Charlotte, you loved 'Shirley' better than any of your other works, did you not?"

"Yes; it was nearer and dearer to me than all. That was why I was so grieved at the severity of some criticisms. They called it coarse,—God forgive them!"

"Charlotte, is God near to you where you dwell? And the Saviour, is it permitted you to see Him there?"

"Yes. He suffered and knows how to sympathize with such as I was. Yes, never think of Him as afar off, but as with you, close to you, hand to hand, and heart to heart,—the elder Brother, the tender, everlasting Friend."

"Can this mode of writing be conducted so as to be really spiritually improving?"

"It could, only for the preponderance of evil influences in the world. It is only occasionally that a person can command an interest from any one spirit, the watchful care necessary for their full development. I have charge over one, to develop her and save her."

"Well, what do you think of this whole dispensation of planchettes. Will it be for good or for evil?"

"Neither; it will be forgotten. Vanity Fair has too many things of interest to think of Planchette."

"Is Mrs. Gaskell with you?"

"Yes; we are friends here, as there."

"Why have you crossed the seas to America to interest yourself in S. T. R., when you must have known so many in England?"

"Because our natures are similar, and I must save her from what I suffered. I know no England, or America, now."

"Had you any commission from a superior power to undertake this charge?"

"Yes; a commission, after I had expressed a choice."

"But how came you to know enough of her to make the choice?"

"I cannot explain so as to make myself understood,

as there are some things I must not tell. But you can understand that natures which would have been in sympathy on earth may still be so, although one is absent from the body."

"Is Thackeray there?"

"Yes."

"I know Thackeray's daughter. Do you, Charlotte?"

"Yes; she is writing herself a name in the world."

"Do you know much of her writings?"

"Not much."

"Do you attend to the course of literature in this world?"

"So far as I am specially interested in any particular subject."

"Have you been interested in the great changes that have taken place in America?"

"Yes, as a whole, but not in detail."

"Do you maintain Thackeray's acquaintance now?"

"Yes; his asperities are softened, and done away with. His slight savageness has disappeared. He is very lovable now."

"Do you have, in that world, anything which corresponds to bodily form in this?"

"Yes."

"And have you local habitations?"

"You must not ask."

"What constitutes your happiness?"

"Each one of us has some peculiar mission. We are happy in that, and we have what to you is an unknown feeling of perfect peace." *

"Whence comes that peace?"

"God gives peace and rest to his weary children."

* But see Is. xxvi. 3. "Thou wilt keep him in perfect peace whose mind is stayed on Thee."

"What must we do to prepare ourselves for peace in that world?"

"Read God's Word, and grieve not."

The following letter comes under this class of communications.

"CENTRE HARBOR, N. H., Sept. 12, 1868.

"REV. C. E. STOWE, Hartford, Conn.

"Rev. and dear Sir: Without claim to your consideration, and knowing you only through your writings, I am still bold enough to ask your advice, and to feel sure that you will not refuse it, although you may deem it strange that I should address you on such a subject.

"In passing through Boston, last July, I bought a tin toy called Planchette, which seemed to be the fashion, and during the summer have been amusing the ladies with its mysterious vagaries, which in public amounted to nothing, its answers to questions being as often wrong as right. But, trying it in private, I had communications which astounded me, from so-called spirits, who give their names and various personal particulars, besides some account of their present conditions.

"Among them are friends who were dear to me when living, and who profess to entertain the same feelings now. All this by the aid of Planchette. But now I am informed that that toy is not necessary, and that simply paper and pencil are necessary; and on placing my hand in position, I find my pencil writing messages and advice to me which astounds and frightens me.

"What is this power which tells me of its spiritual state; which replies to my thoughts; which advises me for my welfare? I close my eyes, and my pencil replies to my thoughts — it tells of persons unknown to me, and how they will be connected with me.

"In order to test it, I asked if it would write the name of our Lord; it at once wrote 'Jesus Christ.'

"Tell me, Reverend Sir, am I possessed of a demon, a familiar spirit, or am I the recipient of communications from the souls of the blessed dead?

"I am not a spiritualist, nor have I heard a rap, or seen a table tipped. I am a member of the Presbyterian Church of Philadelphia."

The following, though having no relation to Planchette, may be inserted here.

"NEW YORK, October 5, 1874.

"MY DEAR MADAM: As requested, I give you the following incident in writing.

"In 1866, business called me to Austin, Nevada. In the late fall of that year I was living on Landon Hill, in that town, lodging in my office. A personal friend — I will call him Foster — had his desk in the same room with mine; and the superintendent of the mine that I had charge of—I will call him Morgan — lodged with me. An expedition was arranged, and undertaken, to prospect for gold in the vicinity of Death Valley, California. Foster was specially active in the matter, and I contributed a portion of the funds. Foster finally concluded to accompany the prospecters, and the party of five left Austin, prepared for a two months' trip. They had been gone twenty days, when, on a moonlight night at about eleven o'clock, as I sat writing at my desk, which was placed near the south window, there came a clear, sonorous knock on the sash, repeated three times. Morgan and myself heard it distinctly, and Morgan at once stepped to the door, unlocked and opened it, expecting to find some friend who wished admittance. The office was a one-story building, and the window within easy reach. He was surprised to find no one, though he went entirely around the building in the moonlight, which was very bright, and there was no place in the vicinity for any one to conceal himself. He came in, looking anxious, and we both stood by the open fireplace a moment, when the three knocks on the sash were repeated. We both hurried to renew the examination out of doors. No one was to be seen or found. We again returned to the fireplace, when Morgan suddenly exclaimed, 'For God's sake, look at Foster's desk!' Looking there, I saw the books and papers in the greatest agitation, jumping and bounding in all directions, and all in a violent confusion, which continued some minutes. We were awe-struck indeed, and I remarked, involuntarily, 'Something has happened to Foster!' and at once made a memorandum of the date and hour. Eleven days thereafter the prospecting party returned to Austin, deterred from further explorations by hostile Indians; but Foster was not with them: he had been shot and killed in an attack by Indians on the very night of the disturbances at my office, and at about the same hour.

"I have had during my life several somewhat similar experiences, and I apprehend that the progress of science will some day reveal the cause. I have never been able to connect the circumstances with what could be deemed a communication from the other world. In my case, death has invariably closed the mysterious connection of mind with mind.

"Yours very respectfully,

WM. H. ADAMS.

"MRS. H. B. STOWE, Hartford, Conn."

CHAPTER IV.

SECOND SIGHT.

IN the present chapter we offer an example of natural seership, or second sight, or spirit-seeing. There is a wide range of very curious facts of this character, ancient and modern, to which it is not necessary more than to refer. The present case lies within the circle of the author's family connection and personal observation. Prof. C. E. Stowe, D.D., is well known to the public, and especially to those who have enjoyed the privilege of being his pupils, as a man of remarkable sagacity and sound common sense.

Distinguished for the accuracy of his scholarship, the extent and variety of his reading, the tenacity of his memory, and his ready command of encyclopedic information, — thoroughly familiar with the whole literature of spiritualism, ancient and modern, — he is the last person one would suspect of being the victim of a hallucination. Yet the fact is that he has been a seer all his life. And although in particular instances, as in those presently to be mentioned, he concedes the possibility of an intra-cranial and non-spiritual origin of the phenomena, yet the general effect, taking his whole life through, has been to intensify his belief in the reality of spirit intercourse. With his permission, the following extracts from "Oldtown Folks" are here inserted, as literal descriptions of scenes in his early life.

"There was one peculiarity of my childhood which I

have hesitated with an odd sort of reluctance to speak of, and which yet so powerfully influenced and determined my life, and that of all with whom I was connected, that it must find some place here. I was dreamy and imaginative, with a mind full of vague yearnings. But beside that, through an extreme delicacy of nervous organization, my childish steps were surrounded by a species of vision or apparition, so clear and distinct that I often found great difficulty in discriminating between the forms of real life and these shifting shapes, that had every appearance of reality, except that they dissolved at the touch. All my favorite haunts had their particular shapes and forms, which it afforded me infinite amusement to watch in their varying movements.

"Particularly at night, after I had gone to bed, and the candle was removed from my room, the whole atmosphere around my bed seemed like that which Raphael shadowed forth around his Madonna San Sisto, — a palpitating crowd of faces and forms changing in dim and gliding quietude. I have often wondered whether any personal experience similar to mine suggested to the artist this living background to his picture. For the most part these phantoms were agreeable to me, and filled me with a dreamy delight. Sometimes distinct scenes or visions would rise before my mind, in which I seemed to look far beyond the walls of the house, and see things passing wherein were several actors. I remember one of these, which I saw very often, representing a venerable old white-headed man playing on a violin. He was always accompanied by a tall, majestic woman, dressed in a strange, outlandish costume, in which I particularly remarked a high fur cap of a peculiar form. As he played, the woman appeared to dance in time to the music. Another scene which frequently presented itself to my eyes was that of a green meadow by the side of a lake of very calm water. From a grove on one side of the lake would issue a miniature form of a woman clothed in white, with a wide golden girdle around her waist, and long black hair hanging down to her middle, which she constantly smoothed down with both her hands, with a gentle, rhythmical movement, as she approached me. At a certain point of approach she always turned her back, and began a rapid retreat into the grove, and invariably as she turned there appeared behind her the image of a little misshapen dwarf, who pattered after her with ridiculous movements, which always made me laugh. Night after night, during a certain year of my life, this pantomime never failed to follow the extinction of the candle, and was to me a never-failing source of delight.

"One thing was peculiar about these forms,—they appeared to cause a vibration of the great central nerves of the body, as when a harp-string is struck. So I could feel in myself the jar of the dwarf's pattering feet, the soft, rhythmic movements of the little woman stroking down her long hair, the vibrations of the violin, and the steps of the dancing old woman. Nobody knew of this still and hidden world of pleasure which was thus nightly open to me.

"My mother used often to wonder, when, hours after she put me to bed, she would find me lying perfectly quiet, with my eyes widely and calmly open. Once or twice I undertook to tell her what I saw, but was hushed up with 'Nonsense, child! There hasn't been anybody in the room. You shouldn't talk so.'

". . . . One peculiarity of these appearances was, that certain of them seemed like a sort of *genii loci*—shapes belonging to certain places. The apparition of the fairy woman with the golden girdle appeared only in a certain room where I slept one year, and which had across one of its corners a sort of closet called a buffet. From this buffet the vision took its rise, and when my parents moved to another house it never appeared again.

"A similar event in my shadow world had marked our coming to my grandmother's to live. The old violin-player and his wife had for a long time been my nightly entertainers; but the first night after we were established in the apartments given up for our use by Aunt Lois, I saw them enter as they usually did, seeming to come right through the wall of the room. They, however, surveyed the apartment with a sort of confused, discontented movement, and seemed to talk to each other with their backs to me; finally I heard the old woman say, 'We can't stay here,' and immediately I saw them passing through the wall of the house. I saw after them as clearly as if the wall had dissolved and given my eyes a vision of all out-doors. They went to my grandfather's woodpile, and looked irresolutely round; finally they mounted on the pile, and seemed to sink gradually through it and disappear. I never saw them afterwards.

"But another of the companions of my solitude was more constant to me. This was the form of a young boy of about my own age, who for a year past had frequently come to me at night, and seemed to look lovingly upon me, and with whom I used to have a sort of social communion, without words, in a manner far more perfect than human language. I *thought* to him, and in return I received silent demonstrations of sympathy and fellowship from him. I called him Harvey, and used, as I lay looking in his face, mentally to tell him many things about the books I read, the games I played, and the childish joys and griefs I had; and in return he seemed to express affection and sympathy by a strange communication, as lovers sometimes talk to each other by distant glances."

To the author's inquiry whether these visions were subject to his volition, the reply was, "Never, in the slightest degree."

"Have you been able to form a decided opinion whether they are objective realities?"

"Some of them I have, and some not."

"Have you ever seen and touched departed friends?"

"Yes. I have seen H., and felt his hand in my own."

CHAPTER V.

VISIONS.

IN the present chapter are offered a number of cases, of somewhat similar character with those in the preceding chapter, some of which have been narrated to the author by intimate personal friends, on whose testimony he places implicit reliance.

When the Rochester rappings first began, the writer was residing at the West, and one afternoon was reading, at a ladies' sewing-circle, an article from the "Tribune," giving some account of the manifestations. While reading, he noticed that a young lady, who at times resided temporarily in his family, was listening very intently, and that she turned very pale. The expression of her face was so singular, that, after the reading was finished, he said, smiling, "Why, A——, did you ever see anything of that sort?" or words to that effect. She replied, in substance, "I don't tell everybody all I see." On returning home, on being questioned, she said she had often heard rustling noises in her room at night, and moving of the furniture, and had seen spirits both male and female, and described their appearance and dress, especially a peculiar sort of head-dress, or covering of the head worn by all the female forms. The writer had not, at that time, seen Dr. Kœrner's work, "The Seeress of Prevorst," nor had anybody in that region ever heard of it. But when he subsequently obtained it, he found that Mrs. Hauffe described the head-dress of the female spirits exactly as A—— had done.

This case was more convincing to the author, as unexpectedly occurring in his own family, to an intimate friend and member of his church, in whose testimony he had perfect confidence, and especially as coinciding so curiously with the visions of Mrs. Hauffe, as above stated.

In this connection the following seems appropriate.

Mrs. Hauffe, in her last illness, said to Dr. Kœrner, "that during her sickness she often saw visions; all sorts of spectral forms passed before her eyes, but it was impossible to express how different these ocular illusions were from the real discerning of spirits; and she only wished other people were in a condition to compare these two kinds of perception with one another, both of which were equally distinct from our ordinary perception, and also from that of second-sight."

Here, also, we may insert the following, narrated to the author by an intimate friend, Miss Sara E. Horner, of Georgetown, Massachusetts.

"About a mile from Haverhill lived my oldest sister, Mrs. W., on a homestead place. A third of a mile toward town was another old homestead, the old Ayer place, where two sisters lived, one of whom married a man by the name of Spiller. In the same town lived a famous nurse by the name of Davis, who had dressed more people for the first and last time than any other person in the county; and who was so strong of nerve that she might have sat for the portrait of Aunt Roxy, in the 'Pearl of Orr's Island.'

"Mrs. S., sickened unto death. Nurse Davis took care of her. After her death, nurse Davis went to my sister, Mrs. W., and said, 'I wish I knew how old lady Ayer looked.' My sister said, 'I don't know; she died before I came here. She must have been tall and thin, I suppose, like Mrs. S. Why do you want to know?' 'Because, the morning Mrs. S. died, I saw sitting just the other side of the glass door that opened out of the room in which she died, a short, stout old lady in a white muslin cap with a broad, black ribbon around it, a white handkerchief crossed over the bosom and fastened behind, and I wondered if it was Mrs. S.'s mother. I saw this the morning Mrs. S. died, and thought nothing of it. I saw it again the next morning, and thought that if it came again I would open the door. I saw it again the third morning, and opened the door, and there was nothing there.' As my sister could not satisfy her curiosity, nurse D.'s part of the story ends here. She made no further inquiries, and soon after died.

"Some months after, while my sister, Mrs. W., was visiting us in Boston, and had told us the story, an aunt of her husband, Aunt Nancy, who was contemporary with Mrs. S., came in, and without telling her that nurse Davis had seen anything, I asked her what kind of a looking woman Mrs. S.'s mother was. She said, 'A short, stout old lady.' My sister, Mrs. H., then said, 'How did she dress?' She said, 'She wore a white cap with a broad, black ribbon around it, and a white handkerchief crossed over her bosom and fastened behind.' Then my sister, Mrs. W., to whom nurse Davis had told the story, asked, 'Had she any favorite seats?' She said, 'Yes. Don't you know that room that opens out of the bedroom, with a glass door? I've seen her sit by that door more than a thousand times and spin, and sing —

"Fly swifter round, ye wheels of time."'

"Now, whom did nurse Davis see? For she did not know how Mrs. S.'s mother looked; and Aunt Nancy did not know that nurse Davis saw anything.

"Mr. Whittier, the poet, said, when I told him this, that it was the best ghost-story he ever heard; and he knew all the parties, which made it all the better."

The same lady gave the following:

"This one was told me by Colonel Apthorp, of Florida, so it only came second to me. Two gentlemen were travelling among the Alps: one was a lawyer, a hard-headed man, of almost infidel tendencies; the other, of a poetical temperament, who might 'see visions and dream dreams.' As they were about to enter a natural tunnel, the lawyer suddenly stopped, and said, 'Who's that man there?' They were on foot. His companion said, 'Where? I see no one.' The lawyer answered, almost angrily, 'Can't see him there?'—pointing his finger. 'No, I can't,' replied his companion; 'how is he dressed?' The lawyer described his dress, height, and looks, severally. His companion replied, 'That's my brother; he travelled all over this region, and he died some years ago,—and—I won't go into the tunnel.' The lawyer replied, 'Well, I will,' and went in alone. After he had proceeded a little distance, he perceived a slight tremor underfoot; he still proceeded until the tremor became so perceptible that he turned about and ran at the top of his speed toward the mouth of the tunnel. He had barely time to step one side of the entrance, when the tunnel was entirely filled with water,—a water-spout having broken back among the hills. The tunnel was so small, it would have been absolutely impossible for two to have escaped with their lives, had they entered, as one did alone. Whom did the lawyer see?"

The following incident was related to the author by Mrs. Jones, of Bridgeport, Connecticut, a daughter of Noah Webster.

"Dr. William H. Goodrich, son of Professor Goodrich of Yale College, was pastor of the First Presbyterian Church in Cleveland, Ohio. Some time previous to his death we were conversing on such subjects, when he said to me: 'One fact I can verify. There was a lady in Cleveland, who had a son who was wild, and lived an irreligious, dissipated life. She had done all in her power to save him, but apparently in vain. She had left Cleveland, and was residing with another son at the West. One evening, this young man in Cleveland retired to rest; he saw his mother standing by his bedside in her usual dress. She spoke to him, expostulating with him on his life, and urged him to repent and embrace Christ, and left him. As soon as she disappeared, he arose and noted down the facts, the time, date, &c. The next morning he went to his pastor, and related the circumstances, and said, "I want to become a Christian; show me the way." In fact, he did from that day reform, and lead a Christian life. At the proper time for a letter to come from the West, he received word that his mother had died at the hour when she appeared to him.' "

A very dear friend, now residing in Italy, last summer told the author the following circumstance.

"It was about the time of the last panic when my husband's fortune was swept away, and when, at the same time, he was absent from me in America, and our son was lying dangerously sick in Indiana. I was very anxious both about my son and about my husband, and became very much exhausted and depressed.

"In my sleep, one day, I seemed to have a vision. The Saviour came and stood at my side; He had my little Eddy in his arms. The Saviour appeared to me most exquisitely beautiful — more beautiful than anything I had ever imagined, or conceived possible. He seemed to bend over me with a sweet smile. He did not speak, but seemed to communicate to me without words a sense of his protecting care. The burden was lifted from my heart in a moment. I awoke and was perfectly calm and tranquil. Ever since that, if I am in the least disturbed or anxious, if I think of how He looked, it takes all my care away."

Now the author is aware what explanation might be given of this by physiologists, somewhat as in the case of that very striking apparition seen by Lord Brougham.* We can imagine Dr. Clarke saying in this case: "Mrs. —— was in Italy, surrounded by beautiful paintings of Madonnas, and angelic forms. She is herself an artist. The cells of her brain must have been stamped with some of those exquisite pictures. Those cells, thus sensitized, like a photographic plate, were laid away in the recesses of her brain. There they were deposited, the hieroglyphic representations" of celestial things, "like a portrait in a garret, or a manuscript in a drawer, ready to be brought out whenever anything should occur to drag them out."

The circumstances of her family, together perhaps with some unusual fatigue and exhaustion, may have produced "a moderate anæmia of the periphery of the brain, and a moderate hyperæmia of the base of the brain, sufficient to bring within the sphere of automatic activity the latent cell-groups; they appeared, subjective vision was accomplished, and she saw the Saviour bending above her."

We admit that this is a possible explanation; but it is hypothetical in the extreme. We know that the retina, and certain nervous ganglia, and the cerebral lobes, exist, and that sight depends on them, and that certain conditions of the inner ganglia are accompanied with pseudopia, or conscious subjective vision. But that is all. That there is any "sending of messages," or "telegraphing," or "stamping," or "photographing,"—that there are any "cells," and that those cells auto-

* Visions, pp. 307–9.

matically appear, — is purely conjectural, and the language even figurative. "Any explanation of the matter," says Dr. Clarke, "must, from the nature of the case, be more or less hypothetical. . . . . The hypothesis of Herbert Spencer is perhaps as plausible and satisfactory as any." "The expressions, 'cell-groups,' polarizing the cells, and some other terms," says Dr. Holmes, in his introduction to this interesting book, "must be accepted rather as a convenient form of signifying an unknown change of condition, than as intended to be taken literally."

Now the hypothesis that the cerebral organism was affected by the actual presence of Christ is as possible, may we not say as "plausible," as the other. We accept it as with a strong conviction that such faith is not unreasonable, or unscientific. Dr. Clarke himself admits that some apparitions may be objective. "Probably all such visions (of the dying) are automatic. Yet who, believing in God and personal immortality, as the author rejoices in doing, will dare to say absolutely all?"

He mentions one case in particular, (p. 277,) where the person, "after saying a few words, turned her head upon her pillow as if to sleep; then unexpectedly turning it back, a glow, brilliant and beautiful exceedingly, came into her features, her eyes opening sparkled with singular vivacity; at the same moment, with a tone of emphatic surprise and delight, she pronounced the name of the earthly being nearest and dearest to her, and then, dropping her head upon her pillow, as unexpectedly as she had looked up, her spirit departed to God who gave it. *The conviction forced upon my mind, that something departed from her body, at that instant rupturing the bonds of flesh, was stronger than language can express.*" *

* The Italics are ours.

Dr. Holmes, referring to this case, says: "Dr. Clarke mentioned a circumstance to me not alluded to in the essay. At the very instant of dissolution, it seemed to him, as he sat at the dying lady's bedside, that there arose 'something'—an undefined yet perfectly apprehended somewhat, to which he could give no name, but which was like a departing presence. I should have listened to this story less receptively it may be, but for the fact that I had heard the same experience, almost in the very same words, from the lips of one whose evidence is eminently to be relied upon. With the last breath of the parent she was watching, she had the consciousness that 'something' arose, as if the 'spirit' had made itself cognizable at the moment of quitting its mortal tenement. The coincidence in every respect of these two experiences has seemed to me to justify their mention in this place."

CHAPTER VI.

REMARKABLE CONVERSIONS.

IN the present chapter reference is made to a class of phenomena, ancient and modern, of a higher grade, and, to the author's mind, of greater convincing power. The following is an extract from the memoirs of a distinguished public man, giving an account of his conversion. The incidents related took place in the back room of a lawyer's office, whither he had retired for prayer. "There was no fire, and no light in the room; nevertheless, it appeared to me as if it were perfectly light. As I went in and shut the door after me, it seemed as if I met the Lord Jesus Christ face to face. It did not occur to me then, nor did it for some time afterward, that it was wholly a mental state. On the contrary, it seemed to me that I saw him as I would any other man. He said nothing, but looked at me in such a manner as to break me right down at his feet. I have always since regarded this as a most remarkable state of mind; for it seemed to me a reality, that he stood before me, and I fell down at his feet and poured out my soul to him. I wept aloud like a child, and made such confessions as I could with my choked utterance. It seemed to me that I bathed his feet with my tears; and yet I had no distinct impression that I touched him that I recollect.

. . . .

"As I turned, and was about to take my seat by the fire, I received a mighty baptism of the Holy Ghost.

Without any expectation of it, without ever having the thought in my mind that there was any such thing for me, without any recollection that I had ever heard the thing mentioned by any person in the world, the Holy Spirit descended upon me in a manner that seemed to go through me body and soul. I could feel the impression, like a wave of electricity, going through me and through me. Indeed, it seemed to come in waves, and waves of liquid love; for I could not express it in any other way. It seemed like the very breath of God. I can recollect distinctly that it seemed to fan me, like immense wings. No words can express the wonderful love that was shed abroad in my heart. I wept aloud with joy and love. . . . . These waves came over me, and over me, and over me, one after the other, until I recollect I cried out, 'I shall die if these waves continue to pass over me.' I said, 'Lord, I cannot bear any more;' yet I had no fear of death." *

Mr. Finney was one of the most honest, artless men that ever lived. His whole life was consecrated. He was a power in his day and generation. He not only planted the germs of religious life in thousands of individual hearts, but he was one of those who educated whole communities, and toned up public sentiment for great reforms, and conflicts with wrong. The experience of such a mind is valuable, though it may be unique. The fact which it impresses upon our belief is, that there was a real objective spirit-manifestation. Whether there was an objective vision of light, and of form, or not, — however the more outward and physical phenomena are to be explained, — there was, it is believed, then and there, a real manifestation of Christ.

It is a case substantially of the same kind with that mentioned by St. Paul in the narrative of his own con-

* Memoirs of Rev. Charles G. Finney, pp. 19–21.

version: "Whereupon, as I went to Damascus with authority and commission from the chief priests, at midday, O king, I saw in the way a light from heaven, above the brightness of the sun, shining round about me, and them which journeyed with me. And when we were all fallen to the earth, I heard a voice speaking unto me, and saying, in the Hebrew tongue, Saul, Saul, why persecutest thou me? It is hard for thee to kick against the pricks. And I said, Who art thou, Lord? And he said, I am Jesus, whom thou persecutest."*

In this connection also, reference may be made to the opening scenes of Pentecost: "And when the day of Pentecost was fully come, they were all with one accord in one place. And suddenly there came a sound from heaven, as of a rushing mighty wind, and it filled all the house where they were sitting. And there appeared unto them cloven tongues, like as of fire, and it sat upon each of them. And they were all filled with the Holy Ghost, and began to speak with other tongues, as the Spirit gave them utterance."† The above have always been regarded by Christians as real spiritual manifestations of great sublimity; and it will be conceded that it is not the outward features of the transaction, the mechanical, or physiological parts, —if the expression may be allowed, — that are of chief importance, but the fact of a real spiritual agency — a power external to, and above, the mortal organism. In the beneficent career of the Wesleys, the physical phenomena in Epworth Rectory, and those accompanying their public preaching, when numbers fell as if shot on the field of battle, however striking, were of inferior importance compared with other evidences of invisible spiritual agency. This principle may be applied, not only to individuals, but to nations. The Jewish nation, for example, may be regarded

* Acts xxvi. 12–15. † Acts ii. 1–4.

as a kind of MEDIUM among nations — an organ of spiritual manifestations. That nation, always recalcitrant, always rebellious, — or, as Stephen expressed it, "always resisting the Holy Spirit," — stoning their prophets, and slaying those sent unto them, — seems yet, throughout its whole course, grasped by a mighty power outside of and above itself, and moulded upon a high ideal. Had they been more plastic and obedient, they would have been more prosperous and happy. For their indocility they were chastised by repeated strokes, and finally dashed and scattered. Their history is a sublime series of spiritual manifestations, in which the outward and physical phenomena, however striking, are of secondary value; and the great fact of real spiritual agency, first. "What advantage hath the Jew? Much every way; but chiefly, that unto them were committed the oracles of God." * The most important class of phenomena is that which is least conspicuous; phenomena occurring in the private life of every believer, — such as answers to prayer, and communion with God. Reference is now made, not to the unusual, but to the common; not to the ecstatic or mystical, but to the average, the commonplace, as it were.

There may be moments of transfiguration in every life, even the most prosaic. Perhaps in some communion-service of unusual emotion, the cup, as it came to your lip, did not seem to contain wine; for an instant, a fleeting moment, it seemed to be filled with blood; but it passed, as all exalted frames must, leaving only an affecting memory behind. Perhaps in some season of distress or exhaustion, in your slumbers, the Saviour has seemed to bend above you, a form of ineffable beauty, the form of some lost darling by his side, and to speak to you words of encouragement. Such moments, how-

* Rom. iii. 1, 2.

ever precious, must be brief; they are, of necessity, exceptional. There is a simpler style of communion with the unseen, resulting in inward peace, tranquillity, and a feeling of health. Is not this, after all, the best and highest form of spiritual manifestation, because it is most suited to the needs of everyday life, and to the capacities of average humanity? "Lord, how is it," said a disciple, "that thou wilt manifest thyself unto us?" "If a man love me," was the reply, "he will keep my words, and my Father will love him, and we will come unto him and make our abode with him." In this way the humblest disciple may have a sweet certainty of things unseen, and sing as he journeys on —

> "So shall my walk be close with God,
> Calm and serene my frame;
> So purer light shall mark the road
> That leads me to the Lamb."

CHAPTER VII.

HISTORIC METHOD.

SCIENCE is but another name for history. The instinctive tendency of modern investigation is to go back to the origin of things. The evolution-theory is simply an effort to answer the question how the universe came to be as it is. That is history pure and simple. The belief in spirits and their manifestations is ancient and wide-spread. It is found in Egypt at a very early period; in Babylonia, and India. That belief is a fact to be accounted for like any other belief. Hence the evolutionist sets himself to give the history of the possible or probable origin of such a conception. It is an interesting endeavor in which the spiritualist may well sympathize, while appreciating the difficulty of the problem. If thought is material, or, in other words, if matter thinks, how came matter to believe in the existence of spirits when there are none?

On the other hand, spiritualists show the same tendency in attempting to account for all phenomena on the hypothesis of spiritual agency. Their writings are largely occupied with the problem how spirits came to be what and where they are, and what their relation to the material system; in short, what is the history of the spirit universe; and no one can really discuss spiritualism appreciatively without either accepting its theory of the history of the universe, or proposing a better one.

It may be thought that the common people are not competent to such an undertaking. To attempt that, one must possess an extensive knowledge of facts, and trained powers of observation, induction, and abstraction. A feeling of scorn is sometimes manifested towards the entire spiritualistic literature, as the product of the uneducated classes. But the fact is, that while the common people may not be able to originate a theory of the universe, they may have common-sense enough to judge one when it is elaborated; and the shrewd judgment of average humanity no philosopher or scientist can afford to despise. He who retires into his own thought-world, however extensive, deprives himself of valuable tests. As merchants take account of stock in trade every year, so minds should take account of stock in ideas. A man who has never abstracted himself from himself has much to learn. He who has never taken out all his ideas, (as a man takes down books from the shelves of his library,) and inspected them, and put them back, may become vain, or morbid, or spiritually hallucinated without knowing it. If a man be ever so learned, he ought frequently to come out of himself and deal with the average needs of humanity. This is eminently sanitary and conservative.

As to the masses, they have been but too willing to abandon religious speculation to professional men. Any movement that really interests them and excites them to think deeply, loftily, comprehensively, however it may be mixed with errors, is, in this respect, beneficial. And without attempting a Theodicy, or undertaking to settle the vexed question of the origin of evil, it will be impossible to deal with the subject of spiritualism, without taking a comprehensive survey, and adopting an historical method, in short, propounding a possible system of the history of the universe.

Analogy would seem to suggest, at the very outset, that the universe of mind is coextensive at least with that of matter. As this material globe is densely peopled, nay, crowded with diversified life, so the unseen may be peopled with equally numerous and various orders of minds. As between all the orbs of space there is a subtile relation, a harmony, so between all intelligent orders it is natural to suppose there is a relation, a kind of moral harmony.

The moral universe has a history. The history of this world cannot remain forever isolate, disconnected with the history of the great whole. As all nations on earth are morally one, so all worlds in space are one. As the pebble falling by gravity attracts the globe, so this village-world, this ant-hill of humanity, affects the entire thought-universe from centre to circumference. The history of nations unfolds not in total seclusion from other worlds. Spirits exist; they operate, they exert influence. History is to be studied with a full recognition of this fact. As well calculate the orbits of planets without reference to perturbations from the attraction of other planets, possibly unknown, as solve the problems of earthly history without reference to the powers of the world unseen. We may be unable fully to penetrate the plans and motives of the invisible orders, but that is not a valid reason for not trying to form some probable conjecture.

And this, at least, we may assume as an axiom, an intuition: that the universe, as a whole, is to be a success. Its history, whenever we do know it, will prove to be a poem, a perfect epic, which will satisfy our highest cravings. Even on the principle that thought, emotion, and volition are strictly material products of cerebral organism, it appears that matter itself is quasi benevolent. Admit that matter thinks, feels, wills; still on the great scale we see a gradual improvement, a tendency towards an ideal. Matter, then, is, even on this extreme hypothesis, essentially good, and has done automatically, and is doing, and will do, all that the devoutest minds have ever attributed to the divine benevolence.

If matter thinks in this world, it thinks in all worlds. If matter automatically evolves moral results here and now, it will do the same everywhere and always. The material system is essentially good and benign, as really so as if it were the work of a good and benign being. So much, even on materialistic premises, seems undeniable.

But if we believe in God, and an intelligent moral universe coextensive with the material, this intuition becomes even more clear in our consciousness. Social happiness cannot exist without confidence. Confidence cannot exist without truth, friendship, and self-denial. The unfoldings of history have in fact been conducted on a plan affording a vast, an exhaustive demonstration of these facts. They will continue to be so conducted until a perfect state of society is reached in this world and in all worlds.

CHAPTER VIII.

ANALOGY.

THE material universe has often been spoken of as a kind of solidification of divine thought — a complex analogon of spiritual relations. It is sometimes supposed that figures of speech are certain creations of the mind. Some nations are literal, and do not create them easily; others are more tropical, and cannot help creating them. But they have no necessary objective basis in nature. It is better, however, to say that the analogies are there in the material system, and that the difference between races is, that some see and enjoy and use them more readily than others. Some, perhaps, carry their use to excess; others employ them too sparingly.

It is often supposed that figures of speech are purely fanciful, in the sense of being governed by no law; that they are mere frolic, froth, mist, moonshine. Doubtless the analogies of the material system have been but imperfectly studied; the action of the mind towards them has been often unregulated and empirical, and, as in every other part of nature, use has degenerated into abuse. But the principles of analogy which underlie all figurative diction are as really objective realities, capable of scientific statement, as are the laws of gravity or cohesion. They are as distinct from mere subjective habits of casual suggestion, hints, association by direct resemblance, as are the laws and formulas of logic.

Mr. Spencer, in his "Studies of Sociology," alludes

to this point. Many assume, he says, that such phrases as "body politic," "political organization," and others which liken society to a living creature, are mere phrases of convenience, not founded on fact; but the truth is "that there is a real analogy between an individual organism and a social organism;" and he asserts that, "without asserting this fundamental kinship there can be no such thing as a science of sociology."*

This is a very important truth. A volume might be profitably devoted to its full elucidation. The great fact is, that *analogy* is an objective law of the material world, as really as gravitation. By analogy is meant a similarity of relations. In arithmetic, a proportion is a numerical analogy, — that is, an identity of ratios, — 2 : 4 :: 3 : 6. Two is contained in four, as many times as three is contained in six. But if we say, As light to the eye, so is truth to the mind, we have not an identity of ratios, but a certain intuitively felt likeness of relations. In every analogy there are four terms, arranged in pairs, — the relation in one pair being more familiar, that in the other less, and the former employed to suggest or illustrate the latter. Every true analogy, fully stated, assumes the form, $a : b :: x : y$. This formula may be as useful in testing analogies as the syllogism is in testing arguments. An illustration which cannot be reduced to this form is not a true analogy.

A metaphor is simply a condensed or abbreviated analogy, as, "I see" for "I think," or "light" for "truth." Now this similarity between the relation of light to the eye and that of truth to the mind is not a creation of the fancy; it is an objective law of nature. In all languages light is used as an emblem of truth, and darkness of error. It is believed that it would be

* Studies of Sociology, pp. 331–333.

impossible to train a generation from birth to reverse this analogy. They might change the word-sign, and call the sun's radiance by the word "darkness," and conversely, but they would think of light itself as the emblem of truth. "Examine language," says Carlyle; "what, if you except a few primitive elements of natural sound, is it all but metaphor, recognized as such, or no longer recognized? . . . . An unmetaphorical style you shall in vain seek for; is not your very attention a *stretching to?*"

Let us try a moment to trace out this analogy of light. Of course, if light is the analogue of truth, warmth is the analogue of affection. The sun becomes the emblem of a mind imparting knowledge, the eye the emblem of the mind receiving (and by the same law, a star, a lamp, a torch, a luminary of any kind). But as sunlight reveals things most perfectly, in their true shape, size, color, and perspective, so the sun becomes the emblem of the most perfect teacher, omniscient, infallible, in whose light we see light. Here comes in a variety of connected analogies relating to the interception of light. Whatever hides the sun's rays resembles analogically the obscuration of truth. Mists, exhalations, fogs, clouds, and night are natural emblems of errors, delusions, doubts, and ignorance in general. "Thus day unto day utters speech, and night unto night showeth knowledge." This analogical language is real, objective, natural, whether expressed in verbal form or not. "Tho' there be no speech, nor language, yet their line is gone out into all the earth and their words unto the ends of the world." Images borrowed from the dawn of day, with all its beautiful phenomena, are transferred to the dawn of life, or infancy, to the dawn of national existence, to the infancy of the race; also to the dawn of love, and to the earliest stages of religious experience. The same is true of the imagery connected with noon, with evening, or with midnight.

In examining this wonderful correlation, we find that it includes all the phenomena of nature, — those of light and shade, of color, of form, of size, weight, hardness, number, time, tune, motion, warmth, fragrance, taste, and others. The rays of heat, for example, in their relation to the comfort or discomfort of the body, to the vital processes of the vegetable kingdom, to climate, to the destruction or preservation of organic structures, are the natural emblems of love, or other strong emotions, with their contrasted effects upon the mind and upon social organizations. Thus arise such familiar expressions as warm-hearted, cold-hearted, love's fire, the heat of anger, the coolness of estrangement, the coldness, and icy frigidity of alienation.

Passing by easy steps to the changes of the seasons, we find all the characteristic features of spring, summer, autumn, and winter, even to the minutest shades and gradations, transferred to corresponding states of individual or social experience, even to those most recondite and spiritual, most abstract and abstruse. And all men in all ages and nations see and feel and use these analogies alike, substantially, and by a law as resistless as that by which they eat bread with relish; and yet there is not one of those outward material phenomena which is not directly or indirectly what it is because light is what it is, because there is nothing on this globe which the sun has not made to be what it is. If we pass into the animal kingdom we find the same law of correspondence everywhere. Every organ of the body, external and internal, — the head, the eye, the ear, the mouth, the lips, the hand, foot, heart, blood, flesh, — is irresistibly representative of analogons realities. And the health or unhealth of each and all, their growth or decay, their cleanness or defilement, their dress or adornment, or nakedness, are equally symbolic. So with everything the body or its members touches or uses, — the dress, the implement of war or of peace, the path, the walk, the steps, the habitation, lying down, rising, turning to the right or left; looking upward, downward, or askance; standing erect, upright; strength, weakness, health, sickness, pain, pleasure, hunger, thirst, eating, drinking, laughing, frowning, sleeping, waking, living, dying, birth, burial, — everything pertaining to the body in all its countless contrasts and uses, is intuitively, necessarily, felt to correspond to something mental or moral, and is so used spontaneously by all men in all ages, and without change or mistake. Scientific definition, abstract statement, metaphysical discriminations, may be misunderstood on these matters; analogies seldom are, because the analogy exists objectively to us, and controls us as gravity controls the body. Pass to the animal kingdom, and the carnivorous races, in their relations to the weaker species, and all, in their relations to the vegetable world and to man, are emblems by a similar necessity. The sinuous coil of the serpent, his envenomed fang, cannot be made the emblem of truth and love; the spider in his web cannot be made the emblem of good neighborhood. The correspondences are established for us; and if the world should vote to change them, they could not be changed. Pass to the vegetable world, and the same law holds good. Leaf, bud, flower, fruit, seed, stalk, trunk, root, sap, branches, growth, decay, seed-time, harvest, are fixed analogues of corresponding mental or moral realities.

Take that very "struggle for existence" everywhere going on around us, and try to interpret it by the law of analogy to illustrate benevolent co-operation. You cannot. It is a picture of selfish rivalry and destructiveness. Certain species are killed out; others survive. The survival of the fittest means, in nature, the survival of the strongest, the most encroaching. It is like the survival, in society, of the most unscrupulous, the most grasping and selfish, who make the most of every casual advantage to root out and throttle and destroy all competitors. Men do not call benevolent, truthful, obliging, and merciful people sharks, wolves, foxes, serpents; they do not call men of opposite traits doves and lambs. It matters not where you touch this material system, you find it like an infinite lexicon, or cyclopedia, of signs. As before remarked, the analogies of nature, like every other good thing, have been abused; yet they have shown a wonderful vitality to resist abuse, and defy misinterpretation.

We may not be able to verify the history of every word in our language, but we can arrive at a moral certainty that they all originated, directly or indirectly, from this intuitively perceived analogy between the material system and the mental, or between one portion of the former and another portion; and this analogy existed anterior to its perception by our minds. The relation of solar light and heat to the greenness and floral beauty of the globe existed ages before there were eyes to see it and perceive the analogy. Can this have been accidental? Mr. Spencer well observes that no religion of humanity can long shut out the thought of "a power which was in course of ever-changing manifestations before humanity was." We reverently ask, must not that power have been intelligent and self-conscious? Can we conceive of such an objective law of analogy as a result of a blind, fortuitous combination of mechanical forces? By what process of struggle for existence, and survival of the fittest — by what more law of selection — is this to be accounted for?

The material system thus becomes to the contemplative student a vast and complex system of signs, — the basis of human language, — so that day unto day uttereth speech, and night unto night showeth knowledge, of the great Author of all.

The mind of man is provided with a constitutional faculty for the understanding of the science of analogy. As causality is the organ of logical reasoning, so comparison is the faculty of analogical reasoning; and these, the reflective faculties, occupy the noblest position in the dome of intellect; and of these, the analogic power is most central, most infallible, most used and most abused, the latest ripened and vindicated of all the intellectual powers of the soul. It has been called fanciful, playful, ornamental; it has been, like ideality, cavalierly set aside as unscientific, untrustworthy, suspicious; but it holds the golden key of millennial knowledge.

When the analogic power is duly honored, vindicated from neglect and abuse, then will this material system be seen in its true light, and its lessons be heard by the deep slumbering soul of man. All nature then becomes our Father's whispering gallery, his school-room, — the walls hung with diagrams and pictures, every object a word of his, every change a phrase, every event a sentence.

"Thou art, O God, the life and light
Of all this wondrous world we see;
Its glow by day, its smile by night,
Are but reflections caught from Thee:
Where'er we turn, thy glories shine,
And all things fair and bright are thine."

CHAPTER IX.

TABLEAUX.

THE principles discussed in the previous chapter suffice to account, in part, for the great influence of the Bible over the most diverse races. The Bible makes a more free, constant, and scientific use of the analogies of the material system than any other book. The more those analogies are studied the better the Bible is understood, and the higher it rises in our estimation. This will readily be conceded, so far as relates to the diction, the style. But there is an application of the analogic principle which a class of minds fail to appreciate. When "types and shadows" are mentioned, some minds revolt with a feeling that such conceptions are visionary and unscientific. That analogic laws may be violated is plain. That they have been frequently violated is equally evident. But the abuse does not discredit the use. There is an application of the law of analogy in types and emblems which is legitimate and scientific. As every argument can be tested by the syllogistic formula and its soundness, or its fallacy demonstrated, so every type or emblem can be tested by the analogic formula.

For example: it has been said that the lion is the emblem of courage. Apply the test. As the lion to other animals, so is courage to the other virtues. Does courage, then, eat up the other virtues? But if we say that a wild beast is an emblem of a conquering world-empire, — Babylon, for example, or Rome, or any other, — then the analogy is manifest. As a wild beast to weaker species of animals, so is a conquering world-empire to weaker nations.

It is the great fault with Swedenborg's correspondences that they do not always correspond. All spiritualists concede that he was a medium; but his communications, like those of all other mediums, ancient or modern, must be tested by logical and analogical rules. In him comparison, or the analogical faculty, was naturally predominant; and when drawing his illustrations from nature, he obeys the objective law in a striking and often beautiful manner. But the action of the faculty is unregulated, especially as linked with excessive wonder and ideality, and when employed in the exposition of scripture.

Too many of the alleged correspondences cannot be reduced to analogic form. They even directly violate analogy; as, for example, when he says, "By Tyre, in the Word, is signified the church." * Now, Tyre was one of the principal polytheistic nations antagonistic to the divine manifestation in Israel. And the prince of Tyre was an embodiment of worldly power, and thus a vivid illustration of the great cosmocratic chief or prince of this world. And the analogy, correctly stated, is: As the prince of Tyre to Israel, so the prince of this world to the spiritual Israel, or the Church.

In many cases the alleged correspondences are purely arbitrary; or they depend on mere resemblance, or association of ideas, — local, casual, incidental, far-fetched. If he had shaken out quantities of nouns from a dice-box, and made those happening to fall in pairs correspondences, it could not have been more haphazard, and non-correspondent. But he is by no means alone in

* True Christian Religion, No. 219.

this fault. It is the main defect with most expositors of sacred emblems, and one great reason why there is so much confusion in the use of terms, so much disputing between "literal" and "figurative" interpreters.

The material system itself has not been sufficiently studied in its analogies. Writers have not sufficiently distinguished between the objective emblem, and the mere words descriptive of the emblem;—have not defined their own terms, and adhered systematically to their own definitions, much less agreed with each other upon certain controlling definitions.

It is said that good usage is the only canon in deciding the meaning of words. But suppose there is no good usage? Suppose that such words as mythical, allegorical, metaphorical, figurative, symbolical, emblematic, tropical, typical, shadowy, parabolical, &c., are used as convertible terms, and as in some vague way opposed to real, literal, historical, prosaic, natural, and the like? Will it not be very difficult to say what good usage is?

No one writer can make good usage or decide it; but he can at least control his own usage, make it consistent, and as far as possible harmonize it with the usage of other writers, provided they have any that is uniform and consistent. Now, if writers would study the analogies of the material system more carefully, and keep more clearly in mind, and apply more rigidly, the analogic formula $a : b :: x : y$, it would be a step in the right direction toward the establishment of a recognized "good usage." If next they would agree to employ certain terms, say emblem, symbol, type, tableau, in an objective sense always,—as denoting an object either seen or conceived of as seen,—and to use the words metaphor, figure, simile, myth, fable, exclusively of the diction, it would be a great point gained.

This distinction will at least be carefully made in the

present discussion. By an emblem, a type, a symbol, a tableau, will be understood something seen with the natural eye, or in a vision, or in a dream; or conceived of by the imagination as if seen.

On the other hand, all figures of speech, of whatever kind, will be considered as pertaining to style exclusively. According to these principles we shall hope not to be misunderstood when we speak of the Eden tableau, or the Eden emblems, or of Adam as a type, or of the transactions in the garden as shadowing some thing. No one will understand us to assert that the account is mythical, fabulous, allegorical, figurative, for these terms relate to the diction, and imply, or are generally supposed to imply, that there was no such objective reality, — no garden, no actors, but pure fable — fiction.

The very definition we have given of emblematic representation demands objective reality. In a tableau we see the objects and actions bodily before us. In dreams and visions we seem to see them. In a cartoon or painting we see an objective imitation of them. In a verbal description we obtain a mental conception of them *as if* we saw them. The garden, the trees, the man, the woman, the serpent, the Lord, the dialogue, the action, the costume or want of costume, the exclusion, must be historic realities in order to be symbolic. We read in Hebrews that the Levitical ritual was a shadow; but there must be a ritual before there can be a shadow. So Eden must be, before it can be emblematic. The group of actors must be historic to be a tableau; it must be vivant to be tableau vivant. A friend suggests that the whole account may be simply a relic of primeval legend, just as the Izdubar (or Nimrod) legend is; and that the advance of knowledge points towards this result. In that case, we should still say that the tableau is described as if objective. It is conceptually objective if not historically so, and the principle of analogic interpretation is the same in either case. The most recent discoveries, however, do not, at least in our judgment, point to this result.

Granting the historical, objective character of the objects described, their typical, or emblematic, character, readily follows. "Adam," we read, "is the type of him that was to come." * There has been an impression more or less general in every age, that such was the fact. And if, as has been shown, the whole material system is itself analogical, and designedly so made by the Creator, why should He not be supposed to use types, and emblems, and tableaux? If the family itself is necessarily symbolic; if the relation man sustains as husband and father is in some respects like that sustained by God on a higher plane of being; then why should it be thought incredible, or unscientific, that God should take a particular man, in some important crisis, and place him on a specially prepared stage, and cause him to act a specially significant part?

And whether we suppose the crisis before us to be the actual first introduction of the human species on the globe, or the introduction of an improved variety, and the inauguration of a new historic era, of high moral importance, why should it not seem in either case a fit occasion for such a proceeding? Is it not at least worth while to ask, if such a garden existed, if such scenes were acted out by such actors, what, according to analogic law, would they mean?

One thing is evident: there is much meaning condensed in very small compass. The objects themselves say more than the words describing the objects. The emblems are a Rosetta stone awaiting Champollion.

* Rom. v. 14. *Τύπος*, type, in the original.

They are like the cuneiform tablets before the key was discovered. A detailed exposition cannot be attempted here; it would require a volume, and may form the subject of a separate work hereafter. At present there are one or two points on which we will briefly touch.

The description given of the garden and its occupants is not figurative nor metaphorical, but literal. The words are simple, the style artless. It is just the language any matter-of-fact traveller or observer would use if he had actually seen such a place and wished to describe it. Let the reader reflect on this. Let him test the truth of our remarks. Let him read carefully Gen. ii. and iii., and see if he can find any metaphors, or other figures of speech. *The hidden meaning, if there be one, is not in the diction, not in the style, but in the objects themselves.* If you could see the scene acted correctly on the stage, not a word being spoken except the dialogue; if you could see it in a dream, or by a vivid exercise of the conceptive faculties, and could forget every word of the narrative (except the dialogue), — the analogic meaning would remain whole and entire. It is not, then, in the language or style at all.

Of the actors, we here mention only two: man (including woman), and the serpent. The one is interpreted for us by the apostle as a type of him that was to come; and the analogy is briefly thus: As the natural creation, with all its races, was put in subjection to Adam, so the moral universe, in all its orders and grades of being, is to be put in subjection to Christ. This is the leading analogy; but there are numerous secondary relations which might find a parallel; but we cannot consider them. The other emblem to which we refer is the serpent. Without entering into details, the idea we have formed is this: The serpent was simply an actor provided for that special tableau — historical objective — and his whole value, so to speak, was in the analogic import of his role in the play. Briefly, it is an emblem of a combination of some kind, — a party, or kingdom in the spirit-world, hostile to mankind. This statement is addressed primarily not to those who doubt or deny the existence of any spirit-world, but to spiritualists, who fully believe in it, and who believe that there are great numbers of spirits that are more or less deceptive and selfish. The point we wish to make with spiritualists is, that the serpent here (and wherever else in Scripture the same or an equivalent form is used emblematically) is the comprehensive emblem of all that is, to use their customary phraseology, *low*, *deceptive*, *selfish*, and in any sense prejudicial to human welfare in the invisible world, conceived of as organized under a great leading intelligence.

For despotic and selfish organizations in the visible world, the customary emblem is a wild beast, as a lion, a leopard, a bear, or some composite wild-beast form. But for selfish and despotic organizations in the invisible world, we have the serpent, or some modification of the serpent-form. That the selfish and oppressive world-empires of the past have been as it were controlled, energized, inspired, from behind the scenes, one would suppose all spiritualists would see at a glance. Kings, emperors, princes, and their armies, have been pieces and pawns on the grand chessboard, but the game has been played from behind the veil.

"Where, then," says Carlyle, "is that same cunningly devised almighty GOVERNMENT of theirs to be laid hands on? Everywhere, yet nowhere: seen only in its works, this too is a thing aeriform, invisible; or, if you will, mystic and miraculous. So spiritual is our whole daily life, all that we do springs out of mystery, spirit, invisible force; only, like a cloud-image, or Armida's Palace, air-built, does the actual body itself forth from the great mystic deep."

Of this, great minds in different ages have seemed to have a more or less vivid impression. What is the spirit of the age, of which we hear so often, but an influence breathed in from unseen minds? "We wrestle not with flesh and blood," said Paul; and surely no man ever had more to do with the organized forms of the visible world than he. But these were not, in his view, even the principal part. "Our wrestling is against principalities, against powers, against the cosmocrats of this present darkness, against wicked spirits in Heaven." *

Such, spiritualist reader, is the literal meaning of the apostle's words. And you admit that Paul was a medium. He had been caught up to the third heaven. He had had transcendent visions. Was he not competent to speak on a point like this? Now, it is this cosmocracy (it is a word we shall frequently use) which we understand to be symbolized by the serpent.

To this general statement one can hardly see how spiritualists can consistently object. And it opens the way to the deepest, the most interesting investigations. We bespeak for those investigations their most earnest and candid attention. But before going on, we wish to say a little more on the historical objective nature of the tableau.

* *Πρὸς κοσμοκράτορας τοῦ σκότους τούτου, πρὸς τὰ πνευματικὰ τῆς πονηρίας ἐν τοῖς ἐπουρανίοις.* (Ephes. vi. 12.)

CHAPTER X.

EDEN.

CAN we with any reasonable certainty fix the locality of the garden of Eden? This is what a majority of Bible readers would desire. Can they do so in good faith, upon evidence usually considered satisfactory in historical inquiries? Is there any lately discovered scientific impossibility in the way? Is there any great improbability, in the commonly received view, driving us, as honest men, into the misty region of myth and legend?

The Mosaic authorship of the Pentateuch is held with undiminished confidence by those who have patiently considered all that has been, or can be, urged against it. Honest Christians and honest Jews can say, if the authorship of Moses be not established, that of Herodotus or any other ancient author is not, and cannot be. That Moses wove into his account of the creation documents he found in the archives of the Egyptian priesthood, is admitted; but this only increases our confidence in the substantial historic credibility of the narrative. Objections have been made on chronological and ethnological and geological grounds; but those objections are obviated by conceding a limited deluge, and the possibility that some tribes may have been outside of its scope; also by the theory that the first chapter of Genesis may describe a volcanic destruction of a limited portion of the earth's surface, and its reconstruction in six natural days, emblematic of six great periods of material evolution past, and six great periods of moral evolution future. Not that this solution is the only one; not that it is to be held as proven. It is simply a possible one, and to some minds probable, even attractive by its beautiful accordance with the great principles of analogy already pointed out. But other solutions are possible, on some one of which, if not on this, the objection may be fairly met.

In favor of the theory alluded to, it may be stated that the words "without form and void" (*tohu va bohu*) sometimes imply the condition into which a populous district is thrown by a wasting invasion; as when Jeremiah exclaims, "I beheld the earth, and it was without form and void." * Perhaps, if the first chapters of Genesis should be printed a little differently, according to modern methods, indicating indefinite periods of time by breaks in the narrative, and the use of asterisks or points, it might assist the reader in forming different associations of ideas in respect to time. And as it is admitted that the first chapters are composite, containing fragments of unknown antiquity, there would be a certain appropriateness in such a method.

Without attempting anything more than a mere hint at what might be possible, let it be supposed the opening narrative presented something of this appearance to the eye: —

"In the beginning Elohim created the Heavens and the Earth. . . . .
. . . .
. . . .
. . . .
. . . .

And the earth became waste and depopulated, and darkness was upon the face of the abyss."

* Jeremiah iv. 23.

The mind would easily learn in early childhood, by the use of such a page, with simple explanations, to form the idea of a period of indefinite duration between the formation of the system and the catastrophe indicated. The rendering "became" does no violence to Hebrew grammar; and the extent of the catastrophe may be limited to a portion of the earth, the same substantially which was afterwards covered by the deluge.

We should then have to conceive that those changes which would naturally take place in six days, in the subsidence of an inundation, and clearing away of volcanic vapors, and recommencement of processes of vegetable and animal life, were successively heralded by some impersonation of Deity, with the distinct purpose of shadowing forth, analogically, grand æonic periods, past and to come.

However reluctant our prosaic occidental minds may be to fall into such a train of associations, can we not conceive that a generation of children (and childhood is always Oriental) trained in this way would naturally work in it? And suppose such an explanation to have been handed down for a thousand or two thousand years, — is it not obvious that the sense of a discrepancy between geology and the sacred narrative would not be what it is now? That feeling of a strong presumption against the narrative which is so common could not then exist. May we not say, then, that there is no necessary conflict; and that nothing in Genesis forbids us to believe, whenever the evidence shall fairly warrant the conclusion, that the earth was peopled both by animals and by man before the so-called chaos in the second verse?

Science is at liberty to prove, if it can, that some nations now existing have descended from pre-Adamic tribes, and to carry those tribes back to the pliocene epoch, or to suppose that some pre-Adamic tribes have become extinct. It need not disturb our confidence in the credibility of the Mosaic history. It has not been shown that the descent of Jesus from Adam is an impossibility. It has not been shown that it is so improbable as to be morally impossible. We can still hold to the substantial reality of the historic line of descent from Adam through Shem, Abraham, and David, to Christ, without being justly chargeable either with ignorance, dishonesty, or superstition.

Even if the extreme theory of evolution should be generally accepted, it is confessedly only a theory, and can never prove it impossible for Nature (which is another name for God) to strike in at any assumed point in the grand succession, to institute a new line of development of a higher order, and with reference to which all preceding evolutions had been preparatory. Minds addicted to a wide range of spiritual and moral speculation would still feel the probabilities of such intervention to be little short of demonstrative in their force.

While thus evading, or neutralizing, the shock of supposed scientific objections, we are influenced by a train of simple common-sense arguments to believe that the Mosaic history was a plain matter of fact. We know that we inherit our civilization from the Roman Empire, and that Rome derived her civilization largely from Greece. Grecian civilization was inherited from Persia, Assyria, and Egypt. The actual development of civilization, then, has been mainly from that region lying between the Mediterranean and the Caspian, and between the Black Sea and the Persian Gulf. And this is the region we suppose to be comprehensively termed 'Eden' in Genesis; and in the highlands of Eden tho Euphrates and the Hiddekel (or Tigris) do now take their rise within a few miles of each other; while a few miles further north two other rivers flow, one to the Caspian, the other to the Black, which may be the Pison and Gihon. In fact, the name of one of them, the Araxes (a dart), is the same in signification with Gihon.

Now, what more probable than to say the garden was in the highlands of Armenia, where these four rivers take their rise? It must have been in a mountainous region,* for four rivers to flow out of it. This region

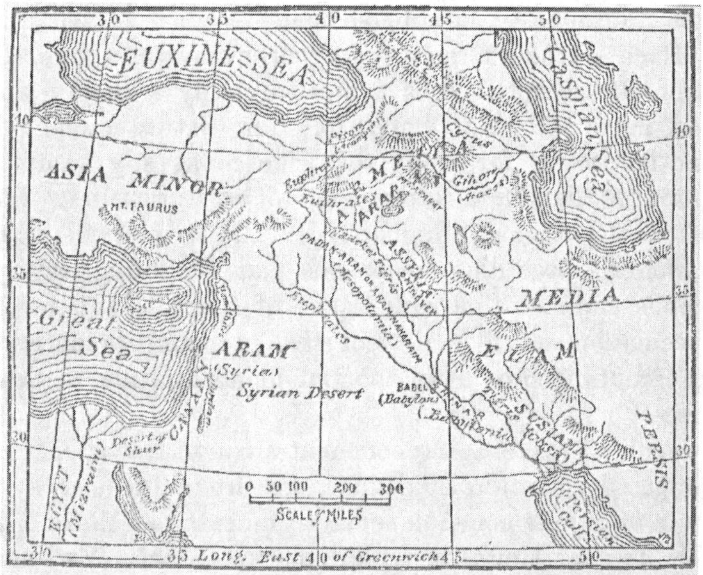

ARMENIA, (OR EDEN) ASSYRIA, BABYLONIA, SYRIA, ETC., IN THE PATRIARCHAL AGES.

fulfils all the conditions; and we can easily conceive that, if this was the general region affected by the deluge, the common source of the four rivers might have been even more marked than it is, though striking enough now.

Suppose the deluge effected by a subsidence of this

* In which case there would be no elephants to calculate for in the ark.

region, and the retreat of the waters by its upheaval,—the configuration of the country, the water-sheds, and the course of rivers would be, with slight modifications, the same. We cannot say precisely where the garden stood, but it was not far from where we see on the map the head-waters of the Euphrates, Tigris, and Araxes springing out of the earth, very near together. The Mosaic history, the map of the country, the names of its watercourses, the development of the great empires from which we mainly derive our civilization, all harmonize together, so that there is really nothing to prevent common readers of the Bible, Jews or Gentiles, from believing, without doubt or misgiving, that this was the scene, and that the garden, and its inhabitants, were realities. All recent discoveries tend to confirm this view. The clay tablets discovered and translated by George Smith contain nothing to invalidate the Mosaic history, but much to confirm it.

There may be those who will object to the idea of a celestial creative or re-creative drama of six days, previous to the introduction of the Adamic family; but spiritualists, for whom chiefly we are writing, cannot consistently be of that number. They believe in spirit manifestations, visible appearances of celestial beings, glorious forms, voices, and physical effects generally. The idea that a celestial being, or some representative of the Deity, should appear on earth after a great volcanic eruption, and by his word of command seem to regenerate the universe, one might suppose would seem to spiritualists as much more probable than the modern phenomena, as such a manifestation would be more grand and benign. The idea that, in commencing a new development of history, he should produce such a garden by the operation of laws to us unknown, and therefore seemingly miraculous, will not appear more incredible to spiritualists than some things they have either witnessed or believed on credible testimony.

Ex-Secretary McCulloch told the writer that, when he resided at Washington, he witnessed at the house or office of Secretary Seward something of this sort:— A Japanese took a flower-pot, filled it with earth, put a seed in it, placed it on the table, and commenced fanning it. Soon the earth was broken, the plant appeared, and in a few minutes grew before their eyes into a bush, budded, blossomed; and the performer picked off the blossoms and gave them to the spectators.

Madame Blavatsky, after describing a performance of this kind, says: "We have witnessed the same experiment in India and Thibet, and more than once we provided the flower-pot ourselves. We filled it with earth with our own hands, and planted in it a small root handed to us by the conjurer, and until the experiment was ended never once removed our eyes from the pot, which was placed *in our own room*."* The result was the same.

Believing in the supremacy of spirit over matter, spiritualists can consistently admit any form or degree of its exercise demanded by any great crisis for great and benevolent results; and if the history of the Adamic family was to contain a series of spiritual manifestations, as spiritualists believe it has in fact done, they can easily see the appropriateness of prefacing that history with an emblematic tableau, throwing some light both on the past and the future. The general statement would be as follows:—

At the time when the Adamic stock was introduced, from which the principal civilized empires of antiquity descended,—Egypt, Assyria, Persia, Greece, Rome,— there were existing in the invisible world, under one

* Isis Unveiled, Vol. I. p. 142.

prince of commanding intellect, great numbers of imperfect and selfish spirits, constituting an organization whose influence was hostile to man. At that time the Eden tableau was enacted by objective materialization, and the account handed down to the time of Moses, and by him incorporated in the Book of Genesis. In this tableau Adam represents the human race, the serpent represents the invisible hostile organization ; and the action is both retrospective and prospective, shadowing forth the race's exile from heaven, the age-long conflict with the invisible cosmocracy, and final victory.

CHAPTER XI.

THEORIES.

WE are now approaching the point at which a general hypothesis may be proposed, to include the phenomena of spiritualism, in connection with all known facts. We suppose the spiritualist to grant the historical objective character of the garden, and its analogical character as a tableau. Nothing is gained by regarding it as merely conceptual objective, for it would still have to be interpreted by the same law of analogy, and the import would be the same. The Bible is the spiritualist's main dependence, — to invalidate its historical character is to break down his best witness. The advantage of the historical objective is, that it gives a real event as subject of the tableau, namely, the entrance on the stage of the race, or of an improved variety of the race. The tableau is to tell us something of their past, and something of their future. It joins on to authentic history. There is no break. It is the commencement of a family-tree, one of whose branches was Israel, one of whose children was Jesus. This tableau is to tell us, in pantomime, something appropriate to such a great historical epoch.

We leave the evolutionist at liberty to prove, if he can, the existence of pre-Adamic races, and pre-Adamic civilization. Here, we claim, is the beginning of a new civilization, — the same, substantially, which now exists.

We leave the evolutionist at liberty to form his theory

of the origin of mental phenomena. It is but a theory. Thought, emotion, and volition, he tells us, so far as observed, are connected with the material organization, — increase with its development, decrease and disappear with its decay and death. Parents survive in their children — not literally, but figuratively. Generations are like waves; the form advances, but the particles constituting the curve do not advance.

Our present object is not so much to controvert this theory, as to examine the theories offered by the spiritualists in opposition to this.

And here we observe, that, though there is no authoritative statement of the belief of spiritualists, there appear to be three theories on this subject more or less widely held. The main body, at least in this country and England, appear to agree in the theory that the soul originates in, and with, the body, but is evolved from it at death. All spirits in the spiritual world, however numerous and exalted in degree, have originated thus. This theory, while it in some degree affiliates with the evolutionist theory, by conceiving of the spirit as originating in the body, and carrying with it out of the body a sort of refined corporeity, yet differs from that theory in a very important respect, namely, the continuity of the self-conscious principle. It is not the mere advance of the wave-form on the ocean of being; the same conscious self will continue to exist hereafter, and will remember. The same self, now conscious of joy and pain, hope and fear, will preserve and recognize its identity forever. But conceding fully the greatness of this difference, it still remains true, that, according to this theory, moral evil is, to some extent, of material origin. And this material world, this corporeal organization, is conceived of as of corrupting tendency, so that the further the spirit is removed from it, the purer and more nearly perfect it becomes. The natural effect of this is to weaken the sense of personal demerit. Insensibly we are led to feel that all our sins are the results of a low stage of physical development; and though they are to be regretted, yet we are no more accountable for them, no more blameworthy, than for the color of the eyes and hair.

There is, however, a school of spiritualists who do not believe that spirits originate in this mortal body. "The spirit-world," says M. Allan Kardec, "is normal, primitive, pre-existent, all-surviving. The corporeal world is secondary only; it might cease to exist, or might never have existed, without altering the essence of the spirit-world." * According to this, moral evil may be of spiritual origin; and this corporeal world in which we now are may be, not only not depraving in its tendencies, but the reverse. In general, M. Kardec is a very clear thinker, and of remarkable precision of style.† Whether spiritualism be true or false, the *Livre des Esprits*, viewed simply as a philosophical, or theological treatise, is admirable, and as deserving of study as almost any work of the kind, ancient or modern. It is not the plan of the present work to construct a theodicy, or discuss the vexed question of the origin of evil, except incidentally, as it may be alluded to by others. Any principle enunciated by such a mind as that of Allan Kardec is worthy of profounder consideration than our present limits allow. For example, having raised the question, "What was the occasion of the different use of free-will — by some spirits to good, by others to evil?" he replies: "God created all spirits simple and ignorant, that is, without knowledge. He gave them each a mis-

* *Livre des Esprits.* Introd., p. xiv. The author's real name is Hippolyte Léon Denisard Rivail.

† "With us," says the *Revue Spirite*, "that which is not clear and precise is not correct."

sion,—to enlighten and progressively perfect them by the knowledge of the truth, bringing them near to Him. Eternal unalloyed bliss depends on this perfection. Spirits acquire experimental knowledge by passing through the ordeals which God appoints. Some accept these ordeals submissively, and arrive more speedily at the goal; others submit with murmurs and remain, by their own fault, far from the promised perfection and felicity." *

Abstractly considered, it must be conceded that self-indulgence cannot lead to individual perfection, either at the beginning of existence, or at any stage of being. Fortitude is essential to nobleness of character at all times; and fortitude is patient endurance. Self-denial is essential to social well-being; and this also implies voluntary endurance. If a harp were endowed with sensation, it might experience pain in being tuned to concert pitch. A mind, with as many faculties as there are strings on a harp, may perhaps necessarily experience some pain in being tuned to perfect moral harmony with itself, and with other minds; and this may be a law, not of minds just beginning, but of all minds. Self-denial, in the sense of keeping the mental and moral strings in tune, may be necessary forever; at any rate, it is necessary now.

Now the ordeal, of which this gifted author speaks, may have been either natural, or artificial, that is, it may lie either in the normal relations of existence, in the spirit-world,—as illustrated by tuning the harp,—or it may be something extra, as it were. In the present life we may find self-denial enough in the natural relationships,—husband, father, neighbor, citizen,—and there is also an artificial self-denial by ascetic methods,—fasts, vigils, flagellations, and various austerities. The ques-

* *Livre des Esprits*, p. 50.

tion is, Does our author locate this ordeal at home, or abroad? in the original normal conditions of the pre-existent spirit-world, or in the secondary world of incarnation? This question is less distinctly answered than most others in this treatise, usually so transparent. From some expressions one might suppose the author thought that spirits in their native and normal conditions began to diverge, and that the severer ordeals of the present corporeal life were then imposed, — being rendered necessary by begun courses of error and self-will. But there are some expressions that are difficult to reconcile with this view of our author's meaning.

"Free-will develops in proportion as the spirit acquires self-consciousness. There would be no liberty if choice were determined (*sollicité*) by a cause independent of the will of the spirit. The cause is not subjective, but objective, in the influences to which it yields in virtue of its freedom. It is the grand reality, shadowed forth in the fall of man, and original sin. Some have yielded to temptation, some have resisted." Thus our author takes his stand with us at the gates of Eden; and interrogates those eloquent emblems. "Whence come the influences which operate on the spirit?"— that is, the tempting influences of this life. The answer which those emblems seem to give him is, "Imperfect spirits, who seek to take possession of him and are happy in making him yield. This it is which has been depicted under the figure of Satan." From this, we should suppose that the author would regard the serpent as an emblem of the combination of such spirits, acting in their original normal world; and that the processes of deterioration, or divergence, had commenced in that world. Thus the question is immediately asked: "Is this influence (of temptation) exerted upon the spirit at the commencement of its existence only?"

And the reply is: "It follows it in its spirit-life, until the spirit acquires such self-mastery that evil spirits renounce the attempt at obsession."

This implies clearly, that in the author's mind, or in the view of the spirits communicating, — for this work is professedly from spirits of the highest grade, — the process of divergence originated in the spirit-world. Yet the further development of the theory casts some doubt upon this important point. The theory is, that the process of conducting all spirits to perfection is by a series of successive incarnations, in this or other globes of the material universe; and in developing this theory, expressions constantly occur implying that matter is corrupting. The lower grades of spirits are "characterized by the predominance of matter over spirit." The highest grade, those which have attained perfection, "have ascended over all the steps of the scale, and have cleansed away all the impurities of matter."

Thus the corporeal world seems to be regarded in general, and from one point of view, as remedial; and yet from another point of view as defiling. In this respect the theory seems not to have been thoroughly worked out and made self-consistent. If this one feature, the defiling tendency of matter, could be eliminated, the theory would be improved, not only in consistency, but in intrinsic probability. For, that God should make this material world as a sin-removing or purifying instrumentality seems more probable, from the author's own standpoint, than that he should make it as a sin-producing or defiling instrumentality.

The theory of reincarnation, in itself, contains nothing impossible, or improbable, carefully limited as it is by the author to the ascending series, and in the human line. It is thus distinguished from the ordinary theory of transmigration. It is a question, however, whether, as presented in the work before us, it is not carried to such an extreme as to convey the impression of extravagance.

To complete the view of the Kardecian theory we may observe, that it distinctly repudiates pantheism; and bases itself, so far as morals are concerned, on the teachings of Christ. Psychologically, it is not unbiblical. Spirits are not conceived of as metaphysically immaterial. The spirit proper (pneuma) has a certain ethereal corporeity (psyche) — the spiritual body. Man is thus a trinity — body, soul, and spirit. At conception the spirit becomes connected by means of the psyche with the body (soma) — dying out, as it were, of the spiritual world. The number of spirits is illimitable; they are conceived of as in three general grades, with ten subdivisions founded on differences of knowledge and purity. The theory admits of no essentially evil or malignant spirits; but there is a very large number of imperfect spirits, ranging from those neither very good nor very evil, to those who are classed as impure, who suffer from envy, jealousy, and other evil passions, and who believe that their sufferings will be without end. It is the will of God that they should entertain this belief as a part of their punishment. All, however, are destined, sooner or later, to ascend through successive incarnations to final perfection.

There is another theory held by a class of spiritualists represented by the Theosophic Society of New York. With spiritualists in general they agree in the reality of the spiritual world and the modern spiritual manifestations. With the Kardecian school they agree in the pre-existence of the soul; the trinity of body, soul, and spirit; and in a possible reincarnation in some instances.

"We are, then," says Colonel Olcott, "generally in

perfect accord with spiritualists. Where we differ is, in the first place, in thinking that it is not good to encourage mediumship under all circumstances, because, especially as actually practised in America, it exposes the sensitives to enormous physical, psychological, and moral perils, and too often produces in the investigator himself a blind credulity, which is quickly transformed into bigotry or dogmatism. . . . . Finally, to comprehend the most serious ground of our disagreement with the spiritualists, one should know how we contemplate man and nature. For us, man is a trinity, not a duality. Inside the natural body, and pervading it, is the *astral* body or soul (psyche), and the two are overshadowed, illumined, spiritualized, by a third element — the divine, immortal spirit (pneuma), — the *Nous* of the Greeks. . . . . We believe that the fleshly man declines, dies, and enters the course of evolution to be elaborated anew and without end; that the astral man, disincarnate, freed from its physical captivity, is followed by the consequences of its earthly deeds, thoughts, and desires. This astral man purges itself from the last traces of its terrestrial grossness, and finally, after an incalculable lapse of time, is indissolubly united to its divine Spirit to live forever. . . . . Or, having been completely degraded upon earth, abases itself lower and lower in matter, and ends by annihilation."

Such a soul, after death, and prior to annihilation, "wanders about among, and enters into human bodies, obsessing the sensitives, gratifying through the organs of another his depraved appetites, till, consumed by his own proper fire, he crowns his frightful career by the dissolution of his elements." These are the *Elementaries* in the nomenclature of the Theosophic Society. "The *Elementals* are another thing. What are commonly termed the forces of nature, the Oriental philosophy teaches, are beings to whom, conformably to our masters, we give the name elemental spirits."

The human spirit, however, by a certain course of initiation, generally of an ascetic nature, is able to assert its original, native, pre-existent superiority over all such elemental spirits. . . . . "The perfectly initiated, or Adept, possesses absolute power over these natural forces, which are vague, incorporeal, unintelligent. Of themselves, these forces have no desire either to help or harm us. . . . . They are the forces of the winds, fire, water, subject to immutable laws; and man, in using them, acts only in conformity with those laws."

There are two forms of this supremacy over elemental spirits, according as the Adept is himself good or evil; the one being what is termed by Orientals "white magic," the other, "black magic." Magical science in general is sometimes spoken of under the general name of Occultism.

Another influential class of spiritualists are the followers of the Swedish seer, styling themselves the New Church. In one respect these agree with the modern movement, or the modern movement with them, namely, as to the earthly origin of all spirits. "There is not any angel that has not been a man." * "The seed of man is conceived inwardly in the understanding, and is formed in the will, and thence is transferred into the testicle, where it clothes itself with a natural covering, and thus it is conveyed into the womb and comes into the world." † "The natural man, viewed in himself as to his nature, differs not at all from the nature of beasts." ‡ "What man is from birth, and what he would be if he were not regenerated, may be seen from savage beasts of every kind; that he would be a tiger, a

* True Christian Religion, No. 121. † *Id.* No. 584.

‡ *Id.* No. 574.

panther, a leopard, a wild-boar, a scorpion, a tarantula, a viper, a crocodile." * "From nativity he is a hell in miniature." †

Man is indeed spoken of as, in a certain sense, "a native of both worlds;" but he has never had any real conscious celestial existence prior to this life. The general aspect, then, of the material system is, that it is something to be redeemed from, — not in itself of remedial design and influence. In fact, the tendencies of the system were such as to threaten the destruction of Heaven itself. "For before the coming of the Lord, hell had grown up so as to infest the angels of heaven, ... nor could even the angels of heaven have long subsisted in their integrity." ‡ "The hells had grown up to such a height that they filled all the world of spirits, which is in the middle between heaven and hell; and thus not only confused the last and lowest, but also assaulted the middle heaven, which they assaulted in a thousand ways, and which would have gone to destruction unless the Lord had protected it." § "Redemption was a battle with the hells, a subjugation of them, and afterwards an establishment of order in the heavens." ‖

The precise relations of this respectable body of spiritualists to the modern movement we have not the means of accurately determining. That Swedenborg was a gifted seer, all spiritualists admit; but, according to their cardinal principle, all his revelations must be tested by reason and the moral sense. Undoubtedly his remarkable system has had a potent influence, preparatory to, and formative of the more modern movement, to which it is yet, in some important respects, antagonistic. While teaching the endlessness of future conscious retribution, the nature and degree of penal suffering is some-

* True Christian Religion, No. 574. † *Id.* No. 612.
‡ *Id.* No. 579. § *Id.* No. 121. ‖ *Id.* No. 126.

what modified by the conception that evil spirits do not realize their condition, but are fixed in the belief of falsehood, and find a kind of enjoyment in evil. The conception of organization of both good and evil spirits in societies, and grades, is prominent; also, of a great conflict between Christ, and all invisible evil organizations, their subjugation, and the establishment of final order. Spiritualists will admit the importance of these general principles, whether they accept in detail the manner in which they are elaborated or not. In respect to the tendency of this material system to produce moral evil, this school does not differ materially from that of later spiritualists. Directly or indirectly, it is from the senses, and this material environment, that all sin and all moral evil arises. Eliminate this element, and the system would be greatly modified. It has recently been stated that Swedenborg held to the doctrine of pre-existence. We have not, however, been able to find the evidence on which such a statement can be defended. From this brief survey of the field, it appears that two schools of spiritualists, of distinguished ability, though inferior in point of numbers, hold to the pre-existence of the soul, and the existence of sinful habits anterior to incarnation; and they assert that the reason why the spirits communicating through mediums of the more numerous schools do not teach this doctrine, is because they are low in the scale, and comparatively ignorant, and incapable of comprehensive thought. We also see that three different theories are entertained respecting future retribution. There is the theory of universal restoration, the theory of conditional immortality (or the annihilation of the wicked), and the theory of endless conscious suffering.

All spiritualists agree in speaking of the material system as in some way, either directly or indirectly, defiling; and of the process of purification, as a cleansing away the stains of this material system; or a subjugation of the external material organism by influences from above. It is at this point that we wish to submit for their consideration a theory more satisfactory to our own mind, and one which seems to us more consistent with the cardinal principles of spiritualism. If spiritualists will pause awhile and reflect, they will see that, on their own principles, there is no good ground for regarding this material world as in fact defiling, however it may be sometimes figuratively so spoken of. We must distinguish between figure and fact. Nature is, in fact, morally salubrious and restorative. We cannot understand sin in a mechanical sense, — if the expression may be allowed. Moral evil is in its own nature internal, not external. It is always the abuse of something good, either by excess or defect. It is excessive self-indulgence, or self-pleasing, or selfishness. Pride is an excess of a good quality; so is ambition; so is avarice, and every other lust. Duplicity, even, is an abuse of powers essentially innocent. "Be ye wise as serpents, harmless as doves," said Jesus.

A self-idolizing spirit can be shown through bodily organs; but it can also be conceived of as shown without them. Spirits may love power over other spirits; they may use that power either selfishly or benevolently, either truthfully or deceptively. It is in this excessive self-pleasing spirit that sin consists. Thus Jesus teaches that "nothing from without entering into a man defileth him; but from within, out of the heart proceed evil thoughts, murders, adulteries, thefts, and all forms of sin, and these defile the man." And this seems to be a point on which all spiritualists can consistently with their own avowed principles accept the teachings of Jesus. It is essentially the foundation of morals and ethics; and there is nothing in his teaching which is repugnant to our highest reason and conscience.

It is not, then, this most divinely beautiful material world which is the cause of moral defilement. It is not one immense, complex, almost omnipotent, sin-producing contrivance. It is just the reverse. It is a sin-removing contrivance. Its influences, if not perverted and abused, are eminently salutary. The nearer we get to nature, the nearer we get to God.

Man is a celestial race, exiled from his native skies, we may not be able to tell precisely how, or when, though we shall know by-and-by. He is abroad on his pilgrimage, — not as a felon incarcerate; not expiating guilt; but for remedial purposes. And that not merely for individual restoration, but with reference to the political regeneration of the moral universe.

That regeneration is rendered necessary on the same general principles that, on a smaller scale, reorganization is rendered necessary in earthly communities, namely, on the principles of truth, humility, and self-denial, as opposed to fraud, pride, and self-indulgence.

The human race — so say the emblems of Eden — is destined to preside over all races and orders of the finally reconstructed universe; but against this, all selfish and jealous principalities in the spirit-world are leagued together under one great intellect of commanding eminence; while to carry it into effect all holy and unselfish spirits are combined, and divinely led. The reason why the scene of conflict should be laid in this world is conceived to be, that the conditions for achieving results so comprehensive did not exist in those spheres of being, where society was older, more settled in its courses, and where antagonisms of spirit and principle may have been more intense; corrupt influences more deeply rooted; and the individual less easily defended against them, and braced up to form habits of truth, meekness, and self-denial.

Most spiritualists admit that spirits in the lowest spheres or grades are practically helpless; that they can only be reformed by being transferred to other spheres; and that spirits from higher spheres have to stoop to their level to do it, and find it an extremely difficult task. The general principle, then, of a need of some change of circumstances is conceded. Incarnation is that change.

As a father, residing in some gay metropolis, seeing his son forming dissipated habits under the influence of convivial associates, might purchase an estate South, or West, or beyond the seas, and induce his son to accompany him, in order to break up old associations and form new ones, in healthy contact with Nature, — so we conceive it to have been, in some measure, with man. Of course this must be a very brief and imperfect statement of an hypothesis, in the nature of the case so extensive, and difficult to grasp in all its bearings. To make it more intelligible, especially in relation to the conservative and salutary aspects of the material system, we will specify more in detail some of the hypothetical reasons for incarnation.

CHAPTER XII.

THE HYPOTHESIS.

HAVING exhibited the several theories held among spiritualists, and briefly suggested an amendment, we now proceed to offer some conjectural grounds or reasons for such supposed incarnation.

1. To render more definite mind's relationship to place. That a change of the sense or feeling of space is possible may be illustrated by the supposition that our eyes were microscopes. We should evidently be, so far as our sense was concerned, living in quite a different world from the present. So if our eyes were telescopes. Or, again, suppose our eyes so made that at will we could use them microscopically, or telescopically, or as we now do, — our space-world would be very much enlarged; but space would be none the less a necessary form of thought. All created spirits probably possess some body, more or less tenuons (psyche), and consequently some relationship to place; and they may possess powers of locomotion very swift, like the electric current, or rays of light. On the supposition that spirits have grown proud, this freedom may need abridgment. The evasive spirit is more restricted in space than previously. This would tend to enforce patience and humility.

2. To render more definite the feeling of time. Time and space are objective realities, or, perhaps we should say, necessary forms of thought; but the sense or feel-

ing of them may vary. We cannot admit the possibility of a mind, at least of any considerable degree of intelligence, without the sense of succession and extension. To assert that a rational mind can exist without space and time as necessary forms of thought, is to assert that a mind can think of a triangle without three sides; for the conception of a triangle (or any other geometrical figure) involves both space and time — space included by the sides, time in counting the sides. But minds may differ widely in the *sense* of time; and in order to a social state some common measure of time is needed. In the spirit-world, it is possible that the sense of duration is less marked, or less slow, or less regulated to a common standard, than here; though still it cannot be proved that spirits are not cognizant of the planetary motions, or provided with other modes of marking time. It may, however, be necessary, for remedial purposes perhaps, to magnify the sense of time for a while, — to render small portions of it more sensible, — so that what might *seem* to spirits a short time shall seem a long one, and so that spirits of unequal rates of succession of ideas by reason of unequal ardors of temper may be reduced nearly to a common rate or sense of succession.

In connection with this may be the making a record or history of individual and social developments, by means of a common graded rate, effected by "the stupendous horology" of the heavenly bodies.

3. Another design may be to increase or diminish sensation, the pleasurable or painful impressions of the material universe. We may conceive all spirits embodied, and more or less susceptible to external impressions. Those impressions, under certain conditions of moral character, may be, some of them too intense, or some too dull. It may be important to increase some,

and diminish others. "The organs of sense may be regarded as limitations of the general percipient faculty of the mind. The animal organization, with its medullary mass and nervous expansion, may be regarded, not merely as a means of sensation, but as a means of abatement, or as a sheath defending the percipient faculty of the mind from the too forcible impressions of the external world." "Perception is a circumscribed faculty." The body is "an envelope, or rough coating." *

The effect of this may be salutary as a check to the audacity of the untrammelled spirit. Ambition and self-esteem receive here an effective rebuff; and the general proportionment of minds together by constitution and temperament may operate to bring diverse spirits nearer to a common average of sensation, and hold them to certain laws, thus chastening their pride and evasive subtlety.

4. A fourth design may be to diminish or increase their power over matter. Some spirits may have too much, some too little. By incarnation they may be brought to an average. Some spirits may be proud on account of their easy control of material phenomena, and may need to be taught patience and submission, and *vice versa*. Such a decrease of power may be plausibly inferred "on the ground that the muscular force is now felt to be a power restrained,—a faculty equal to much more than is as yet permitted to it; and perhaps with not a few individuals the conscious mechanical energy is strictly analogous to that of a strong man handcuffed and fettered, who meditates what he will do when set at large. Is there not a latent, or half latent, instinct in the mind which speaks of a foregone liberty of ranging at will through space?" †

5. A fifth design may be to discipline the imagina-

* Physical Theory of Another Life. Isaac Taylor. † *Id.*

tion. Perhaps the imagination may be far more exuberant, more creative, more intense, in the spirit-world than here; and if spirits have become proud and self-pleasing, the wings may need clipping, and through the analogic forms of this wondrous world the imagination may be schooled to sobriety without being disabled or degraded. And if in any classes of spirits it had happened that imagination had become morbid in any way, so that the intenser expressions of divine beauty and moral perfection might be too painful (as sunlight to an inflamed eye), it might be desirable to protect or shield the spirit organ, so that while the heavens declared his glory, the mental eye might not be blinded by excess of light.

6. Another supposable reason for incarnation might be the clearer defining of individuality. The very existence of society seems to demand some power of privacy on the part of the individual, especially if the idea of contrast of character in the spirit realm be allowed; but it is conceivable that originally there was much less privacy than we are accustomed to. Spirits may have been more transparent to each other when love was young and confidence unimpaired. But if pride and ambition and self-will be supposed to have supervened, then the mastery of spirit over spirit might be too great, and if processes of reformation were to be instituted, it might be expedient to increase the privacy of the individual. "The body is not the bower or tent of the soul; it is its castle, from which all other minds may be excluded."* If we reflect, in this connection, upon the present construction of the material universe, we shall not wonder that profound thinkers have declared it "plainly marked with the intention to prohibit intercourse."†

* Physical Theory of Another Life, p. 40. † *Id.* p. 178.

If diphtheria or some malignant disorder shows itself in a large family of children, how quickly is that family scattered! — one here, another there, far and wide apart from the centre of contagion. So it may be God's family has been scattered from the contagion of pride.

7. A seventh reason may be to curb somewhat and discipline the plastic power. It is conceivable that spirits may have a power of assuming forms at will, by a quasi creative power over the elements, and that indulgence in this power in a self-pleasing spirit may have degenerated into a kind of masquerading habit, illusive, protean, deceitful, and so immoral. Now in the mysteries of incarnation mind may unconsciously build its own cell, like the chrysalis, and during life carry on automatically the vital processes. The child unborn may affect the mother more, sometimes, than the mother the child. The great law of heredity may be more complex than has been frequently imagined — involving something from the father, something from the mother, but something from the idiosyncrasy of the incoming spirit elaborating an organism suited to its own peculiarities. Thus the body may indeed be the soul's own house, being elaborated by it; and the vital principle, so much speculated upon, may be only the mind's creative power reduced within prescribed boundaries. Thus, as a man's house and grounds are in some degree a revelation of his character, so the body may be an expression of the spirit architect that builds, and repairs, and vitalizes, and clothes, and feeds it. The tricksy, masquerading spirit is thus taught that, if this world be a stage, life is not a mere farce or light comedy, but deep tragedy, demanding its profoundest energies.

8. Another supposable reason may be the temporary suspension of discouraging memories. It is easy to conceive that spirits may have entered on unfortunate

courses, and done deeds and formed habits they would wish to forget. In order to reformation, it may be necessary to suspend memory for a time and begin again. And there is much in the phenomena of memory in the present life to suggest such a conception. Memory in this life is "a partial exercise of a larger power, which, in adapting itself to the occasions of active life, forfeits or holds in abeyance its plenary prerogatives. . . . . The power which in its original capacity might fill a broad field does in fact only beat a narrow path, and gropes its way backward over the ground it has traversed." "Perhaps, if our memories of the past were not in some such manner abated and borne down, or obscured and obliterated, there would be in most minds certain vivid recollections which would continue to usurp the entire consciousness and so exclude the present." Hereafter the mind may "repossess itself of its entire past existence; however such full consciousness of the past might seem to exceed in kind as well as in amount our present partial and fallacious recollections, it would nevertheless be only the same power of the mind set free from physical obstructions and infirmities."

"Moreover, it is reasonable to believe that whereas, in the present state, the heterogeneous elements of mind and matter as consorted within the animal organization are held together as by force, and so as to occasion a vague feeling coming over us at times as if we were dreaming, or as if our very life were an enigma, ... on the contrary, when (hereafter) the corporeal nature has become nothing but the vehicle and instrument of the mind, ... that then there shall attend us an incomparably more vivid sense of reality, then we shall perceive things with a sharp intensity, and shall have a bright, vivid consciousness of life, such as shall make us think of the gone-by period of animal life as if indeed it had been a dream. It is so that a man may have groped his way, hour after hour, across a marshy level, veiled in fogs, till he comes to the foot of a steep, where after some arduous steps he gains a height, and not only overlooks the mists of the swamp, but beholds a wide illumined landscape, and the clear sky, and the sun!"* That wide illumined landscape may be our celestial fatherland; that sun is God.

9. Another supposable reason for incarnation would be to interrupt certain trains of association of ideas which might have become habitual and irresistible. If the condition of society in unseen realms be supposed to be mixed, if reformation be an object, it is conceivable that habits must be interrupted — that minds must be for a time brought back as near as possible to their starting-point, so as to take a new departure.

Now, there is a contrivance in the material system to set up and keep going trains of association, very various, ever fresh, and all of them (except as the system is abused) of a healthful or sanitary kind. The associations of infancy, of home, of maternal influence, of brothers and sisters and playmates, how sweet and sacred they are! The spirit must do great violence to nature to go downward to crime and ruin. The following beautiful passage from a well-known writer is in point: —

"But what was most valuable in my home education was unconscious infiltration from a good home atmosphere. This is an influence of incalculable importance a thousand times outweighing all the schools. It is that for which God established the family — the one single possible real and efficient means of well bringing up the young; and whatever shades of repression, misunderstanding, ungeniality, restraint, may have sometimes

* Physical Theory of Another Life, pp. 66–68, 152.

troubled me, still I constantly feel and fully know that that pure, calm, quiet, bright, loving, intelligent, refined atmosphere of my home silently and unconsciously penetrated and vivified all my being." *

10. Another supposable design is to reveal to the spirit its own weakness. It may be that spirits are unconscious of fatigue. Their corporeity, whatever it is, may be such as to need no sleep, no rest, no relaxation, no nutriment by food, and thus it is possible the sense of weakness and dependence may need to be increased. Under such a state of things it would be more difficult to effect a change of temper and spirit if pride had once crept in. Pride is very subtle, and self-knowledge very difficult. "Under such an economy the good might be better than they are here, and the bad might be worse. We may therefore readily surmise the reason of the actual constitution of human nature in this behalf as fitting mankind for a state wherein good and evil are in conflict, and the object is to give victory to the former." † The conditions of reformation, as consisting in meekness, gentleness, dependence, are more favorable in such a world as this than in any other.

11. Another supposable reason is to check pride of intellect, and enforce docility. It may be that in the spirit-world minds can do two things at once — or three, or four — without exhaustion. The mind possesses this ability here to some extent, but is proportionately fatigued by its exercise. In the other life, all the faculties may have marched abreast, in skirmish line, instead of, as here, going Indian-file.

The mind may have had exalted intuitional vigor, or insight into truth, without the need of study or painful process of deduction or induction. The mind may not

* Childhood: A Study. F. B. Perkins.

† Physical Theory, p. 78.

have prized knowledge so easily won. The appetite may have grown dainty. Self-conceit and elation may have wrought unhealth. The very truthfulness of the mind itself might be endangered through the quasi insanity of self-worship. Therefore confinement under a system where usually one thing must be learned at a time, and where at every step the pupil must believe what it is taught, might be necessary. Thus the spirit learns to value knowledge by working hard for it, and to be humble and teachable in view of its own limitations. Thus while perforce plodding our weary way, by induction and by logic, towards the heights, we yet feel the slumbering intuitional power stir within us; we beat against the bars of our cage like birds untamed; we have clairvoyant glimpses; we grow at times prophetic, enthusiastic, inspired; we dream; we rave. Then, "taking our happiest moments as a gauge of the original power of the mind, we feel that we need to be only a little more disengaged from organic imperfections," in order to seize the most remote abstract truths by intuition. If the question be, what might the mind achieve, thus set free, we are to judge from, not the average, but the maximum of its present powers. "The rarest and most admirable performances of the favored few who have far outdone their competitors are to be assumed as the measure of the abstract powers of the human intellect; and even this measure ought probably to be regarded as too low, as the most vigorous and clearest mind still labors under considerable disadvantages of a corporeal kind." *

12. Another supposable reason of incarnation may be to restrain, and discipline, and purify the power of expression. What the languages of the celestials may be, we know not. Possibly they may communicate directly,

* Physical Theory, p. 89.

without intermediate signs; or they may have a language of surpassing compass and power. But that mode of communicating thought and emotion may be the thing most injuriously affected by any spiritual disorder, like pride or self-conceit, or any other form of selfishness; and if we admit the conception of society in its higher and complex forms, — thrones, dominions, principalities, and powers, — if we admit the idea of conflict, of controversy, of combinations, and of wide-reaching disorders, — we may conceive that a reformation of the tongue might be most fundamental and most difficult. It may be true in other worlds, as in this, that the tongue "setteth on fire the course of nature," and that if a being, of any grade or race, offend not in word, that same is a perfect being, and able to bridle the whole spiritual body.

Now, it is remarkable that "language, while it facilitates in one sense our mental operations, does also in another *impede* and *limit* the play of our faculties, and especially of the highest of those faculties." Language, "a consequence of our corporeity," is the point of contact where mind and matter most intimately blend; "mind imparting to the modulations of sound several hundred thousand distinctions, which nothing less than the boundless refinements of its own conceptions could to such an extent multiply and fix," while matter imposes on mind its own limitations. The mind which invents and employs a machine is immeasurably superior to that machine; but of all machines, language is the most "elaborate in construction, copious in material, nice in its evolutions." "Yet this vast apparatus, compared to the wants of mind, is scanty, rude, inpliable, inexact, and poor; it is nothing better than a material machinery; but matter falls vastly short of being commensurable with mind." A language is "an operose and cumbrous engine;" but a mind that speaks four or five languages can shift from one to the other at will. This is "not a proof of great ability in the individual, but a sure indication of the immeasurable (not indeed infinite) inherent power of the human mind." *

Can we not all appreciate the immense chastening effect of such linguistic discipline on the hypothesis in hand, and the amazing enlargement and enhancement of the power of expression, when, purified, humbled, restored to health, the soul shall regain its own real language, its native tongue, commensurate with its immortal faculties?

13. Finally, another supposable purpose is to deprive the spirit for a time of an obsequious and perfect instrument of its will. Such we may conceive the spiritual body to have been. But the spirit being supposed more or less imbued with pride, may need to be for a time deprived of the unrestricted use of that body; not deprived of that body itself, but of its unrestricted use. We may understand that the spiritual body becomes incarnate as well as the spirit; that it is within us now, but in a sense bound and imprisoned. The animal body seems to us as though it had a will of its own. "The body serves the soul in order that the soul may more effectively serve the body; *as if a brute held a man in bondage* whom it compelled to lend his superior intelligence, and whom, for its own purposes, it would cheerfully carry and help at bidding." †

Such are some of the supposable reasons for the theory of incarnation. The facts of our present life, the facts of consciousness and of mental philosophy, are as if the soul were older than the body. In stating these points the author has done little else than follow in the track of Isaac Taylor, in his "Physical Theory of

* Physical Theory, pp. 93–104.

† *Id.* p. 106.

Another Life." He reasons from the facts of our present life to a future life ; we simply take his premises, point by point, and often in his own language reason to a possible past life. And it must be apparent to every one, that, revelation apart, the argument for a future existence must be just equal to that for a past. If the facts are as if the hypothesis of a future life were true, the facts are as if the hypothesis of a past life were true. And so striking is this, that our author, although professedly regarding this life as our initial state of existence, continually talks as if it were not, but as if the soul were held in captivity in a foreign land.

We may observe further, respecting this hypothesis, that it has a manifest bearing on the most interesting problems of the age. On education, because, as Socrates taught, all learning is a kind of reminiscence ; on physiology and psychology, and all kindred topics. Thus in dreams we may suppose, in addition to automatic cerebral action, a possible partial liberation of the spirit from the bonds of incarnation, and a recovery of imperfect glimpses or gleams from a former existence. In clairvoyance we may see a still further liberation of the spirit, and partial resumption of primeval modes of action. In the fact alluded to by physiologists, that visions are more characteristic of the earlier and later stages of life, we may see a revelation of that primeval power just circumscribed in infancy, and just about to be disenthralled in old age. In all the phenomena of mediumship we see possible traces of an imprisoned spirit corporeity more or less acted upon by forces from its own native state or sphere ; and finally, in death we see the falling down of the temporary tabernacle, and the unloosing of the spirit. If, then, we look at the actual facts of this material system, especially as actually applied under Christian auspices, and as we may easily conceive them applied when rescued from abuse and consecrated, what do we behold?

We find that there is, on the whole, a certain isolation of man from the direct control of spirits. They do invade; they do penetrate; but they are manifestly to a great degree as it were dyked out. This they confess, and all spiritualists admit. At the same time, the very highest classes of spirits, in virtue of their supremacy over matter, are able to manifest themselves so far as may be needful. Then, the natural relationships of the family, and of society, are adapted to teach meekness, benevolence, and obedience. The proud, evasive, subtle spirit is confined within its own house, or tent, or tabernacle, by the law of gravitation. It is weak; it is dependent; it is subjected to an amazing amount of tuition, the effects of which our hypothesis permits us to suppose permanent. To have controlled this mass of matter for threescore years and ten, — to have governed it by the golden rule, — to have thought through it, with prodigious outlay of vital and volitional spirit-dynamics, — may be found of itself to have chastened, and disciplined, and every way improved the character. Even those not reformed by it may not be as bad as they would have become otherwise.

The family state is especially adapted to the results contemplated by the hypothesis. While husband and wife are drawn together by the master passion, the relation is one requiring self-control and self-denial. The beauty of it is that it tends to teach these things. Love itself is teacher. The most exquisite felicity rewards every act of true nobleness and self-devotion; and for fifty years two spirits made one in this holy union are learning the elements of heaven. And the ingenuity of the contrivance! — the exquisite moral mechanism of it! It is the masterpiece of Infinite skill.

Then the parental relation. The father and mother are, by analogy, to their children what God is to his children. Thus, in an additional and impressive sense, man is made in God's image, not merely, as all rational spirits must be, by reason, affection, and will, but by being placed in a quasi creative headship of a household or kingdom. Thus the parent is being taught by experience to appreciate the emotions and principles of God, and how the behavior of his creatures must affect Him. He is also taught — and by a long, long schooling of years — the necessity of self-control, self-government, self-denial, condescension, in order to control children. All the qualities which we may suppose by the hypothesis selfish spirits were deficient in, are here taught, and taught by love. Parental feeling is so sweet, the beauty of childhood so winning, the joy of doing right so heavenly, that parents are won to better things by almost irresistible motives.* And the infant all the while, supposing father and mother to carry out the divine idea, in worshipping them is indirectly worshipping God. Its docility, its faith, its petitions, its adoring love, its grand pride in father and mother, are all the very elements of the feeling due to God, and easily transferred to him as

* "The rearing of offspring affords the highest discipline for the faculties. The parental instinct is everywhere that which calls out the energies most persistently, and in the greatest degree exercises the intelligence. . . . . Parenthood produces a mental exaltation not otherwise producible. . . . . Men who were random grow steady when they have children to provide for; and vain, thoughtless girls, becoming mothers, begin to show higher feelings, and capacities that were not before drawn out. In both there is a daily discipline in unselfishness, in industry, in foresight. The parental relation strengthens from hour to hour the habit of postponing immediate ease and egoistic pleasure to the altruistic pleasure obtained by furthering the welfare of offspring. There is a frequent subordination of the claims of self to the claims of fellow-beings; and by no other agency can the practice of this subordination be so effectually secured." — H. Spencer's *Studies of Sociology*, p. 371.

the powers expand, and He is made known as the true father of all.

Then come society, the state, the church, agriculture, commerce, finance, science, art, — in all which, such is the analogy between the material system and the larger moral universe, man is indirectly studying the problems of eternal empire, and developing quasi creative faculties proper to the heir of God and joint-heir with Christ.

That such a system could be abused is manifest. The hypothesis is such that it not only could be, it would be, it must be, as certainly as the gallant ship will be abused by the tempest which it yet outrides. That the abuses of such a system would naturally be precisely those abuses which we actually see in the history of this world, it is easy to show. On no other hypothesis can it be so readily shown why the majority of the race, antipodes in place as in character, and philosophy, and system, should agree in a dogma so painful as transmigration. On no other hypothesis can the universal prevalence of sacrifice, of oracles, of spirit-manifestations, of hero-worship, of nature-personification, be so consistently explained. No other hypothesis comports so well with what we may call the experimental nomenclature of the Bible, the phraseology of religious experience.

Religion — a rebinding of the soul to God.

Redeemr— to buy back into liberty.

Restore — to replace a lost treasure in the treasury; a lost sheep in the fold; a diseased body in health.

Renew — to make over an old thing, as it was when first made.

Return — to come back again to one's place.

Reconcile — to reunite alienated hearts in their old affection.

Revive — to bring to life again, life being the necessary logical antecedent of death.

Regeneration — a second natural birth by reincarnation; and a second spiritual birth into the original celestial state and character.

Resurrection — a term perfectly synonymous with the preceding, in its full extent.

Repentance — recommencing to do right. Only a being once holy can repent.

Reform — bring back into the form which was first.

Remember God — implies that men have known him once, but have forgotten him.

Restitution of all things — literally, to set things up as they were before they fell down.

To awake — to be roused out of sleep. Nobody can be "asleep" who has not first been "awake."

To wash, cleanse, purify — imply the removal of contracted defilement.

Atonement — the Hebrew word is 'cover,' implying a state of nakedness and exposure which is to be covered.

Justification — every creature is presumed innocent till proven guilty. To justify is to restore one to his original good standing in law, either by disproving the charge, by pardon, or by execution of penalty.

There is an abundance of experimental terminology in Scripture which we cannot particularly examine. We are wanderers, exiles, orphans, lost sheep, astray on the mountains in a dark and stormy day; we are foreigners; we are mariners unmooring for the home voyage. Everywhere the same general conception: God is our father, heaven our home. We seek fatherland (πατρίδα). Jerusalem above is mother of us all. There the old family mansion is pictured as standing; there is the dear old family record, our names in Father's handwriting, not blotted out yet by all our sins. We have forgotten home, but home has not forgotten us. Every name is where Affection inscribed it the day we were born. There is joy there when one sinner repents, —

> "And angels in their songs rejoice,
> And say, 'Behold he prays!'"

We are asleep, and dreaming; we are not ourselves; we are delirious; we wander. But we shall come to ourselves; we shall awake; we shall remember; it will all come back to us. Perhaps it will not seem so very, very long as it looks to us now. It may seem as though a thousand years were but as a watch in the night. We shall remember all that went before; we shall remember all of our earth-life that we wish to remember. Our sins and our crimes God will enable us to forget; He will blot them out forever. And, O how thankful shall we be to that Love that has patiently waited and expected through the long tragedy of ages, and that says, "It is meet that we should rejoice, for this my son was dead, but is alive again, and was lost, and is found."

We commend this hypothesis, then, to the consideration of spiritualists, as one already in part taught by an influential section of their own body, and as largely sanctioned, as to its main feature of pre-existence, by the suffrages of the masses of mankind in all ages, and by some of the sweetest poets (those truest seers and singers) of the world, teaching us that—

> "Our birth is but a sleep and a forgetting;
> The soul that rises with us, our life's star,
> Hath had elsewhere its setting,
> And cometh from afar:
> Not in entire forgetfulness,
> And not in utter nakedness,
> But trailing clouds of glory, do we come
> From God, who is our home."

CHAPTER XIII.

PRIMEVAL SPIRITUALISM.

IF now we have succeeded, in any measure, in leading our spiritualist readers to regard patiently our hypothesis, we invite their attention to some of its prominent historical bearings.

If the Eden tableau was exhibited, as we have supposed, at a great historical crisis, either at the introduction of the incarnate race, or at the introduction of a late and improved variety, or family of the race, then it would be natural to expect some institution of religious worship at the threshold.

This, in common with many eminent expositors, we do find in the simple announcement: "And he placed at the east of the garden of Eden, cherubim, and a flaming sword, which turned every way to keep the way of the tree of life." * Now, we wish to show, that, although from the extreme conciseness of the narrative the cursory reader might not be aware of the fact, yet we have here a record of the institution of a system of religious worship.

The Israelites were familiar with statues of complex animal forms, which were stationed at the gates of Oriental temples. Moses himself had superintended their construction for the tabernacle, and mentions them briefly as though perfectly well known.

* Gen. iii. 24.

The following is the command given to Moses in reference to their construction: "And thou shalt make two cherubim of gold, of beaten work shalt thou make them, out of the two ends of the mercy-seat. . . . And the cherubim shall stretch forth their wings on high, covering the mercy-seat with their wings, and their faces shall look one to another; toward the mercy-seat shall the faces of the cherubim be. . . . And there I will meet with thee, and commune with thee, from above the mercy-seat, from between the two cherubim which are upon the ark of the testimony, of all things which I will give thee in commandment." * This mercy-seat, or golden cover of the ark in which was deposited the ten commandments, or law of love, was simply the throne of God in Israel. And when the tabernacle was erected, we read: "Then a cloud covered the tent of the congregation, and the glory of the Lord filled the tabernacle. And Moses was not able to enter into the tent of the congregation, because the cloud abode thereon, and the glory of the Lord filled the tabernacle." †

The radiating point from whence this intense lustre, this glory proceeded, we conceive to have been from over the mercy-seat, between the cherubim. We can imagine a lambent flame, so bright, so dazzling, so penetrating in its effulgence that it transfigured, as it were, the whole structure, causing it to shine and glow afar. "For the cloud of the Lord was on the tabernacle by day, and fire was on it by night, in the sight of all the house of Israel throughout all their journey." Now, if we conceive of this intense illumination from within, as emitting flashes of light, as coruscating, streaming afar with broad beams or blades of splendor, we can conceive what impression the Israelites might receive from the words, "a flaming sword that turned every way." And

* Exod. xxv. 18–22.

† Ex. xl. 34.

we may also conceive what they would understand by such an expression as "he tabernacled at the east of the garden of Eden cherubim." They would understand he enshrined the cherubim in a tabernacle, with the dazzling glory of the Lord shining forth on all sides, from the mercy-seat between the cherubim.

Now this is precisely the expression Moses does in fact use. "He tabernacled the cherubim at the east of the garden of Eden." Says Kitto: "The word rendered by our translators 'placed,' signifies, properly, 'to place in a tabernacle,' an expression which, viewed in connection with some incidents in the after history of the primeval family,* seems a conclusive establishment of the opinion that this was a local tabernacle in which the symbols of the divine presence were manifested."

The brevity of the statement implies a general familiarity with the objects mentioned. Complex figures were so common, and so constantly associated with temples, that the idea of any explanation being needful could not arise. Moses had just erected "a tabernacle." He had just placed cherubim in it; and if he incorporated in his narrative extracts from ancient documents, which he found in Egyptian archives, documents handed down, possibly, from before the flood, from a time when that primeval tabernacle might be yet standing, the significance of such a picture-word as "tabernacled" to his own mind, and to the minds of the Israelites, becomes strikingly manifest.

Hence, in reading the narrative, the Israelites would naturally understand that this was done, substantially, for the same general purposes aimed at in their own tabernacle system. For example, their own tabernacle, with its cherubic mercy-seat, was an oracle. The apostle mentions it as one great advantage pos-

* Gen. iv. 14–16.

sessed by Israel over other nations, that "unto them were committed the oracles of God." * And Stephen says they "received the lively oracles." † This is the use they actually saw made of their own tabernacle. "And when Moses was gone into the tabernacle of the congregation to speak with him (Jehovah), then he heard the voice of one speaking unto him from off the mercy-seat that was upon the ark of the testimony, from between the two cherubim." ‡ Unto this oracle all matters of controversy were to be referred, as to a supreme court of last appeal. "If there arise a matter too hard for thee in judgment, between blood and blood, plea and plea, stroke and stroke, then thou shalt get thee up unto the place that the Lord thy God shall choose; . . . and shalt come unto the priests and inquire; . . . and the man that will not hearken unto the priest that standeth to minister there before Jehovah thy God, . . . even that man shall die." § Naturally, the Israelites, in reading of a cherubic tabernacle at Eden's gate, and of "going out from the presence of the Lord," ‖ would think of that as an oracle of the same kind.

In the temple of Solomon we find the holy of holies called by this name: "the oracle he prepared within, to set there the ark of the covenant of the Lord." ¶ It was an apartment about thirty feet in length, breadth, and height, overlaid with pure gold; "and they stretched forth the wings of the cherubim so that the wing of the one touched the one wall, and the wing of the other touched the other wall, and their wings touched one another in the midst." On the doors and walls there were carved and on the hangings embroidered cherubim, and palm-trees, and flowers. Into this oracle was brought the original ark made by Moses, and placed

* Rom. iii. 2. † Acts vii. 38. ‡ Num. vii. 89.
§ Deut. xvii. ‖ Gen. iv. 16. ¶ 1 Kings vi. 19.

under the wings of the cherubim. Here, then, there were two sets of cherubic figures: those originally made of beaten gold, of one piece with the cover of the ark; the others, of larger size, made of olive wood overlaid with gold, on high above the ark. This, perhaps, may account for the fact that Isaiah seems to see seraphim above the ark; * — the same objective emblems being reproduced in vision, but with certain modifications, and intensifications, proper to the ecstatic state. The seraphim thus would be simply the larger and loftier pair of cherubim, — two different names for substantially the same symbol.

In his dedicatory prayer, Solomon indicates in a most impressive and beautiful manner the design of this edifice; and among other things, that it is for all nations, — "that all people of the earth may know thy name and fear thee, as doth thy people Israel." So Christ afterwards said, It is written "my house shall be called a house of prayer for all nations." Now, at the close of this sublime dedicatory prayer, "the glory of the Lord filled the house, and the priests could not enter into the house of the Lord because the glory of the Lord had filled the Lord's house."

If now we understand that the central point of illumination was as before that lambent flame above the mercy-seat, and that the whole temple was, as it were, interpenetrated, transfigured with its effulgence, we can conceive what Israelites would understand by the brief statement, "he tabernacled cherubim and the flaming sword at the gates of Paradise." And the same element of catholicity might suggest itself to their minds, that that was designed as a place of prayer for all nations; that that was a "lively oracle," where men might seek responses from the living God. Hence Jehovah was de-

* Isa. vi.

scribed as "The Lord of Hosts, that dwelleth between the cherubim." * And in devotional exercises this expression became common: "O thou that dwellest between the cherubim, shine forth." † "The Lord reigneth, let the people tremble: he sitteth between the cherubim, let the earth be moved." ‡ "O Lord God of Israel, which dwellest between the cherubim, thou art the God of all the kingdoms of the earth." §

Hence this inner sanctuary, or oracle, was called "holy of holies," and is explained to be a type of Heaven.‖ Hence the ark was God's throne or mercy-seat; Jerusalem was styled the holy city, or city of the great king; and God was said to place his name there, to dwell there, and as it were to make it his home, — "the place of my rest." The entire Hebrew ritual was based on this idea of a divine home, or house of the Lord, and that from that centre of love, and domestic attraction, sin was the only excluding power. The Lord could not thus intimately dwell among men, unless they repented of and confessed their sins, and obtained forgiveness. This was the design of all the sacrifices and ceremonial purifications. Every sacrifice was a confession of sin, and a covenant with a forgiving God. Well then might Jewish writers say that the cherubim were "the foundation, root, heart, and marrow of the whole Levitical dispensation." Would it not be inevitable, then, that the Hebrew mind, in reading that brief sentence, "he tabernacled cherubim and a flaming sword," should receive the impression that the Lord instituted a system of worship, in some respects at least like their own, especially when the historian immediately speaks of Cain and Abel bringing their offerings?

Thus far we have found the cherubim described as

* 1 Sam. iv. 4. † Ps. lxxx. 1. ‡ Ps. xcix. 1.
§ 2 Kings xix. 15. ‖ Heb. ix.

objects formed by man. There are three cases in which they are described as seen in vision, namely, in Isaiah,* in the opening chapters of Ezekiel, and in the Apocalypse.

These visionary figures are still emblematic, as really so as those made of beaten gold. The difference is, that being exhibited in vision, the representation is more impressively majestic and mysterious. They burn, they glow, they sparkle, they are covered with eyes; there are awful wheels; there are explosions as of thunder; the rushing of their wings is as the noise of a host; the whole pageant seems alive; it moves up or down, this way or that, like lightning. Two pairs of wings only are visible when the throne is in motion, three when it is at rest. Manifestly, however, it is one and the same emblem with additional elements suggestive of intensity of life and power. No such shapes exist. It is by analogy we are to interpret them. By analogy they denote, not individuals, but certain organizations in the spirit-world intimately connected with the divine administration. Further than this we cannot go, consistently with the scope of our present work.

We merely observe, that it is not necessary to suppose that an Israelite of Moses' time, or of the time of Samuel, or of the age of David and Solomon, in reading the passage in Genesis, "he tabernacled cherubim," would naturally think of such forms as Isaiah, Ezekiel, and John describe, for those descriptions were not then extant; but they might have conceived of forms such as Moses and Solomon made. Whether the forms actually enshrined in the Eden tabernacle were of human construction, or a kind of spirit materialization, we cannot decide.

The usual conception, probably, of the casual reader,

* Isa. vi.

at the present day, is purely conventional, — that the cherubim were angels stationed in broad daylight, with blazing swords in hand, to keep Adam and Eve from getting back into the garden. This is not the idea Moses must necessarily have meant to convey. If a later Jewish writer, of the age of Solomon, had said, "Moses tabernacled the cherubim at Sinai," every child in Israel would know what he meant. So every child in Israel to-day can see that Moses may have meant substantially the same thing as occurring in Eden, namely, that God erected a house of worship, and instituted a cherubic oracle, and appointed sacrifices and other rites of confession of sin and worship. There was indeed the idea of temporary exclusion from the tree of life, but inseparable from it the idea of a return to that tree. To keep the way of the tree of life, was not to keep it shut forever, but for the present, while strongly suggesting its being hereafter opened again. It was to keep it from being shut forever. The word implies, to watch, to guard, as if a treasure; to keep safe, to protect, to preserve, to retain, reserve, &c. And if we suppose that to Adam, the first priest and patriarch of this Eden tabernacle, some explanation was given of these emblems, and by him handed down, we can see how in one most impressive sense that tabernacle did "keep the way of the tree of life" from total oblivion, in the traditions and sacred rites of all ages and all nations, and how that sanctuary and that ritual was the original religion, from which, by corruption on the one hand, and additional revelation on the other, have flowed all subsequent religions of the great historic races.

The farther back we go in the ages, and the nearer we approach the most primitive times, the more we find certain grand features impressed on the monuments of the nations. Their temples are often on high places, connected with graves and gardens, and sacred fountains and streams; they have holy places and most holy places; they have in many instances various constructions resembling a serpent and a sacred tree; and above all, they have complex images, more or less corresponding to the cherubic forms, and often of colossal size, impressive even to sublimity, at the gate-ways of their sacred enclosures.

Moses lived on the Nile. That imposing Egyptian system, claiming, perhaps, to be the original Eden system, was before his eyes every day. He did not need a page to describe what he meant. One picture-word was enough. The Eden tabernacle stood before his mind's eye, and stands before ours, filled with the glory of the Lord, all ablaze with His majesty, transfigured as it were, and its beams of splendor shooting out on every side. It was the presence of the Lord, — "a house of prayer for all nations." We appeal to all true spiritualists to admit this beautiful conception. If you believe in the manifestation of higher powers now, you can believe in it then. If it is called for now, when the world is so advanced in science and knowledge, it was then, when civilization was less mature. If to you the responses of your household circle seem precious, if the "materialized" forms of the departed are in your view wonderful and admirable, surely the responses of this first family oracle, and the splendors of a manifestation essentially divine, will seem to you far more glorious!

CHAPTER XIV.

THE DAWN OF PROPHECY.

IN nature we behold the "struggle for existence" everywhere going on; certain species being gradually killed out, and certain other species surviving. Geology shows that this has been the case in all ages. The world is, and always has been, in both vegetable and animal kingdoms, in air, earth, and sea, one wide battlefield.

Into this battlefield, under these analogies, the sacred historian in Genesis ushers new combatants. Man, the latest, highest, noblest species, appears, in conflict with a serpent, or dragon enemy,—and the survival of the fittest is again to be exemplified as the result of age-long development in antagonism. As if to lend intensity to the conception, a dramatic scene is improvised. The stage a terrestrial paradise, fitted up with most significant scenery; and after a vivid tableau vivant, the Creator of the whole system appears upon the stage to announce in few words the plot, or plan of the coming drama of ages, in a declaration of war. He who has been depicted with matchless brevity as re-creating the heavens and the earth, and all races therein, plants and animals in all their varieties, now stands forth as if to declare, "I have made this world to be a battlefield," and here shall the struggle for existence between man, and orders older but less worthy of survival than he, be fought out to its conclusion. "I will put enmity between thee (the serpent) and the woman, and between thy seed and her seed; thou shalt bruise his heel, he shall bruise thy head."

Sixty centuries have rolled away since that announcement. How has human history unfolded? Has it been in keeping with material analogies, and with this impressive announcement? Has not the human race had a dim impression of an unfriendly agency in the invisible realm? And do we not, as we look back, perceive that there has been a war upon man? And is it not a striking fact that the powers unfriendly to man have struck at man through woman? There may have been some attempts, in ethnic religions, to elevate and ennoble woman, but in general she has been degraded. In some systems it has been taught that woman has no soul. In most cases, she has been made a sensual toy, or a servile drudge. Classic civilization, however beautiful in some of its conceptions, and however we may give it credit for trying to honor woman, never truly and permanently ennobled her. Knight-errantry, with all its chivalrous extravagance, failed to think honorably of woman.

Modern civilization has too often insulted woman, in the act of crowning her queen of fashion and goddess of love. Is there no latent hostility to woman in the constant caricature of her whole being by the laws of fashion? What is woman, according to the teachings of the Parisian demi-monde, who must tell Christendom how the wives and daughters of Israel ought to behave? How does Fashion paint her portrait? She too often disfigures the beauty of face and form, injures the health, poisons the complexion, and makes her dress such that each generation appears ridiculous to the next. In all time the arrow aimed at man's well-being has transfixed woman's heart.

The necessary consequence of this has been the apparent war on childhood. Degraded as the human race may have become, the parental instinct would seem to be strongest of all, and to have retained most of its original sacredness. Yet in spite of maternal fondness, a strange invisible power has blighted the fair blossoms, so that half the race die in infancy. Some cast wailing into the fires of Moloch, some thrown to the crocodiles of the Ganges, some exposed on the hills of classic Greece, some slain in war, some slain in the womb, and some gasping out their sickly lives in countless forms of malady and distress. Half the race dying in infancy; and those that live, do they not sometimes live in spite of the education they receive? There are localities under Christian auspices where childhood is happy, where education is a little like what it should be; yet those localities are but a small part of the whole globe, and even at the best, education is imperfect. The best parent feels most acutely his own deficiencies in this respect. But take the world through, savage, barbarous, half-civilized, and civilized, and through what a sad and painful ordeal do children come up into life! And if you look at this with the eye of a philosopher, you will see a method in the madness, a plan underlying the age-long campaign, as if a skilful general were striking at the race in its weakest point, — the very secret of the art of war, — by striking at woman and her seed.

And when in the fullness of time there appeared on earth that wonderful child Jesus, in whom humanity was to recognize its ideal, and who constantly spoke of himself as the Son of Man, that promised seed around whom the age-long conflict must revolve in closer and closer circles, do we not see tokens of invisible attention fixed upon him — portentous — malign? Is there not a power behind the scenes striking at him from first to last?

Witness the massacre of the innocents by Herod, the temptation in the wilderness, the agony in the garden, the scenes of Calvary, — do we not see in all this the enmity against the woman and her seed brought to a focus upon the person of that Just One? And ever since, that same hostility has manifested itself, not only against woman, the family, and childhood, but against the larger family formed among believing households, a few believers associating for mutual help and for worship, a little circle of love, a church. Wherever there is one that is really happy and heavenly, a home of the soul, how soon does something strike at it, and leave it bruised and bleeding! Or else, by outward ease and prosperity she is beguiled, deceived, and changed into an organization of corruption and oppression. Thus in all ages and world-empires there has been a false and persecuting Church, drunk with the blood of saints, represented under the form of a woman riding upon a wild beast, and on her forehead, "Mystery, Babylon the great Mother of Harlots, and abominations of the earth." And in her, that is in the city of spiritual confusion and despotism, "was found the blood of prophets and of saints, and of all that were slain upon the earth." As much as to say, the corrupt hierarchies of Egypt, Babylon, Persia, Greece, Rome, and all great world-empires, are substantially one; certain general principles characterize them all; they are modulations of one sombre theme, and in connection with civil despotism have been the instruments of moral war against the true woman and her seed. So has been fulfilled, and so is fulfilling to-day before our eyes, one part of the primeval declaration of war.

How, then, does history exhibit the other side of the great contest? One thing we see, that woman was ennobled, and marriage sanctified from the beginning, by the patriarchal Jewish, and Christian economies. Polygamy indeed crept in, but in violation of law. "From the beginning it was not so," said Jesus. De Coulanges, in "The Ancient City," shows how in the most ancient Aryan races marriage was a sacred institution created by religion. The Hebrew law was express: "Thy king shall not multiply wives unto himself." The general tendency of the Mosaic legislation was to protect, refine, and ennoble woman and the family; and notwithstanding the repeated apostasies and ultimate rejection of the nation, such has been the effect of the system. The Hebrew wife and mother, and home, is for purity and sanctity, above the average of the nations in the midst of which that remarkable race is captive.

One cause of this has been the constant and scientific use of the nomenclature of the marriage covenant to represent by analogy the relationship between the Lord and his people. The nation is now "the virgin daughter of Israel" espoused to the Lord; and now, a bride, a wife, a mother. "Thy Maker is thy husband." So constant and copious a usage must have had an ennobling effect upon the ideas and associations of the people. Woman, wife, mother, daughter, father, son, the family, the house or home, all were imbued with dignity and sacredness by this constant divine impersonation. And this is brought to a climax in the scenes of the incarnation. In a world where every thought connected with marriage had been extensively corrupted, where ascetic ideas were widely prevalent, teaching the impurity of matter, and defiling the mind by the notion that the sexual relation was in itself sinful, — in such a world, a virgin daughter of Israel, a betrothed bride, becomes, without prejudice to her nuptial vows, a mother by the power of the Holy Spirit. "The Holy Ghost shall come upon thee, and the power of the highest shall overshadow thee, therefore, that holy thing that shall be born of thee, shall be called the Son of God." The tendency of this to ennoble woman and maternity has been incalculable. And in spite of the corruptions and apostasies of the era following, it has had its effect. This has been one marked feature of the defensive part of the war;—shielding woman and her seed against the attack, and nourishing her even when chased by the dragon into the wilderness for twelve hundred and sixty years. Side by side with this defensive war there have been significant premonitions of a final offensive campaign.

Clarence King, in his late address before the Sheffield Scientific School, shows that the line of geologic science lies midway between Catastrophism and Evolution, or gradualism. Cuvier and the old geologists went to one extreme: all past changes in earth's strata had been sudden and violent—catastrophic. Lyell and modern geologists have gone to an opposite extreme: no sudden and violent crises; no convulsions, cataclysms, upheavals; all strata formed slowly as we now see them in process of gradual deposition, through almost infinite periods. In a masterly way Mr. King shows from the rocky records of this continent, that the truth lies between. There have been long ages of gradual formation, and there have been crises of swift and violent activity.

So in what we may term the Moral Geology of the past. Christ compares it to a field tilled and sown and then apparently forgotten; until in time of harvest suddenly the sickle is thrust in.

The field was tilled and sown when the Lord tabernacled the cherubim at the gates of Eden. There is condensed in four or five words the church history of an epoch. He set up a ritual of worship. Then, through the antediluvian period things were left apparently to gradualism, until the harvest of iniquity ripened, and the earth was filled with violence, when suddenly there was a rush of waters and an ark on the face of the deep.

That was an effective stroke of moral military catastrophism, dealt at the head of the dragon enemy. Again the field was tilled and sown, and another long interval of seeming neglect, until idolatry became universal, but one family being left uncontaminated. From that family Abraham is called; one reason being given, "I know him that he will command his children, and his household after him, to keep the way of the Lord." That is, in his line, family government and training would retain some vitality.

How corrupt the rest of the world had become, is shown in Sodom; and in the fate of the Cities of the Plain we have another instance of moral catastrophism. "The Lord rained fire and brimstone upon Sodom and Gomorrah, and the smoke of the cities went up as the smoke of a great furnace." And the apostle says those doomed cities were set forth an ensample, an emblematic specimen. To the eye of imagination those fires are ever falling, and the smoke rising up to heaven.

Then follows another long period of gradualism, and apparent neglect, until, at the Exodus, moral catastrophism again bursts upon us. We see Israel (the woman and her seed), with loins girt, staff in hand, at midnight, eating the paschal lamb, in houses every one marked with blood on the door-posts, and the angel of the Lord abroad in the land passing over those houses, and in every Egyptian house the first-born dead!

The whole period of the life of Moses and Joshua was catastrophic, a period of what is called supernaturalism, (which on the divine plane of thought is eminently natural,) when a shock was given to the world, and (as has been said of Waterloo) the universe changed front.

This alternation of gradualism and catastrophism was repeated all through the era of the Judges. We see it exemplified, from time to time, in the history of the great world-empires, down to the time of Christ. Now, Jerusalem herself, after a long period of gradualism, is the field overgrown, and apparently neglected. Jerusalem becomes herself the corrupt persecuting power. Messiah is slain; the Church persecuted, and scattered, until suddenly, the city is besieged by Titus, destroyed with unexampled horrors, and Israel led away captive into all nations.

There was a mighty blow at the dragon power. The teachings, life, death, resurrection, and ascension of Christ, all together, were an immense development of moral catastrophism. Great as the effect has been in this world, the effect in worlds unseen was greater. Its greatest effect in this world is yet future. Its first sublimest effect was in realms unseen, the higher spheres of celestial existence. The dragon was vanquished and cast down, and we hear the shout of victory pealing through the empyrean, "Rejoice ye heavens and ye that dwell in them; for the Accuser of our brethren is cast down, that accused them day and night before God!" This was a tremendous blow at the head of the dragon.

The defeated powers, expelled from other realms, retreat upon this world, which thus becomes, not merely a battle-ground, but the battle-ground on which is to come the shock of battle of the great day of God Almighty.

Then follows another long period of gradualism, the woman and her seed flying to the Wilderness, — and the great apostasy running its course. God seems to sleep. The ages are dark. The world seems given over to civil and ecclesiastical despotism. But the seals are opening, the trumpets sounding, and the vials being poured out, till a period of catastrophism arrives more tremendous than all preceding. The dragon is bound, shut up in the abyss, and the atmosphere of human thought is purified. Here the sublime epic pauses, and again we are surrounded by the emblems of Eden, the tree, and river of life, the paradise of God; and in the midst of the garden, on the banks of the river, a marriage festival is celebrated. "The marriage of the Lamb hath come, and his bride hath made herself ready."

There is a new heavens and a new earth, because the material system being now understood in its pure and purifying influences, and spiritual analogies, it is to man as new as if he had never seen it. Till now it has been abused by hostile powers of air. Now for the first time it is used by those in the unseen for whom it was made, and by them with infinite skill applied to the renovation of the nations. The family state is new; wedded love is new; maternity new; childhood new; there is no more dragon enmity against the woman and her seed; woman has no wrongs, infancy no tears; therefore man is redeemed. God wipes away all tears. And he that sits upon the throne says, Behold I make all things new. And yet it is the very same world; the same solid ground; the same bright sky; the same continents; the same dear familiar scenes; — new, because perfected, idealized. New, because all husbands are loving, all wives faithful, all parents in the image of God to their children, and children in loving them love God. New, because sickness, disease, and death disappear, earth overflows with populations of more than antediluvian longevity, and generations of children rise more beautiful than painter dreamed, to be trained for heaven, and translated without tasting death. Then will science, art, literature, and wealth be stimulated and vitalized, and consecrated, and progress accelerated beyond all we can now imagine. And far beyond all this, the climax, when man, the Race Elect, purified and ennobled by suffering, shall be enthroned in the dominion over the Moral Universe, the interrupted work of creation be resumed, race after race spring into being, forever and ever.

CHAPTER XV.

THE TITANS.

WITH this brief glance at the actual outline of earthly history, we return to attempt an examination of some of the principal crises of development. Our idea of human history is, that it is from beginning to end a sublime process of spiritual manifestation. And however our view may be shut within "the flaming walls of this life," we recognize the fact that the controlling forces lie largely without those walls, even as the forces that control the tides of ocean are not mundane forces, and as the changes of seasons, and the phenomena of growth and reproduction, are controlled by forces exerted millions of miles away. It has been suggested that meteorological changes may depend upon a universally diffused atmospheric medium, so that the change of a barometer here may be but the echo, as it were, or vibration of a change in Sirius, and in every other star in the universe.

True, the innate forces of individual souls, and of families, and races, are immense. The mainspring coiled up in every human breast is tough, elastic, and of prodigious strength of recoil. So also are the forces of environment great, from climate, food, social organization, and the many influences represented in that single word, education. We do not lose sight of this, nor undervalue it in studying the problems of history; but while individuals and nations have strong idiosyncrasies, and while social forces originating here are potent, there are spiritual forces of great power exerted upon individuals and nations by intelligences unseen, — and these are on the great scale the grand historic forces; so that while men are pieces and pawns on the chessboard, the game is played from behind the veil.

We have spoken of the cherubic tabernacle system instituted at the gates of Paradise. The design of that system was "to keep the way of the tree of life," to preserve the knowledge of man's celestial origin, his temporary exile, and his final restoration, and to furnish him in the meantime with an oracle, or means of reliable intercourse with the spirit-world from which he was an exile, at the same time fencing out all unfriendly spirits as far as practicable. It was necessary to do this so as to interrupt trains of association, arrest the formation of selfish habits, suspend discouraging memories, provide the soul with a castle of privacy, the body, — place it in a world of material analogies of spiritual truth, of immense stimulating power, — and in family and social relations, all of them teaching the first principles of self-denial and humility, thus giving the young prodigal a chance to take a new departure.

Yet, lest he should slumber too deeply in animalism, it was wise to reveal to faith, though not to memory, the fact of his lofty origin, and his predestined return; to kindle a glorious beacon-fire at the threshold of the emblematic paradise to light his pilgrimage through the night-watches of time. Thus the Lord virtually says to him, "Hear what the heavens are telling of me, by day and by night; listen to my voice in the soul; and if these do not suffice, if you are in doubt and need an infallible teacher, here in this tabernacle you may call, and I will answer. All other teachers, visible or invisible, are fallible, and may mislead; here is absolute truth and certainty. Me you can trust in the last resort, and me only."

It is from this source that we conceive all the varied religions of the principal historic nations have sprung; and many of the beautiful traits of classic mythology are but faint gleams of that cherubic glory, — alas, how faint! — and overshaded by clouds of fable, and nature-personification, and legendary lore. Yet it did keep alive all over the world some dim notions of an original righteousness, of a golden age now lost, but destined to return. All churches to-day, — Roman, Greek, Nestorian, Armenian, Protestant, — though they have lamentably sunk the antetype in the type, do affirm, while they cannot explain, the sublime truth of man's original righteousness (without which our views of sin inevitably become superficial), so that the cherubic tabernacle did keep, even for us, the way of the tree of life.

Now, by our hypothesis we are constrained to form some conception of the motives influencing the cosmocratic powers in their treatment of the material system; some conception of the policy they adopted and why they adopted it; and its possible relation to the policy of organized bodies of spirits friendly to man; and how these interacted, and how far they modified each other.

In addition to the intrinsic difficulty of such a task, all spiritualists will see at a glance, that we pursue it under some special difficulties of considerable delicacy, being exposed, as it were, to a cross-fire of criticism on the one hand from scientific schools, on the other from the various schools of philosophy and religion. To neither would we wish needlessly to expose ourselves. Yet, reasoning as we do with spiritualists on premises held by us and them in common, (and how else can reasoning be carried on except on common grounds?) we must shape our arguments accordingly, and not resort to some lines that might be legitimate if we were dealing directly with either of the above-mentioned classes of thinkers.

All spiritualists will readily see that in attempting to conceive of the plans and motives of celestial orders however hostile, we must try to look at things from their point of view, as if not abstractly right, at least justifiable on some grounds of expediency. Spiritualists do not admit the conception of an unmixed or absolute malignity, or wickedness; they conceive of sinful passions and habits as being substantially the same in that world as in this. Hence they can easily conceive of such a thing as a hostility to the divine plan, which should be as it were latent, and unconscious, as in this life selfish people are enemies to God's benevolent plans, often without being aware of the fact. It will not be difficult for spiritualists to conceive of leading intelligences being actuated by a self-righteous spirit, by ambition, by pride, by resentment of supposed wrongs or affronts; and as either justifying the use of deceit, at least for good ends, or of being so habituated to it as not to realize its sinfulness.

If, then, the question be, Why should a combination of powerful spirits hostile to man exist, what could be their motive, and what the objective of the age-long campaign? it is not difficult to suggest possible answers. The fact of such evil spirits existing in great numbers, more or less harmful to men, all spiritualists admit. It is easy, in a general way, to conceive that the leaders may have been threatened with removal from high official stations, which they had corrupted by pride and a self-righteous spirit, and that this occasioned resentment, jealousy, and a natural effort to defend their administration while clinging to power.

It is true that spiritualists generally, so far as our reading has extended, ignore the existence of any such being as the devil or Satan is usually considered to be. Now, Whately well remarks that there is no proposition against which objections, and possibly unanswerable ones, may not be urged. The question is, whether the same or even stronger objections could not be urged against every alternative proposition.

Now suppose a proposition something like this: — Satan's power is official or political power, not yet entirely taken away, but in the process of being taken away, by disclosure of the evil effects of his principles. Concede, now, that objections, and even unanswerable ones, might be started against this proposition, what are the alternatives?

1. No devil at all, and no evil spirits, — theory of mere materialistic evolution.

2. An eternal evil principle, — Zoroastrian and Manichean hypothesis.

3. Any and every theory that conceives of him as a convict escaped from prison.

4. Theory of immense numbers of spirits more or less depraved, but without organization, — an army without a general, a community without a head.

Are there not more numerous and equally unanswerable objections against every one of these four alternatives, particularly the last? If so, then, according to the principle stated by Whately, spiritualists would, consistently with their own principles, fall back on the proposition previously stated. Let us endeavor to study the developments of history from that theoretical standpoint. And let us bear in mind that it is very useful for a pupil at the blackboard to work out his problem to the end, even if there be an error in the statement. The problem of history has been studied from the point of view of the alternative propositions; let us try and look it through from this. The cosmocratic powers, the *haute noblesse*, or aristocracy of the skies, may be supposed to look upon the exiled race with something of that mingled feeling of scornful pity with which people of rank, and noble blood, and aristocratic habits, have regarded the vulgar herd, — the feeling of the Pharisee for the publican and sinner; the feeling of the elder brother, in the parable, for the prodigal. Perhaps they looked down on mankind as the sweepings of heaven, — the offscourings, the scum, and *canaille;* they possibly felt as moral people feel about "the criminal classes." It has often been noticed that the character exhibited by Satan in the Book of Job is not that of wilful malice, but rather that of the censor, or public accuser. The Pharisees were zealous for the law, and severe in their condemnation of sinners. May it not be in this respect that Jesus told them they were of their father the devil, namely, that that strict, self-righteous, unmerciful spirit they breathed was substantially like his spirit, so that if we want to know what sort of a being he was, we look at them.

They did not hesitate to plot and scheme, and employ all the arts of intrigue, just as men in official station always have done, without much consciousness of guilt. May it not have been so with higher principalities and powers?

Now, on any such hypothesis, man being in some measure withdrawn from the full effects of their censure, their scorn, and by incarnation shielded against them, how might they be inclined to treat the system? Suppose it may possibly have been intimated to them, that they ought to use the system reformatively; that they ought not to cherish scorn; that they ought to feel compassion, and exercise self-denial; how might they regard such counsel, not merely towards men as individual offenders, but towards a vanquished political party, — a rival race, conquered, expelled, disgraced?

We might conceive of their admitting the abstract truth of the intimation, and undertaking to act accordingly, yet with a certain rancor lurking in their hearts. They might still resent the proposed exaltation of man to universal dominion, even though apparently forever defeated. Might they not have latent misgivings whether it was forever defeated? Might they not ponder the import of those Eden emblems, and that declaration of war? But if such a conception as that of man's exaltation be supposed to seem to them too improbable to occasion a moment's disquiet, yet the mere suggestion might keep alive a certain smouldering jealousy, a certain proud and contemptuous resentment.

Certainly, they would be good friends of the abject race, but it must know its place. We may conceive they felt towards men somewhat as the princely planter of the South, even the most genial of them all, feels in accepting the situation towards his quondam chattels. This may be a very imperfect comparison. Let it not be pressed too far. Suppose something approximating to this — analogous to it.

Of course it is conceivable that the supernal orders might in some respects be unceremonious and unscrupulous towards men. They might feel that men had no rights which angels were bound to respect. And the mere fact of being somewhat shut out from access to them, whether for scorn or for friendship, might tempt them to interfere, and to trespass. And, possibly, the idea might suggest itself to some of the more adventurous, on seeing these their quondam celestial associates moving about in material forms, to wonder how it must seem, and to think of trying the experiment. Not by the, perhaps, painful process of birth; for, as has been suggested, possibly a spirit must painfully die out of that mode of life, to enter the grave-like womb, and rise from the dead by birth; — not in that uninviting manner, but by the exercise of creative or semi-creative sway over matter, assuming a human organism more or less permanent, and condescending to the level of the abject race. In which case there might be attractions such as have been known to exist between different races in this world, patrician and plebeian, prince and peasant, master and slave, so that "when men began to multiply on the face of the earth, and daughters were born unto them, the sons of God saw the daughters of men that they were fair, and they took them wives of all that they chose." *

There was nothing in the conception of such a connection inconsistent with ancient modes of thought. Angels were conceived of as possessing celestial bodies, and endowed with power to assume forms of flesh and blood at will. It is only in comparatively recent times that a different philosophy has prevailed, leading expositors to put a different construction on the above passage. Many of the most eminent recent interpreters, however, have returned to the ancient construction. The phrase "sons of God" having been in other passages of the Old Testament understood to mean angels,† no good reason can be assigned for giving it a different meaning here. Some manuscripts of the Septuagint so translate it, and this reading was followed by Philo, by Josephus, by the author of the Book of Enoch, and by Peter and Jude. This reading is found in the Alexandrian manuscript, which is followed in the edition of the modern Greek Church, sanctioned by the Synod of all the Russias; also, by the edition of the English Society for Promoting Christian Knowledge.‡ In the Epistle of Jude we read of "the angels that kept not

* Genesis vi. 1–4.

† Job i. 2; xxxviii. 7. Ps. xxix. 1; lxxxix. 6.

‡ History of Opinions on Future Retribution. E. Beecher, D.D., pp. 88–91.

their first estate (or principality), but left their habitation;" and this is characterized as a "going after strange flesh," or forming connection with a foreign race or species.* In the Second Epistle of Peter, also, we read that "God spared not the angels that sinned, but cast them down to Tartarus, and delivered them into chains of darkness, to be reserved unto judgment." †

It is mainly on these two passages, and possibly one or two others,‡ that the conventional notion of the Devil and his angels as being already convicts, in a penal state, rests. A small foundation for so large a doctrine. Not only do not Peter and Jude identify the angels by name and title, but the latter makes a quotation from the Book of Enoch, showing the train of association of ideas that was passing in his mind. Now the Book of Enoch limits the number to two hundred, and mentions their names; but Satan is not among them. The Bible, therefore, is not responsible for a theory which would practically represent the Divine government as carrying on a war of ages against a convict escaped from penal incarceration. The Bible, by any fair principles of interpretation, knows nothing of such a theory. On the contrary, Paul, who, as all spiritualists admit, was a seer, and had enjoyed abundant revelations of things unseen, and who was well qualified to testify on a point like this, expressly locates the leading spirits hostile to humanity in Heaven.§

As to the question of the reality of the angelic marriages, we really cannot see why spiritualists, for whom chiefly we write, should deny their possibility, or even their probability. It would simply be a case of materialization on a larger scale than has been yet witnessed in modern days. The only question is, whether, on the

* Jude vi. 7. † 2 Pet. ii. 4.
‡ Is. xiv. 12; Lu. x. 18; Rev. xii. 7–9. § Eph. vi. 12.

hypothesis proposed, an adequate cause or occasion for such a development can be conceived of as existing?

Grant, then, that the material system is designed, as shown in previous chapters, to be a kind of shield to the exiled race, and to dyke out currents of undesirable influence, what more natural than an effort to break in? What more natural than that it may have been done by subordinates, possibly only connived at by the chief cosmocratic princes? Political leaders cannot always control their subordinates in this world; and the more fiery spirits of a party or a people may initiate a war or a revolution in spite of their rulers. It may not have been even connived at; but having come to pass, (like a raid across the borders between two empires,) the celestial cabinet may have inly pondered how to turn it to account. They may have conceived the idea of a magnificent world-empire under these novel conditions, in which a certain immortal vigor should blend with mortality, and the infant race burst into splendid precocity of genius, in the arts, sciences, and their manifold applications to social development. What would this be but the swollen current overleaping the barrier, or bursting through it at every crevice? It would be in one sense, as seen from the higher point of vision, natural that spirits should do such a thing, under the supposed circumstances.

Would not this also naturally account for much that we find in classic tradition and poetry?* Might it not also assist in accounting for the very early development of certain races in the arts and sciences? It was the constant tradition of antiquity that the angels taught their brides the elements of superhuman knowledge. On such a supposition, might not Egyptian and Babylonian art and science, and in especial magical science, be

* How many heroes and great men claimed to be Jove-born!

accounted for, without materially extending the received Scripture chronology? With angelic instructors and pupils of millennial longevity, progress would be rapid. And it is a fact often noticed, that the further back we go in the history of the Adamic family, the more we are impressed with a sense of the high development in art and science to which they had attained. We seem to meet man on a down grade from previous high culture.

It is obvious, also, that such a development, under such auspices, might be expected to grow corrupt. Where there was no fear of death, where there could be little to humble pride, or to repress ambition, or quench the fires of passion, it would be natural that the earth should be filled with violence. And this again might serve naturally to account for the catastrophe of the deluge.

The needed isolation of the race had been interfered with — practically nullified. Without catastrophism, without some signal retribution, it might be impossible to prevent such abuses in future, and to carry out the beneficent design. But if we suppose the offending angels suddenly stripped of the power to lay off the bodies they had assumed; immortals caught as it were in a trap and exposed to a form of death peculiarly dreadful, in circumstances so arranged as to make the whole a sublime type * or tableau; then we see that not only would such incursions be checked, but impressive meanings be shadowed forth by analogy for the instruction of all future generations. And if we conceive of the cherubic tabernacle as still standing through all this period, we shall find little difficulty in imagining the antagonism of feeling indicated in the prophecy of Enoch: "Behold, the Lord cometh with ten thousand of his saints, to execute judgment upon all, and to convince

* 1 Peter iii. 21, speaks of the preservation of Noah's family in the ark as "a type."

all that are ungodly among them, of all their ungodly deeds, which they have ungodly committed, and of all their hard speeches which ungodly sinners have spoken against him." *

* This is not the proper place to discuss the physical objections which have been made to the account of the deluge. We claim that they may be met by the theory of a limited area, and a limited number of animals preserved mainly for typical purposes. A few leading species of a given district would be, typically, or representatively, all species. The difficulty has arisen from overlooking the typical and emblematic nature of the catastrophe.

CHAPTER XVI.

RISE OF POLYTHEISM.

IF the view we have taken of the Eden tabernacle be admitted, it will be found, on reflection, eminently suggestive. What was it? It was a domestication of the Lord; it was a domestic religion. The tabernacle, or tent, was the Lord's dwelling-place; He kept house there. There was the altar, the speaking flame, the daily meal, or show-bread. That was "the presence of the Lord." In the immediate vicinity of that tabernacle Adam, as patriarchal priest, lived; he may have lived in it. The priests were indeed excluded from the Levitical tabernacle as an abode, and only entered it on specified occasions to minister. That exclusion possibly may not have characterized the Eden tabernacle, since it was from the garden man was then excluded, and that idea of exclusion did not need to be repeated.

The Septuagint, instead of saying, "he tabernacled the cherubim," says, "he drove out Adam and housed him (κατωκισεν αυτον) before the paradise of the tree of life, and established the cherubim." Perhaps the fact was that the Lord "housed," or tabernacled, both the cherubic speaking flame and Adam. In the genealogy of Christ, it says, on tracing it back to Adam, "which was the son of God." The fact indicated may be that the Lord and Adam dwelt together. In Revelation, where the Eden emblems seem to rise around us, we read, "Behold, the tabernacle (ἡ σκηνὴ) of God is with men, and he will dwell (σκηνώσει) with them."* The picture is of father and son dwelling in the same tent. Perhaps it was so at the gates of Paradise. The Lord (by his speaking flame) lived there, in the same tent, perhaps, with Adam (the son of God) and with Eve, and "wiped away all tears from their eyes," —tears wrung from them by exclusion from the beautiful garden.

It was a domestic religion then; and it was in Adam's case a true ancestor-worship, for was he not the son of God?—not the worship of a deceased ancestor. but of a living One, as most beautifully symbolized by that speaking flame. It was not in the first instance a public worship, external to their dwelling. They did not go forth from their tent to seek a temple or to raise their eyes to the sky. The direction of their thought in worship was toward the interior of their own tent, the penetralia of their own home; the object of their adoration was within —*penitus*, whence the term "penates," for household gods.

In this worship Eve participated, as one with her husband; for he called their name Adam, and she was "bone of his bone and flesh of his flesh." Hence the sacred, the religious character of marriage, since it not only made woman a wife, but a priestess, man being by the idea of this domestic worship the priest of the family. Hence Jesus, in restoring marriage to its original divine simplicity and purity, goes directly back to Adam, when he said, "For this cause shall a man leave father and mother and cleave unto his wife, and they twain shall be one flesh."

When the Titanic marriages were formed, it is conceivable that primitive customs were rudely innovated upon. - The lovely daughters of men may have been seized by bright flashing forms, and borne with songs

* Rev. xxi. 3.

and illuminations to their new abodes. Hence possibly the singular marriage rites in some nations running back to an unknown antiquity, — the πομπη, or bridal procession, with torches, and music, and certain songs, — ὦ ὑμην ὦ ὑμεναιε, the derivation of which is utterly lost. Hence the pretended violence with which the bridegroom carried the bride, after a feigned resistance, into his dwelling, being careful not to allow her foot to touch the threshold. May not all this be a faint reminiscence of angelic courtship in the days before the flood?

It may be possible that those angelic marriages were at first regarded as a most rapturous and sacred manifestation. Far from perceiving the consequences that would flow from them, men may have regarded them as something divine, something ecstatic and holy. Hence the words used by the celestial visitants, on such occasions, might be caught up and employed on similar occasions, and handed down as a ritual, at least in some lines of descent, and linger among men — the last faint vestiges of the "tongues of angels" — ages after their origin is buried in oblivion.

If, however, it be conceived that the cherubic tabernacle itself was not the actual dwelling of Adam, then we can conceive that the Lord "housed" him in a separate tent, in close proximity to the cherubic tent; and in that tent we can easily conceive an altar on which an imitative flame was kept ever burning, — a flame kindled, perhaps, from the cherubic fire. In this case the same things would be true; that altar and that flame would symbolize the same living presence, and every meal would be a sacrifice, when a portion of the food, or a libation, might be consumed by the ancestral fire.

If, now, we conceive of the children of Adam, we shall see what ideas they would naturally have. The idea of the *interior* would be associated with worship. The interior, the within, the penates, would naturally come to be suggestive of the altar-flame, and the living ancestor, whose emblem it was; and as time rolled on, and population increased and extended on every side with a wider frontier, we can conceive what changes would be natural — in fact inevitable.

The further away in time and space, the more they would confuse and confound together elements associated by ties of veneration and affection. Two opposite modifying causes would work: in some households, the progressive stimulus of Titanic civilization; in others, the conservative tendency to cling to forms, and rites, and usages, with the gradual loss of vitality, and the sinking down from the spiritual reality to the material sign or emblem, — a process inevitable as they felt the tendencies to barbarism inseparable from frontier life. Thus, while the sacred fire might be cherished in each tent, it might come to be regarded as itself divine; and when the mortal ancestor died, so long and intimately associated with the Lord, the living ancestor, his shade, or manes, might easily be associated with that living ancestor, and confounded with him as an object of domestic invocation. Thus the flame, the penates, would come, as time rolled on, to denote, in some families at least, the deceased ancestors, and thus a polytheistic worship gradually spring up.

We have already shown that the sun is a divinely created emblem of Deity, in its relations of light and heat to the natural world, — even as man himself is an emblem, by his relations to the household; these two emblems would easily be confounded, and thus we should find the worship of ancestors and of the heavenly bodies associated with the hearth in the tent, the altar-flame, the penates, and manes, and the worship of the dead.

This view of the subject throws light on the prophecy of Noah after the deluge: "God shall enlarge Japheth, and shall dwell in the tents of Shem;" or, as the Targum of Onkelos has it, "and will make his glory to dwell in the tabernacles of Shem." That is, he will continue in that line the primeval domestic religion with somewhat of primitive purity, resisting the corruptions which assailed it, and at length reinstating it with special features in the Levitical system.

Now it is curious that the idolatry so infectious to the Israelites, and traces of which run back to the family of Abraham in Chaldea, is such as this view would lead us to expect. It was both a domestic ancestral worship, with its teraphim, or penates, gods of the interior, and a worship of fire and of the heavenly bodies; and it is curious that, if we examine the languages of Greece, and Rome, and India, we find certain words, certain rites, certain laws, very much alike, pointing backward to a very remote antiquity, when these three peoples — explain it how we may — had the same language, and laws, and religion.* But the striking fact is, that at the very earliest period to which we can ascend by an examination of language, rites, and laws, we find a domestic religion substantially such as we have shown would naturally result from the Eden tabernacle. We merely glance at the fact here, reserving a more full consideration for a future chapter.

Thus regarded, we can conceive of the ancient polytheism as in one sense the original divinely revealed religion. It had elements of eternal truth and heavenly beauty. Its votaries could sincerely regard it as of divine origin and sanction; and however "the fine gold might become dim," — however gross the corruptions might in time become, — traces of the original beauty

* See The Ancient City. De Coulanges. (Lee & Shepard.)

and truth would still be there, and the process of change, being gradual, would not be noticed. That process would be substantially the same in all the Adamic races, with such diversities of detail as would easily spring from mental idiosyncrasy and from environment.

It has even been maintained by some that the worship of the dead, or nether gods, preceded the worship of the greater or supernal deities; but the reverse is quite as probable, to say the least. It is quite conceivable that the family deities displaced the older celestial divinities, just as we see the invocation of saints in the middle ages largely displace the worship of God. It is easy to see that at an early period in the very remote past a similar process might naturally go on more rapidly, and result in a total loss, in some families at least, of the worship, and even of traditional memory and titles, of the true God. In other families, or races, these might be retained, and in different degrees according to circumstances. And it is only by keeping in mind these various causes, all of them of great power, — (1) the original Eden emblems handed down and corrupted; (2) the analogies of the material system; (3) innate idiosyncrasies; (4) instinctive cherishing the memory of deceased parents; (5) the direct agency of spirit-communication, — that we can account for *all* the phenomena of ancient polytheism. Attempts have been made to solve the problem by some one or two of these causes, but in vain. We need them all, especially the last. Admonished by the shock of the deluge, the cosmocratic powers must seek other methods of controlling the course of empire. When by degrees the worship of ancestors had crept in, a way was open by which to control the living in a less direct and perilous manner. The extreme antiquity of necromancy and magic in all their forms is shown more and more clearly by every fresh discovery in Assyrian and Egyptian remains. That the cosmocratic powers may have designed by such means to found great and imposing empires of worldly splendor, is easily conceivable; but facts showed it was an instrumentality they could not regulate. They could not prevent abuses from creeping in, from the waywardness of the spirits communicating, and from the selfishness of men. Their oracles would degenerate, would become tainted with fraud, would be prostituted for gain and the gratification of the passions.

Earthly rulers have often tried to rule well simply from selfish motives — to enhance their own grandeur and obtain renown. Is it not conceivable that the same should have been the case with the invisible principalities? Spiritualists, at least, cannot consistently object to such a view.

Such motives may appear to work well for a season. They may generate strong governments, with much splendor; but they tend to corruption. Ignorant and selfish masses cannot be really well governed without sincerity, pity, and a self-denying spirit. Pride, fraud, and brute force cannot be made to work as well as the opposite qualities. The cosmocracy perhaps thought they could, and the Lord allowed them ample time and scope for the experiment.

CHAPTER XVII.

"THE FRIEND."

THERE are two conceivable ways in which Divine benevolence might deal with the nations when the primitive Eden religion had become corrupt: one coextensive with the race, and aggressive; the other limited in range, and as it were defensive. The latter was the method, in fact, adopted. A single nation was selected, not because essentially better than other nations, for they were "a stiff-necked people;" they were centrally located, and through them the original Eden system was revived with increment, with a view of finally influencing the race by a morally aggressive movement.

We read: "The living God in times past suffered all nations to walk in their own ways; nevertheless he left not himself without witness in that he did good, and gave us rain from heaven and fruitful seasons, filling our hearts with food and gladness." * The field was tilled and sown, and apparently neglected; but it was only a seeming neglect, for a divine friendliness characterized the whole arrangement. The whole material system, with its sunshine and rain, was ever benignly inciting to gratitude, and its analogic language stimulative to the moral nature. A fair field was left for the innate development forces of man himself, and for the skill and beneficence of cosmocratic powers, if so be they chose to rule wisely and benevolently. And when men showed that they "did not like to retain God in their knowl-

* Acts xiv. 16.

edge," he did not obtrude himself upon them, but let them please themselves, postponing their case for the present. "The times of this ignorance God winked at." * But yet, while seemingly inattentive, he had a plan, which was never lost sight of, even in their territorial distribution or colonization.

Thus when on the plains of Shinar there was a tendency to centralization, when the expansive instinct grew sluggish, and men shrank from the privations and perils of migration, it became necessary to quicken the centrifugal forces. And this was easy, on our hypothesis. Languages are innate. They lie back, forgotten, somewhere in the hiding-places of the soul. The Lord only needs unlock a cabinet or two, swing open a little ivory or ebony door in the soul, and out they come, in Babel jargon, or in pentecostal tongues. Varieties of races exist in the spirit-sphere antecedent to incarnation. He who sends them in, knows how to contrive either to repress or to develop those idiosyncrasies. "Two nations are in thy womb," he says to Rebekah; as if those nations were then waiting, while these their avant couriers led the way, one supplanting the other, and grasping him by the heel. The one, a red man, hirsute, wild; the other fair and delicate: the savage Edom, the civilized Israel!

So when as yet "all the earth was of one language and of one speech" on the fertile banks of Euphrates, and in the unseen all the tribes of the tenth chapter of Genesis were waiting at the door, how easy, while sending in precursors of the several races, to relax a little the bonds of oblivion from the faculty of language, so that in the course of a few years a confusion of tongues would arise, and the diverse families, yielding to the innate impulse, resume the outward march to their predestined homes.

* Acts xvii. 30.

In this dispersion, however, naught was left to chance, whether in respect to time or place. The Lord had "determined the times before appointed, and the bounds of their habitation; that they should seek the Lord, if haply they might feel after him, and find him, though he be not far from every one of us."* Their location had reference to the order of time in which they should successively feel the effects of the development going on in the central nation, and respond to it by seeking the Lord.

Compare this with the statement of Moses: "When the Most High divided to the nations their inheritance, when he separated the sons of Adam, he set the bounds of the people according to the number of the children of Israel. For the Lord's portion is his people, Jacob is the lot of his inheritance."† Call to mind, also, the many passages in which God is spoken of as having a "purpose" or plan, a "counsel," a "mystery,"—that is, a comprehensive plan or outline of human development, faintly sketched in prophecy, but not fully revealed to mankind,—and this plan pivoting upon Israel and the Holy Land. Then glance at the map, and see how Palestine is nearly the geographical centre of three continents; and how the great historic nations have in fact arisen successively at increasing distances from that centre,—Egypt, Assyria, Babylon, Medo-Persia, Greece, Rome; and how between the system of thought at that centre, and the systems of these nations, and through them others outlying still more remote, the great law of action and reaction has gone on from age to age,—and we shall feel that, imperfect as our chronology may be, we have the key to the actual historical development of our present civilization. Outside of these territories and these nations lie shadows and chaos; here in Israel, and the

* Acts xvii. 26, 27.

† Deut. xxxii. 8.

great nations surrounding, light shines out of darkness, and order is educed from confusion. Central as it was, however, it was a strong military position mainly in a defensive sense, and in a great spiritual campaign of centuries. By what law of natural selection was that geographical centre fixed upon, to be the centre of spiritual development which it in fact has been? To "inherit" that land is, in an impressive, spiritual sense, to be "the heir of the world." By what law of evolution, or natural selection, was that inheritance determined in the line of Shem, and to the descendants of the Chaldean sheik Abram?

Our answer is, that it was a moral selection, in which spiritual motives came in play. It was indeed a problem of higher politics; it was also a problem of affection. A government of love, truth, and meekness was to be initiated there, on the only principles on which a family, neighborhood, state, world, or universe can be happy; and a selection is made, not of an existing nation, not of a colony, or church, or state, but of a single genial, noble-minded man, to lead the way as pioneer. Here forces come into play that are not mechanical, not ponderable, not subject to chemical analysis,—the forces of moral affinity, of sympathy, of congenial tastes and aspirations.

Among all the populations of the earth, what was one man? A mere mustard-seed—a mere speck of leaven. But it was that germ, that moral seed, the Lord was looking for, and found. The Lord wanted something more than a mere agent, more than a machine, more than a great mill-wheel,—He wanted A FRIEND, one whom He could love, and who could love Him,—and that was a very Natural Selection for Him to make, who is Nature's very self.

"The God of glory appeared unto our father Abraham in Mesopotamia," says Stephen.* The God of glory, who by the Shekinah flame had tabernacled with Adam, who had promised to dwell in the tents of Shem, appeared to the man of His choice. It was a spiritual manifestation, and (on the highest plane of thought) a perfectly natural one. "Get thee out from thy country, and from thy kindred, and come into the land which I will show thee."

It is the first mention of that land which, by common consent, is known all over the world as the Holy Land. And when he entered the land, the Lord appeared to him again, and said, "Unto thy seed will I give this land." Yet Stephen is careful to remind us "he gave him none inheritance in it, no, not so much as to set his foot on. Yet he promised that he would give it to him for a possession, and to his seed after him, when as yet he had no child." He was there as "a pilgrim and stranger." He sojourned in tents. He went through the land in its length and breadth. He visited Egypt, the nearest and first in order of the great world-empires involved in the plan. He returned. Wherever he went he builded an altar. Several times the Lord appeared, and each time the promise grew more emphatic and comprehensive. "All this land which thou seest, to thee will I give it and to thy seed forever. And I will make thy seed as the dust of the earth!"

Wherever he goes, we find him building an altar and offering sacrifice, and receiving communications from the Lord. In this connection, the appearance to him of the Prince of Righteousness, after his return from the rescue of Lot, ceases to be anomalous. It was simply an instance of materialization. "Abraham rejoiced to see my day," said Jesus afterwards, "and he saw it and was glad." Then he saw it when the Prince of Peace in

* Acts vii. 2.

person, on the site of the future Moriah, presented him the eucharistic emblems, and doubtless explained to him their import. "He saw it and was glad."

There was a divine friendship manifested towards Abraham in these repeated interviews, which is peculiarly attractive. "Fear not, Abram," said the vision, "I am thy shield;" and again and again the Lord appears to him in this friendly manner, repeating the promise with increasing clearness, entering into a covenant with him by the customary solemnities, and in one memorable instance seeming almost to tabernacle with him in a materialized form. He rests under a tree near the tent, while the meal is being prepared, with two other guests. Abraham washes his feet. The meal is set before the three men, and Abraham "stood by them under the tree, and they did eat." Then comes that matchless scene, unequalled in human literature, where Abraham intercedes for Sodom, but vainly, because in his charity he felt sure there must be as many as ten righteous persons there.

Then comes the supreme ordeal, the sacrifice of Isaac. On Moriah, then a wild jungle, where ultimately the Temple should be built, or in its near vicinity, on what was after known as Calvary, the patriarch binds his son, and is in the act of completing the sacrifice when interrupted by the heavenly voice. It showed that he believed in the reality of that divine manifestation, and that nothing commanded by that Divine Friend could be wrong. Nor could the promise fail, for He could instantly raise Isaac up to life again, "from whence also he received him in a figure." And here it is, after this supreme ordeal, that the promise expands to the widest dimensions, — "In thy seed shall all the nations of the earth be blessed." The system centring in that land is a system of love, of good-will to men, of real kindness, and it will prove itself such by deeds of disinterestedness and self-sacrifice which cannot be equalled.

God treated Abraham as Jesus told his disciples he should treat them. "I call you not servants, but friends." He showed a true divine friendship to Abraham, as though he really cared for him, as though he *liked* him, — just as Jesus did to John, who leaned on his breast, and is spoken of as "the disciple whom Jesus loved;" — and He made such an impression of reality on Abraham's mind, and excited such feelings of responsive friendship, that he was ready to do whatever He said, without question; it would all come out right somehow. And it is pleasant to know that among Eastern peoples, not only those descended from Abraham, but others, the patriarch is known by the simple title THE FRIEND, to this day.

How far the promise, in its future outreachings, was unfolded to Abraham, we cannot here attempt to consider. But that he knew more than modern thought is wont to give him credit for, both of a celestial existence past and of one to come, is not only probable, in view of what has been already said, but seems plainly asserted. "By faith Abraham, when he was called to go out into a place which he should after receive for an inheritance, obeyed; and he went out, not knowing whither he went. By faith he sojourned in the land of promise, as in a strange country, dwelling in tabernacles with Isaac and Jacob, the heirs with him of the same promise: for he looked for a city which hath foundations, whose builder and maker is God. Through faith also Sara herself received strength to conceive seed, and was delivered of a child when she was past age, because she judged him faithful who had promised. Therefore sprang there even of one, and him as good as dead, so many as the stars of the sky in multitude, and as the sand which is by the sea-shore innumerable. These all died in faith, not having received the promises, but having seen them afar off, and were persuaded of them, and embraced them, and confessed that they were strangers and pilgrims on the earth. For they that say such things declare plainly that they seek fatherland (πατρίδα). And truly, if they had been mindful of that fatherland from whence they came out, they might have had opportunity to have returned: but now they desire a better fatherland, that is, a heavenly: wherefore God is not ashamed to be called their God; for he hath prepared for them a city. By faith Abraham, when he was tried, offered up Isaac: and he that had received the promises offered up his only-begotten son, of whom it was said, That in Isaac shall thy seed be called: accounting that God was able to raise him up, even from the dead; from whence also he received him in a figure." *

The outline sketched in vision to Abraham we see filled out in the history of his descendants,—in the beautiful story of Isaac and Rebecca; of Jacob and Rachel; of Joseph and his brethren;—scenes from real life which no mere literary artist has ever equalled, or can equal.

That which gives the Hebrew annals their chief charm, is the reality and truth of that same divine friendship, ever and anon manifested; — to Jacob, in his vision of angels ascending and descending the ladder or stairway between heaven and earth, the Lord himself standing at the top; also in the nocturnal materialization scene, when "there wrestled a man with him till the break of day." Through all the family history of Isaac, Jacob, Joseph and his brethren, in the scenes that led to the descent into Egypt, and the exodus therefrom, the idea of the divine friendship for Abraham is ever prominent.

* Heb. xi. 8–19.

Even in the history of Ishmael the wild man, "his hand against every man, and every man's hand against him," — yet "dwelling in the presence of all his brethren," as we see to this very day, — this divine friendship for Abraham expresses itself; much more, however, in the history of the covenant people.

As Abraham lies in a deep sleep, his posterity seem individualized as an actual present reality, though he is yet childless; — Isaac is not yet born; — yet they are spoken of as going down into Egypt and returning again. "In the fourth generation they shall come hither again." Again? When not even Isaac was there? "Thy seed shall be a stranger in a land that is not theirs." This land, then, this central land, the moral key of the globe, *is* theirs, before even one of them has come through the gates of birth! "I will give unto thee, and to thy seed after thee, all the land wherein thou art a stranger, all the land of Canaan, for an everlasting possession; and I will be their God." *

Men for the most part are such poor creatures, so wilful, so unreasonable, that one can hardly imagine how God can love them much except with a kind of parental instinct. Jesus exclaimed to the Jews, "How long shall I suffer you!" John was finer-grained. There was a little something in him which Jesus could take comfort in. So with Abraham. The Lord "had pleasure in him." And it was above everything his implicitness of belief, his spontaneousness, his clinging fidelity, that made him so agreeable to the divine sensibilities. He clung to God. He did not doubt, or dispute, or hesitate. He did not speculate, nor ask why, nor demand excessive demonstration. He did not relapse into incredulity, and have to be convinced every time by excessive proof. He had seen Him who is invisible, and once was enough.

* Gen. xvii. 8.

"He endured as seeing him" all the time. He felt that any one who had seen Him was blessed. His inmost heart thrilled and vibrated like an Æolian harp as the breath of God swept across him, saying, "I am thy shield, and thine exceeding great reward."

It is this element of implicit credence, instant compliance, clinging fondness of docility, which the Lord craves in all his children, which he needs, which he must have; the want of which has made all the trouble in this, and all other worlds where there is trouble. What can He do with children who will not believe him, will not trust him, will not come within arm's-length of him? Here was a child, of noble qualities, who responded instantly, who never for an instant kept aloof, but gave heart and soul and mind and sense at His lightest call. And the friendship the Lord felt for that man enveloped all his seed, in spite of their dreadful waywardness, — and envelops us even, envelops the whole world, — for a similar implicitness of faith makes us Abraham's seed; and the Lord says, "I call you not servants but friends!"

CHAPTER XVIII.

THE EXODUS.

MOSES was of Hebrew blood, but of Egyptian birth and education, trained in all the learning of the royal and priestly class. Whatever there was of the original Eden system remaining uncorrupted in the temples of the Nile, he was so situated as to know. Whatever of the primeval revelation was of record in the archives of the priesthood he could select and preserve. Whatever was preserved of any valuable secrets, of science, or art, or literary culture, which the "sons of God" may have taught the daughters of men, were necessarily at his disposal. He was undoubtedly initiated in the mysteries, and could appreciate at their full value the esoteric teachings of the Adepts. He was eye-witness of their sacred pageantry, and better situated than we are to judge whether there was anything really noble in their worship of animals, which seems to us so base, and which Paul declared "without excuse." He was perfectly familiar with the doctrine of transmigration as then held, and was better situated to judge of its origin than we are at this late day. All those scenes in the passage of the soul through Hades, its conflicts, its justification, its final glory, were far better known to him, than the picturings of the recently translated Book of the Dead have made them to us. He knew whether the system was pantheistic or not, — a point on which eminent Egyptologists are not entirely agreed. He was perfectly familiar with the belief of the existence of evil spirits combined under one great head, — a doctrine which the Israelites are sometimes said to have acquired during the captivity in Babylon, but which the Book of the Dead brings out in bold relief. The tradition handed down through the tabernacles of Shem was purer, more authentic, than that through the tents of Ham or of Japheth, or through any supposable mingling of those lines with lines of extra-diluvial, or even pre-Adamic origin.

What prevented Moses from inculcating the belief in transmigration? Was it not probably his belief in a celestial pre-existence, in purer, more primitive form, kept alive incorrupt by the constant intercourse of the Lord with the descendants of Shem, and especially with Abraham "THE FRIEND"? Was not their knowledge that they were "strangers and pilgrims," "seeking a celestial fatherland," well adapted to prevent their embracing the degrading belief of transmigration as it was held by their oppressors?

What prevented Moses from appealing to fears of future retribution in his legislation? Was it not because it was given him to know that those motives were weaker than those pertaining to this material system, with its analogies, made by divine Love for the express purpose of restraining and reclaiming selfish spirits? Did he not know, as Jesus subsequently declared, that if men would not repent and live good lives from the motives which could be evolved through the material system, they "would not, though one rose from the dead" to drive them by the terrors of the unseen? He saw that those motives had been appealed to, to the utmost extent. Human imagination cannot conceive of anything more terrific than the pictures in the Book of the Dead. What good had they done? The Egyptian lived to worship;

but his religion was sombre, and unable to resist the progress of social corruption.

Forty years Moses was familiar with all the knowledge, science, art, architecture, and worship of Egypt. But then his education was but begun. Forty years more, he was at school in the Wilderness of Midian, learning the healthful lessons of a pastoral life. Perhaps he thought, when he fled from the wrath of the king, that his career was ended, his life's work done. Perhaps he gave up all his patriotic dreams and ambitions, and concluded he should never do anything more, except be a shepherd. He did not know that he had not entered on his public career. He was now at school to Nature; being invigorated in body by pastoral toils, and brought closer to God in Nature, and the pure analogic teachings of the material system. At eighty he graduates from the desert. His diploma is put in his hand by Him who tabernacled in the tents of Shem, and he is confronted with the magicians of the Nile. He, the representative of the living God, Jehovah, whose name, and whose self-manifestation in the burning bush, was significant not only of life but of intensity of life, purity, power, glory. They, the representatives of the gods of Egypt — deified heroes, spirits of the dead, elemental spirits and angels, emanations from the infinite spirit. He, the representative of Redeeming Love, the same Love that revealed itself in the tabernacle at the gates of Eden — coming now to re-enact the tableau on a new stage, — a God of compassion, sympathy, tenderness, claiming the ear of his captive people, claiming their exclusive attention to his manifestations. They, the representatives of unfriendly invisible powers, selfish, proud, deceitful, under whose auspices the civilization of the Nile had come to be the pitiless, corrupt, despotic thing it was. The contest was brief. "For they cast down every man his rod, and they became serpents; but Aaron's rod swallowed up their rods." The same thing took place when Aaron smote with his rod the waters of the river and they were turned to blood. "And the magicians did so with their enchantments." So also with the next plague, "the magicians did so with their enchantments, and brought up frogs upon the land of Egypt." In the next plague, however, they failed. "The magicians did so with their enchantments to bring forth lice, and they could not. . . . . Then the magicians said unto Pharaoh, This is the finger of God."

The spirits operating through the magicians were of inferior grade, their control over matter limited. The spirit operating through Aaron was divine; hence the confession, "This is the finger of God." The plagues came to their climax on the passover night, in the death of the first-born, when God said, "Against all the gods of Egypt will I execute judgment." The great idea of redemption of a suffering race, by breaking the power of an older and oppressive race, is here acted out in a sublime tragedy. The blood on lintel and door-post; the victim eaten in haste, staff in hand, sandal on foot, loins girt about; the midnight death-wail; the tumultuous march; the pursuit; the passage of the Red Sea; the pillar of fire and cloud; the catastrophe; the song of Moses, — all are so contrived as to shadow forth by the strictest law of analogy a higher exodus — of a spiritual Israel from a moral Egypt, through the redeeming interposition of Infinite Love, prostrating the principalities and powers of evil.

CHAPTER XIX.

THE TABERNACLE.

IN the heart of the Arabian peninsula, embosomed among mountains, approachable only through narrow, winding defiles, there is a crescent-shaped plain, about two miles long and nearly a mile in width. At the southern side of this plain rises the rocky front of Horeb, more than a thousand feet in perpendicular height. So abrupt and sheer is the ascent that the traveller can advance to the foot of the cliff and touch the mount with his hand. On this plain, before this mount, a nation of escaped bondmen were encamped, thirty centuries ago, to receive from Jehovah the impress of national organization. Let us ascend the course of ages, and place ourselves in their midst. Early on the morning of the third day after their arrival, the slumbering multitudes are aroused by unwonted signals. The darkness is illumined by incessant flashes of lightning, and the ground beneath their feet trembles with the explosions of thunder. They rush from their tents. That mountain, so still in its majestic repose but yesterday, now presents an awful spectacle of intense excitement. Above its summit vast clouds of inky blackness are rolling, while flashes of electric light dart in piercing brilliance from every part; the mountain is alive. Conscious of the descending God, it melts, it burns, it is all on a smoke. A trumpet, blown by no earthly lip, pours its blast long and loud. Aghast the multitudes bear back from the sight.

"Speak thou with us, and we will hear; but let not God speak with us, lest we die!"

"Fear not, for God is come to prove you, that his fear may be before your faces, that ye sin not."

Then from the midst of the thick darkness, audible to the remotest part of that hushed assembly, came forth the voice of the Eternal, revealing the law of love.

"I am the Lord thy God, which have brought thee out of the land of Egypt, out of the house of bondage. Thou shalt have no other gods before me. Thou shalt not make unto thee any graven image, or any likeness of any thing that is in heaven above, or that is in the earth beneath, or that is in the water under the earth: thou shalt not bow down thyself to them, nor serve them: for I the Lord thy God am a jealous God, visiting the iniquity of the fathers upon the children unto the third and fourth generation of them that hate me; and showing mercy unto thousands of them that love me, and keep my commandments. Thou shalt not take the name of the Lord thy God in vain: for the Lord will not hold him guiltless that taketh his name in vain. Remember the Sabbath-day, to keep it holy. Six days shalt thou labor, and do all thy work: but the seventh day is the Sabbath of the Lord thy God: in it thou shalt not do any work, thou, nor thy son, nor thy daughter, thy man-servant, nor thy maid-servant, nor thy cattle, nor thy stranger that is within thy gates: for in six days the Lord made heaven and earth, the sea, and all that in them is, and rested the seventh day: wherefore the Lord blessed the Sabbath-day, and hallowed it. Honor thy father and thy mother; that thy days may be long upon the land which the Lord thy God giveth thee. Thou shalt not kill. Thou shalt not commit adultery. Thou shalt not steal. Thou shalt not bear false witness against thy neighbor. Thou shalt not covet thy neighbor's house, thou shalt not covet thy neighbor's wife, nor his man-servant, nor his maid-servant, nor his ox, nor his ass, nor any thing that is thy neighbor's."

So much the Eternal would himself proclaim in tones none might mistake or dispute. This was the nation's organic law, its magna charta, its constitution.

The design of the Lord is clearly avowed. "Lo I come to thee in the thick cloud, that the people may hear when I speak with thee, and believe thee forever. Ye have seen what I did unto the Egyptians, and how I bare you on eagles' wings and brought you unto myself; now, therefore, if ye will obey my voice indeed, and keep my covenant, then ye shall be a peculiar treasure unto me above all people, for all the earth is mine, and ye shall be unto me a kingdom of priests and an holy nation."

The design was to make Israel the pioneer of civil and religious liberty for the world,—one that should take the lead of the religious development of the race; the oracular nation, organ of divine communication; an educational nation, finally furnishing the world with the great teacher, Jesus. "What advantage hath the Jew?" exclaims the apostle. "Much every way; chiefly that unto them were committed the Oracles of God. To them pertaineth the adoption, and the glory, and the covenants, and the giving of the law, and the service of God, and the promises, whose are the fathers, and of whom as concerning the flesh Christ came, who is over all, God blessed forever."

This design, so simple, so intelligible, was by no means easy of execution. Egypt was then first-born among nations, the mistress of the world's literature,—architecture, religion, arts, arms, being early ripened by her torrid clime into full flower. How great she was, those can faintly conceive who have stumbled over the ruins of her grandeur. What must have been the geometric science that built the pyramids on a plan in some way connected with astronomic laws and calculations! What that mechanic skill that cut, polished, transported hundreds of miles, and laid up without mortar, with joints almost imperceptible, those Cyclopean blocks, which modern appliances can with difficulty handle!

If the chaotic remains of an Egyptian temple, with its vast spaces, court within court, its cherub-guarded gateways, its sublime colonnades, now impress the mind with awe, what must have been their effect when filled with the enchantment of a mysterious and gorgeous ritual, — claiming, probably, to be the original divinely-appointed system handed down from Eden's gates, with traces of Titanic agency upon it, — with its pomps, and processions, and skilful appeals to every deepest instinct, whether of fear, of wonder, or of sensual desire! How almost infinite the power of that absolutism embodied in the person of that monarch "whose form is ever enshrined in the inmost adytum, to whose hands the gods are represented on the monuments as delivering the falchion, with the command to slay, and slay, and slay!" How difficult the design to set aside Egypt from the intellectual and religious primacy of the world, and substitute the Hebrews in their stead! — the Hebrews, who came into Egypt some seventy souls, a petty tribe of Bedouin shepherds, an abomination to Egyptians, — who, though now numerically increased, had never been a nation, nor possessed a territory, nor capital, nor form of government, nor laws! — the Hebrews, who were not even free, but who had been born in cruel bondage, over whose depressed souls both the government and the gods of Egypt had exercised a dreadful fascination, making them both slaves and idolaters, yet intoxicating them with the licentious orgies of that burning clime, and brutifying them by the abundance of sensual delights, the memory of which only the death of a generation could extinguish! How great the difficulty to overcome the *vis inertiæ* of the Hebrew mind, mould them into form, and qualify them for the spiritual birthright among the nations! It was indeed difficult to unclench the grasp of despotism; it was more difficult to unclench the grasp of ignorance. It was all but impossible to make Egypt give them up; it was quite impossible by ordinary human means to make anything of them after they were given up. To dash Egypt from the summit of power, and doom her to become the basest of nations, was a superhuman undertaking; but it was light compared with exalting Hebrew refugees to national intelligence, spirituality, and moral supremacy.

By what means was this to be effected? Evidently not by moral suasion. Egypt was not to be revolutionized by argument. Public opinion did not exist. There were no means extant for forming public opinion. The only conceivable way was the way by which the record says she was made — by the high hand and outstretched arm of God. Where natural means avail not, supernatural means become natural, because necessary.

By merely natural means the Hebrews could not be moulded after being rescued. There was to their minds something really divine and awful in the deities of Egypt they had learned to adore. We can feel the penumbra of that eclipse as we stand in the shadow of those tremendous fanes after ages of desolation. They could not be reasoned out of their superstitious awe; mere words would be wasted on them. They must see something more awful, more sublime, — something both impressive and pure, both terrible and good, transcending all Egypt could boast, yet sincere and true in every line and lineament.

Therefore God brought them into a temple his own hands had piled from creation's dawn; he stationed them before Horeb's front, even in its own naked majesty more grand than the pyramids, and on that mount the Lord descended in fire and darkness, with angelic myriads; and as they gazed, all Egypt's grandeurs faded and grew pale. In the presence of real truth, purity, benevolence, accompanied with a few manifestations of divine intensity of life and power, the counterfeits of Egypt stood detected, never again permanently to assert their enslaving power.

It is astonishing that such reluctance should be felt to admit the idea of supernatural intervention. What is natural? The natural order of things is God's customary exercise of power. The laws of nature are the habits of God; miracles are his occasional volitions. We have somewhere read of a cathedral clock so constructed as to strike the hours and also to chime the centuries, having one bell which rang out once in a hundred years. Now suppose a gray-headed peasant has heard that clock strike the hours all his life, — now arrives the day when that heavy centennial bell tolls out. The old man cries, "A miracle!" That clock he has heard since he was a boy. The existence of the century-bell has been forgotten; no man living ever heard it before; yet it is the same weight which impels the complex train of wheels ringing familiarly the hours, half-hours, quarter-hours, day and night, and which startles a generation once a hundred years by an unheard-of prodigy. So it is the same divine power moving the intricate wheels of the vast benevolent plan, familiarly unfolding itself in the growing grass or blooming rose, and occasionally manifested in the sublimities of Horeb, or in the mighty works of Him who bore our sicknesses and carried our diseases.

The only question is, whether the design was a good one — worthy of such an outlay of occasional force. Look, then, for a moment at the accomplished result. Behold Israel when at length nationally organized and complete. The law has been read to the people with the customary emblems of a covenant; for though Jehovah might reign arbitrarily, without the consent of the governed, it is not his method or wish so to do. The constitution was submitted to the people, and they answered, "All that the Lord hath said will we do, and be obedient." Hence that law was usually called the covenant, and Israel the covenant people. Suppose this transaction past, the tabernacle built, the priests consecrated, the ritual established, and the nation on their march to the promised land.

We behold an immense square encampment, the twelve tribes, three on a side, each under its own banner. In the middle of the encampment there is a court, with cherubim embroidered on hangings at the east end, the entrance. Within that court there is a large tent, or tabernacle. Within that tabernacle there is a holy place, and within or behind that, a holy of holies. In that holy of holies is the ark with its golden cover, overshadowed by the golden cherubim. That cover is the mercy-seat, or throne of Him who dwelleth between the cherubim. Within that ark is the law of love, the golden rule. The nation, at once an army, a school, a state, and a church, is completely organized. And what is the central idea? Is it of a supreme executive reigning by absolute, arbitrary power, or is it of a supreme executive reigning by law, — an authority founded on essential truth and benevolence, Himself the impersonation of the law he enjoins? To ask the question is to answer it. The use of the ceremonial system was to bring the nation into such attitudes of penitence and faith that the Lord could consistently dwell among them.

Apply now the principle of interpretation in which all spiritualists agree. Moses was indeed a seer, a medium. He received communications from the spirit-world. Those communications, and the spirits bringing them, are to be judged by the principles of our rational and moral nature. Will not this law stand the test? Christ also is admitted by spiritualists to have been a seer. He condensed the whole Mosaic legislation into supreme love to God and impartial love to man. Is not that intuitively seen to be right, and is it not felt to be the necessary law of happy society in all worlds? Can spiritualists, then, consistently with their own principles, impute deception either to the medium or to the spirits communicating? And will they not joyfully accept the conviction these oracles are indeed from a high and pure source? There was here a real opening out of the highest spiritual sphere. That law was given and that nation was organized substantially as stated. It was one elaborate, complex, sublime SPIRITUAL MANIFESTATION. And as the communications in the most solemn manner claimed to be from the Lord, we have every reason to receive them reverently as such, and to study the system there elaborated in all its details, and trace it in its bearings upon the history of the world. We shall be richly repaid. It is replete with ingenuity and artistic invention ; it is characterized by plain, practical common sense in its adaptations to every-day life ; yet it is full of analogies, tableaus, types. In this respect it is like the material system, and bears the stamp of the same contriving mind. It was a system that for fifteen centuries stood the shock of battle, and the nation it moulded, although long scattered and broken, has lived to see every empire matched against them go down ; and it may yet live to repossess its ancient land, and play an important part in millennial history.

CHAPTER XX.

BALAAM.

WE have seen the Egyptian magicians and diviners. We now meet with those of Aram, from the East. As nations diverged from the ark, our theory is that they built temples commemorative of Eden and its tabernacle, and for a time, doubtless, received responses from the Lord. As they grew more and more selfish and corrupt, they more and more repelled the highest order of spirits from communicating, while other spirits drew nigh and gave responses, still pretending, however, to speak with divine authority. This was what rendered it so difficult to distinguish the true prophet from the false. The psychologic conditions were the same. The ethnic ritual was in fact derived from a primitive divine source, and claimed divine sanction, as the original revelation. The spirits communicating could personate deity, — and thus the deceptive power was very great. The truth was, however, that the diviners, as a class, had become very corrupt. This all spiritualists admit, and it is abundantly manifest from the magical formulas, charms, incantations, and imprecations found on the recently discovered clay tablets of Assyria. They had reached such a stage of degeneracy that the divine Spirit could no longer use them for his communications. Hence, as Israel draws nigh Canaan, a most interesting contrast of the two styles of oracular manifestation is brought to view.* Balak sends an em-

* Num. xxii., xxiii., xxiv.

bassy to Balaam — "with the rewards of divination in their hands" — with the invitation, "Come, curse me this people! For I know that he whom thou blessest is blessed, and he whom thou cursest is cursed." Balaam replied, "Lodge here this night, and I will bring you word again, as the Lord shall speak unto me." Balaam intended to seek a response in the usual manner. Such responses had originally come from the true God. They were still considered to do so. And had Balaam been pure in heart, he might still have received the divine spirit.

In such a crisis it was proper that the Lord should interfere, and discriminate against the oracles he was discarding for their corruption, and in favor of that he was reinstituting. Hence Balaam receives a communication from God, — "Thou shalt not go with them; thou shalt not curse them, for they are blessed." A second embassy is sent still more honorable, with promises of greater rewards. Balaam replies: "If Balak would give me his house full of silver and gold, I cannot go beyond the word of the Lord." In this Balaam spoke the truth. He believed in the reality of his own converse with the Unseen. Yet he may have secretly wished to go. He may have hoped the spirits would let him go. At any rate, there was something in his state of mind offensive to the Spirit of God; for although he permitted him to go, he stood in the way with a drawn sword to slay him. And the ass saw what the man, although a seer, failed at first to see. It is well known that animals are sometimes clairvoyant, and strangely affected by the presence of forms invisible to mortals. Nor will it seem to spiritualists incredible that one of the brute species should even be made for a moment an instrument of spirit control, and seem to speak in human accents. Something corrupt there must have been in the seer's motives, since the Lord distinctly told him, "Thy way is perverse before me." It must be that Balaam's heart was set on gaining those rewards, if he could in any way procure a response from unseen sources permitting him to do what Balak wanted. Does it not suggest that he had done such things as that? That he had at times procured responses such as he wanted — or slightly changed, or added to or taken from them, so as to suit his selfish purposes?

He submits in a moment. "I have sinned. . . . . Now if it displease thee, I will get me back again." "Go with the men," is the reply, "but only the word that I shall speak unto thee that shalt thou speak." As if he had been meditating how to speak something else. Hence on arrival, when Balak reproaches him for not coming sooner, saying, "Am I not able indeed to promote thee to honor?" he replies, "Have I now any power at all to say anything? The word that God putteth in my mouth that shall I speak."

On the morrow Balak brought him "into the high places of Baal." It is the first mention of a deity, or deities, destined to be so antagonistic to Israel's life. "Build me here seven altars, and prepare me seven oxen and seven rams," said the seer. It was to be a solemn religious invocation. It was a summoning of all that was most earnest, most venerable, most conscientious, to resist and destroy that which was conceived to be dangerous and destructive to the best interests of society. "And he took up his parable, and said, Balak the king of Moab hath brought me from Aram, out of the mountains of the east, saying, Come, curse me Jacob; and come, defy Israel. How shall I curse, whom God hath not cursed? or how shall I defy, whom the Lord hath not defied? For from the top of the rocks I see him, and from the hills I behold him: lo, the people shall dwell alone, and shall not be reckoned among the nations. Who can count the dust of Jacob, and the number of the fourth part of Israel? let me die the death of the righteous, and let my last end be like his!" In this response, the idea of national isolation is prominent. It is a disclosure by the divine Spirit, of a great moral strategic principle to which we have already referred, — the occupation of a strong central position, its fortification, and defence, against great odds, through a long campaign, or series of campaigns.

After a renewal of sacrifices, another attempt is made with like result. "Stand by thy burnt-offering," says the Aramæan seer, "and I will go; peradventure the Lord will come to meet me." He went, "as at other times, to seek enchantments." That is, he went to throw himself into that peculiar psychologic state in which he usually obtained communications. "And he took up his parable, and said, Rise up, Balak, and hear; hearken unto me, thou son of Zippor: God is not a man, that he should lie; neither the son of man, that he should repent: hath he said, and shall he not do it? or hath he spoken, and shall he not make it good? Behold, I have received commandment to bless: and he hath blessed; and I cannot reverse it. He hath not beheld iniquity in Jacob, neither hath he seen perverseness in Israel: the Lord his God is with him, and the shout of a king is among them. God brought them out of Egypt; he hath as it were the strength of a unicorn. Surely there is no enchantment against Jacob, neither is there any divination against Israel: according to this time it shall be said of Jacob and of Israel, What hath God wrought! Behold, the people shall rise up as a great lion, and lift up himself as a young lion; he shall not lie down until he eat of the prey, and drink the blood of the slain." Here prominence is given to the idea that the Lord is dwelling in Israel as a king; that there is the true ORACLE from which reliable responses can be obtained; (as contrasted with deceptive "divinations" of other lands;) and intimations are given of an ultimate offensive policy in the moral war.

A third attempt is made. Though Balaam sincerely believed the responses to be from God, one cannot resist the impression that he had often found "the Elohim" more complaisant. By varying the "conditions," he had been able to obtain more acceptable responses. This mixture of full belief in the reality and divinity of the responses, with latent elements of finesse and subtilty, may be strange, but it is, unhappily, too often witnessed in our own day. But finding no symptoms of compliance, he yields, and goes straight forward to his work.

"And when Balaam saw that it pleased the Lord to bless Israel, he went not, as at other times, to seek for enchantments, but he set his face toward the wilderness. And Balaam lifted up his eyes, and he saw Israel abiding in his tents according to their tribes; and the Spirit of God came upon him. And he took up his parable, and said, Balaam the son of Beor hath said, and the man whose eyes are open hath said; he hath said, which heard the words of God, which saw the vision of the Almighty, falling into a trance, but having his eyes open: How goodly are thy tents, O Jacob! and thy tabernacles, O Israel! As the valleys are they spread forth, as gardens by the river's side, as the trees of lign-aloes which the Lord hath planted, and as cedar-trees beside the waters. He shall pour the water out of his buckets, and his seed shall be in many waters, and his king shall be higher than Agag, and his kingdom shall be exalted. God brought him forth out of Egypt; he hath as it were the strength of a unicorn: he shall eat up the nations his enemies, and shall break

12

their bones, and pierce them through with his arrows. He couched, he lay down as a lion, and as a great lion: who shall stir him up? Blessed is he that blesseth thee, and cursed is he that curseth thee."

He is struck by the beauty of the spectacle, as he sees the distant encampment, with its majestic pillar of fire and cloud. A revelation is made to his spirit of that beauty which the divine Eye sees in that spectacle; and which our eyes, instructed by the Spirit, can see as we look back through the ages. It is another Eden tabernacle! Another Garden of Eden, with its living waters, and trees of healing, planted by the Lord! It is the primitive Eden ritual rescued from profanation, and re-instituted with added elements suited to the emergencies of the age. There is also another strong intimation of a final offensive in the moral war. No further attempt was now made to procure the desired responses; but before his departure the seer unfolds to Balak a vision of the future. "And he took up his parable, and said, Balaam the son of Beor hath said, and the man whose eyes are open hath said: he hath said, which heard the words of God, and knew the knowledge of the Most High, which saw the vision of the Almighty, falling into a trance, but having his eyes open: I shall see him, but not now: I shall behold him, but not nigh: there shall come a Star out of Jacob, and a Sceptre shall rise out of Israel, and shall smite the corners of Moab, and destroy all the children of Sheth. And Edom shall be a possession, Seir also shall be a possession for his enemies: and Israel shall do valiantly. Out of Jacob shall come he that shall have dominion, and shall destroy him that remaineth of the city. And when he looked on Amalek, he took up his parable, and said, Amalek was the first of the nations; but his latter end shall be that he perish forever. And he looked on the

Kenites, and took up his parable, and said, Strong is thy dwelling-place, and thou puttest thy nest in a rock. Nevertheless, the Kenite shall be wasted, until Asshur shall carry thee away captive. And he took up his parable, and said, Alas, who shall live when God doeth this! And ships shall come from the coast of Chittim, and shall afflict Asshur, and shall afflict Eber, and he also shall perish forever."

This prophecy of the Star out of Jacob and a Sceptre out of Israel, we can conceive to have had a profound effect on the Oriental imagination. We hear its echo at a later day in the inquiry of the magi: "Where is he that is born King of the Jews? for we have seen his star in the east, and are come to worship him." Would that all the magi, of all the ages, East and West, would show the same believing, tender, loving, loyal spirit!

There is more instruction in this brief history of Balak and Balaam, touching the philosophy and physiology of spiritual manifestations, than in many a pretentious treatise of modern times. Balaam was really a remarkable man; his closing predictions (which we do not attempt to discuss) extend to times later even than the present; and there are in all his utterances, traces of original elevation of spirit. Yet there was that mingling of good and evil, of truthfulness and sinuosity, of nobility with sordidness, which is the saddest, as it is the most mysterious and perplexing problem of history. Only Omniscience can fully solve that problem.

CHAPTER XXI.

CANAAN.

THE hypothesis we are considering implies that the material system is pure and purifying; and that to grow up healthily in a healthy body, regulating the natural appetites, and fulfilling the natural relations of the family and of society, in a healthful way, involves such a golden-rule training as goes far towards the cure of innate selfish habits, especially when complemented by the secret monitions of the Spirit, the emblematic rites of religion, and the direct oracles of God from the mercy-seat.

What, then, would be the attitude of the cosmocracy towards such a system? This is undoubtedly a difficult problem to solve completely; and the utmost we dare attempt is to find some way of thinking it through conveniently. The solution is in brief this: they would assail the system, not directly, but indirectly. Supposing two great political parties to exist in the empyreal realms, both would attempt to use this material system according to their respective views, and make political capital out of it. And supposing the human race exiled in disgrace from their native celestial seats, the great parties on high may differ as to the manner of governing them; somewhat as in our own case parties may differ as to the proper mode of governing the freedmen.

Yet, if it be supposed that man had been nominated to the succession in office, and in some way defeated and driven into exile in disgrace, it is easy to conceive there-might be a certain element of jealousy lurking in the mind of prominent leaders, somewhat as an element of resentful jealousy might animate a great national party towards the freedmen, whom they had driven from short-lived political ascendency. We are conditioned, then, by our hypothesis, to conceive of the course pursued by the cosmocracy, not as a conscious, overt "drawing off" or "rebellion," or "unfurling the banner" of "treason" or "revolt," but rather as a course strenuously defended by partisan rhetoric, on grounds of a specious but unsound political morality, the badness of which could only become adequately manifest by a long course of development; — that the credit of whatever was good in the successive world-empires was claimed by both the great political parties, and the responsibility for what was bad thrown upon their antagonists, or upon man himself, — which was an indirect way of throwing it upon the party of whom man was, as it were, client and *protégée*. It is conceivable that the cosmocracy should try to keep men in order by severity, — by intimidation; and finding it no easy matter, should be led to increase severity to cruelty; and enhance intimidation by appeal to threats of future torment, and by various superstitious terrors, — as all ancient remains show, and as all spiritualists admit they did in fact do. And it is conceivable that when nations became grossly corrupt, the cosmocracy should be implacable towards them by exaggerating every fault. Thus the dragon-power is represented as accusing man before God night and day; — while, on the other hand, we can conceive of man's Mediator and Advocate as pleading their cause, and arguing that the remedial system was not properly applied, and that, blameworthy as men might be, the responsibility was very largely with the hostile principalities.

These reflections have been occasioned by expressions of surprise in certain quarters, that any one could imagine such developments as those in Sodom, or those in the seven nations of Canaan, or other degraded nations, could have occurred under the auspices of high celestial principalities, and those principalities still maintain their hold of power, and not be instantly hurled down.

Our conception is, that the problem of government is essentially one in all its main elements in all worlds, and all grades of being; in this nation before our eyes, and in the highest empyrean; in this age and in all the ages of the past.

It is as easy to account for the genesis of polytheism, on this hypothesis, as to account for the questions now agitating this nation in view of the principles of Christianity, and of the Declaration of Independence. What that genesis was, we have partly shown. Polytheism was a wonderful system of mingling elements; simple at first, gradually corrupted; protean, deceptive, awe-inspiring, cruel; yet seductive, alluring, licentious; yet claiming divine origin, and wielding the fearful sanctions of eternal retribution. Such the system of the seven nations of Canaan had actually become. How, by the hypothesis, would this development be met on the earth-plane? What would be the next move on the political chessboard? What the next stroke of moral strategy? Being thrown for the time on the defensive, the Mediatorial economy might contract its lines, and concentrate on some quadrilateral. The policy would naturally be to reinstitute the original Eden system on a healthy basis, and prohibit all degenerate systems. Nay, having so done, and trained a single nation to physical hardihood and prowess, the Lord might commission them as high-sheriff of the nations, to execute capital sentence on some community where the corrupted scheme had worked itself out to its ripest fruits. This would be not merely allowable, but almost inevitable, unless the beneficent, all-embracing plan was to be abandoned.

This, then, is in fact the course that we conceive was taken. The whole Levitical system is adapted with divine ingenuity to incarnate sound minds in sound bodies, with pure family relations, tribe relations, and national relations, in a healthful country and clime, with healthful avocations, and a ritual wonderfully instructive by its facts and its analogies; and above all, an Oracle for direct responses from the Living God.

At the same time, the Author of the system, — not Moses, for surely no man educated as he had been would have done such a thing if left to himself, — the spirit-Author of the system, deliberately and intentionally eschewed all *post-mortem* terrors. They had been so misused, so abused, and had proved so inadequate, that it was probably deemed inexpedient to rely upon them. At all events, they were practically ignored. The appeal was in fact made to temporal rewards and punishments. And yet, by promise and covenant, and type and emblem, the grand ideas of a future resurrection and redemption were preserved. He "kept the way of the tree of life."

And there on the hills of Canaan, the seven nations had gone on since the days of Sodom, four hundred years, more or less, filling up the cup of iniquity. They were fearfully corrupt in the days of Abraham. What must they have become in four centuries of debasement! Let us beware, in the abounding liberality of our happy ignorance, that we do not apologize for what we do not understand, and that of which we must blush to think humanity ever could have been guilty. Look, then, at the statute; — "When thou art come into the land which the Lord thy God giveth thee, thou shalt not learn to do after the abominations of those nations. There shall not be found among you any one that maketh his son or his daughter to pass through the fire, or that useth divination, or an observer of times, or an enchanter, or a witch, or a charmer, or a consulter with familiar spirits, or a wizard, or a necromancer. For all that do these things are an abomination unto the Lord, and *because of these abominations the Lord thy God doth drive them out before thee.*" * "Thou shalt not let any of thy seed pass through the fire to Moloch, neither shalt thou profane the name of thy God. I am Jehovah. Thou shalt not lie with mankind as with womankind: it is abomination. Neither shalt thou lie with any beast to defile thyself therewith: neither shall any woman stand before any beast to lie down thereto: it is confusion. Defile not ye yourselves in any of these things: for in all these the nations are defiled which I cast out before you: and the land is defiled: therefore I do visit the iniquity of the land upon it, and the land itself vomiteth out her inhabitants." †

Now, Israel is taken in hand,. moulded, formed, a church, a state, a school, a camp, — the army of the Lord. Israel is led forty years through the desert. A whole generation, effeminate by birth and breeding on the Nile, drop off, and the new generation are inured to toil. They are healthy. They are sons of the desert. They are disciplined. They are veterans — ironsides. God gathers them in his hand and hurls them with crushing impetus upon that Moloch-worshipping mass. Such is the counter-move on the mighty chessboard; such the strategy of the offensive-defensive moral campaign. The position he designs to fortify, — the key of three continents, — to inherit which is to be heir of the

* Deut. xviii. 9–12. † Lev. xviii. 21–25.

world, must first be carried by storm, — purged with fire and sword, and fortified under intense moral antagonism against all the loathsome abominations of the hostile powers. For loathsome as they are to God, they were, alas! but too alluring to the Egypt-born generation, as they showed by their licentious orgies even at the foot of Horeb, and in the march, and in repeated instances from generation to generation. They must be taught to fight against a system that would otherwise entice, allure, corrupt, and destroy them. They are espoused to Jehovah. He is their husband. To yield to the blandishments of the daughters of Midian, the seers and priestesses of Baal; to eat the sacrifices of the dead; even to "seek" unto, "inquire" of, or "consult" those necromantic oracles, was a spiritual unchastity; — and "I the Lord thy God am a JEALOUS God." It was, it must be, high treason, — a capital offence, — a crime against their whole law, against their own bodies, the family, the state, the oracle, — against God himself enthroned between the cherubim. "Whosoever he be of the children of Israel that giveth any of his seed unto Moloch shall surely be put to death; and the soul that turneth after such as have familiar spirits, and after wizards to go a whoring after them, I will even set my face against that soul, and will cut him off from among his people." *

And if it be said that Israel was in fact infected, if she apostatized about once in every generation, if for a thousand years until the return from Babylon the Lord seemed fighting a losing battle, — every moment pure religion seeming on the point of being swept from the face of the earth, — we see that at last the defence won the game; and we see that nothing but such a destructive onset and such an intense antagonism could have

* Lev. xx. 2.

done it. The moral momentum of that aggressive movement under Joshua was never entirely lost. It is not lost even now, for Israel has yet a part to play on the chessboard of nations. And this view, it is important to observe, flows naturally and consistently from those principles in which all spiritualists agree. Indeed, it would be easy to adduce quotations from leading spiritualists of every school, substantially necessitating these results. And we have carefully endeavored to keep within the limits warranted by the universally conceded premises of the movement.

CHAPTER XXII.

THE JUDGES.

THE period from Joshua to David is peculiar. The divine impulse was apparently suspended; catastrophism was reduced to a minimum; gradualism set in; the forces of environment came into play. "So is the kingdom of God, as if a man should cast seed into the ground, and should sleep and rise night and day, and the seed should spring up and grow he knoweth not how." * Would the good seed grow in the newly-ploughed field, or would the weeds, whose rootlets filled the soil, eat it out? The vine was planted in the vineyard in a fruitful hill: would it bear grapes, or wild grapes, or even grapes of Sodom? It was a small country. Would this divine republic rise to the primacy of nations, or relapse to barbarism, being broken up into small fragments — neighborhoods, families, tribes, factions, in districts, nooks, and corners? Entering into a rich land, receiving houses they built not, wells they digged not, acquiring sudden wealth, would the young saint (Jeshurun) "wax fat and kick?" † Sparing a remnant here, contrary to divine command, and a remnant there, of the Canaanites, with the Philistine on the coast, and Moab, Ammon, and Midian on the east, would the antipathy God had cultivated yield to infection?

The problem is complex. The history is fragmentary; — a raid here, a foray there, a border war, a guerrilla campaign, sometimes in one district, sometimes in

* Mark iv. 26–29. † Deut. xxxii. 15.

another, — almost never the nation in whole, always in parts, — samples, as it were. As in our own newly-settled states one may find families of refinement and families of semi-barbarism within a stone's throw, so there might be idyls of Ruth and Hannah within a stone's throw of massacres of Benjamin and raids of Dan.

If souls in fact came pure into life, — if each generation was a generation either of prim Puritan or of placid Quaker, — if each generation brought with it latent habits of self-restraint and virtue, — the problem would be simpler; there might be a gradual rise, a gradual amelioration. But little flasks of nitro-glycerin, explosive, evasive; animated globules of mercury; a shower of silver shot; — what then? Spirits subtle, proud, wilful, swift, with coiled-up habits of self-will, like watch-springs; how then? Every fresh generation would witness a fresh complication; — here a flash, there an explosion; here an anomaly, there a neglect or total upsetting of the ritual; here a compromise, there a transient penitence, a catastrophic reformation. Every generation would witness a declension. It is what we actually see. The profoundest problem of moral government is to know good and evil; to bring good out of evil; to organize a good system with partially evil materials; to use selfish men for benevolent ends, — yet never compromise principle nor sanction sin. It requires a discrimination of which only Omniscience is capable.

Look at it in our own affairs. How can a great party act together without concert? and how can the honest men of a party act with the dishonest, without conniving at dishonesty? God knows, but we do not; and it will be some time before we find out. But, on the hypothesis we are considering, it was the only problem left to Benevolence to try. He must either wipe out as with a wet sponge all selfish orders, or he must organize a world where benevolent results should be aimed at, with selfish material. By the hypothesis, the body, family, and social state, materially considered, are pure and purifying. By the hypothesis, the divine republic is hurled crushingly upon the corrupt seven nations. The new system is there; it is lodged in its mountain fastnesses, in its vale of Esdraelon, and in a thousand glens and wild caves. It is there; it cannot be dislodged. It must undergo the ordeal of attack from without, and of development from within. Each Israelite is not a nicely turned and sandpapered little chessman — a pawn or a knight; — alas, he happens to have moral gunpowder inside of him. His heart is tinder, and sparks are flying. Of course polytheism is repulsive; — he ought to feel antipathy to the filleted priestesses of Venus Astarte, but he is too easily mollified. Clusters of Sodom ought not to grow on such a vine; but while Christendom makes the amorous songs of Corydon and Alexis a classic in every college, Christendom ought not to wonder that obscure localities in Israel should witness shocking developments of passion.*

Now what we in fact see in the era between Joshua and David is the nation fairly lodged, clinging tenaciously to its hold, — often overrun, often reduced to extremity, at times even hiding in caves and glens, destitute of sword or spear, and dependent on the Philistine even to sharpen plough or mattock; yet surviving, with a tolerably healthy physique, and certain habits of language, and family life, and religion, and national feeling. But the system itself, as embodied in the tabernacle, is sadly dilapidated and needing reinstitution, — the tabernacle in one place, the ark in another, the She-

* Like those, for example, recorded in Judges xix., xx., and xxi.

kinah glory nowhere; the divine housekeeping at Shiloh interrupted; Jehovah on the cherubic throne as king rejected; a mortal monarchy inaugurated; a half-dozen imitation tabernacles or houses of God, one at Laish or Dan, one at Mizpeh, one at Nob near Jebusi, and the old tabernacle at Shiloh; the ship a seeming wreck; government and worship reverting to first principles; patriarchal altars, patriarchal sacrifices, patriarchal prophets, and schools of prophets, seers, second sight, and all the phenomena of clairvoyance, under the auspices of Samuel, the prophet of Jehovah; and, lurking in private families and out-of-the-way resorts, occult practices of incantation, divination, consultation of familiar spirits, and necromancy generally.

The causes of this apparent shipwreck (though David got the ship off the breakers) were simple. The unsubdued remnants of the seven nations multiplied and regained strength; the old generation of desert-born warriors died off. The new generation came on the stage — as the first generation born in New England did — with no taste for the rigid antagonism of their fathers. They thought the garlanded priestesses charming; they visited the groves and the festivals; they intermarried; they were ensnared. Of course the priests of the groves had specious arguments, and could prove that theirs was the original Eden system, the very same that came out of the ark; their gods Baal and Astarte the very same substantially that their ancestors, the family of Abraham, worshipped beyond the Euphrates, in Mesopotamia; and Israel's system was nothing but an innovation. So they yielded, and were punished by captivity, and repented, and were forgiven; and yielded again, and were enslaved; repented, and were forgiven, about once every generation.

The result was, a temporary failure to establish a virtual republic under the law (summed up by Christ as the golden rule) as constitution and the Shekinah oracle for supreme court and executive. Feeling the evils of anarchy, and deficient in faith in the Lord's power to unite them, the people ask a king. Their request is granted, though with reluctance and a vivid delineation of what the character of the monarchy would be.

Meanwhile Saul is crowned. The usual development of ambition follows. Saul usurps the prophetic prerogative, equivalent, as things were, to the judicial and sacerdotal functions; he forfeits the crown; a successor is anointed; then follows an instructive story of jealousy, persecution, delirium, necromancy, defeat, suicide. Of course, as the principles of misgovernment are and must be essentially the same in all worlds, visible and invisible, it is supposable that in the story of Saul there may be shadowed out a dim reflection of higher realities when the celestial principalities found themselves threatened with loss of power by the anointing of man; also that in the story of David there may be a certain similarity to that of the Anointed, which is commonly expressed by saying that David was a type of Christ. Precisely here, then, at this juncture so appropriate, there bursts forth a development unparalleled in the ages — the Psalms. To say they have never been equalled is to say but little. They have never been approached; there is nothing like them in human literature. The secret of this is found in that analogy of which we have spoken. There is a profound significance in them; and as we are in fact exiles from our celestial fatherland, the vibrations of those harp-strings thrill so deeply in our souls that we can at times hardly bear the exquisite pain or pleasure of the touch. We weep when we remember Zion.

"They come as half-forgotten dreams
From that eternal land;
The sound of its celestial streams
And shores of silver sand!"

Is it possible we can be so oblivious as to remain insensible? Deeply are we buried indeed, if such be the case. Or can we be interested chiefly by the mechanism of the manifestation, the psychologic or physiologic phenomena, and ignore the grandeur of the ideas and emotions expressed, the sweetness and awfulness of the revelation of love divine, love absolute, unconditioned, eternal? The greatness of the MANIFESTATION at Horeb was not in the flaming summit, nor in the thunder, nor in all the material phenomena, august as they were; but in the revelation of the spirit of love, as the essential law of God's being and government. So the greatness of the MANIFESTATION in the Davidic era was in the still richer revelation of that love, in relation not merely to all governmental needs, but to the myriad and manifold needs of sinful, sorrowful, struggling hearts, yearning for their native clime, or suffering under the oppression, the contumely of proud and scornful foes, not merely in the visible world, but in realms unseen.

How can we think it is mere matter that defiles and distresses us! How can we think that to put off the last particle or trace of matter, and be absorbed into the immaterial light, is what we sigh for! It is not matter that pains us: it is selfishness; it is pride; it is that palsy of the spirit that makes us feel with acute pain that we are not like Jesus, and that we cannot endure the crucifixion we need. That, and not matter, whether gross or refined, is what distresses us. This makes us cry out: "As the hart panteth after the water brooks, so panteth my soul after thee, O God. My soul thirsteth for God, for the living God: when shall I come and appear before God? My tears have been my meat day and night, while they continually say unto me, Where is thy God?" This makes us exclaim: "O God, thou art my God; early will I seek thee: my soul thirsteth for thee, my flesh longeth for thee in a dry and thirsty land, where no water is; to see thy power and thy glory, so as I have seen thee in the sanctuary. Because thy loving-kindness is better than life, my lips shall praise thee. Thus will I bless thee while I live: I will lift up my hands in thy name. My soul shall be satisfied as with marrow and fatness; and my mouth shall praise thee with joyful lips; when I remember thee upon my bed, and meditate on thee in the night-watches. Because thou hast been my help, therefore in the shadow of thy wings will I rejoice. My soul followeth hard after thee: thy right hand upholdeth me."

More and more, as we study the actual MANIFESTATIONS of the Spirit in all ages, at the gates of Eden, on Horeb, or in the Psalms of David, we shall perceive the great truth bodying itself forth in various forms, that the health both of nations and of single hearts, both on earth and in the very highest heaven, is in loving divinely and being divinely beloved; and as this dawns upon us, the language of our restful heart will be, "As for me, I will behold thy face in righteousness: I shall be satisfied, when I awake, with thy likeness." "Thou wilt show me the path of life: in thy presence is fulness of joy; at thy right hand there are pleasures for evermore."

CHAPTER XXIII.

SOLOMON.

THE temple of Solomon, like the tabernacle in the wilderness, was a reproduction, in more durable form, of the original Eden tabernacle. As in Genesis we read, "He tabernacled the cherubim on the east of Eden;" and as at Horeb we might epitomize the Mosaic legislation by saying, "he tabernacled the cherubim anew, with additional ritual observances;" so here, we may comprehend Solomon's work by saying, he tabernacled the cherubim a third time, on Mount Moriah, in a temple whose foundation-courses were built for all time. As Moses took what Egypt had kept of primeval records, so Solomon now took what Tyre had preserved of primeval mathematics and geometry and architecture, — whatever Egypt, or Chaldea, or any other nation far or near, knew of art, of embroidery, of brilliant dyes, of carving, moulding, and gilding, — and brought them to a focus in the temple. It was one and the same original system, with such variation of detail, and expansion of scope, as befitted the time, and stage of development of the divine benevolent plan.

But while the principle of isolation was by no means abandoned; while the system was being impregnably fortified, for a moral defensive of a thousand years, — there were adaptations in it to ultimate expansion and catholicity. The relation of the system to other nations is distinctly indicated, and the educational primacy of the Israelite people reasserted. The Temple was a National Oracle for times then present, where responses might be sought and obtained from Him that dwelt between the cherubim; but it was also to be a house of prayer for all nations.

In the dedicatory prayer we find the clearest recognition of this, together with the most solemn sense of the divine omnipresence and spirituality. "But will God in very deed dwell with men on the earth? Behold, heaven and the heaven of heavens cannot contain thee; how much less this house which I have built!" * It is in this prayer that the idea of Heaven as His dwelling-place is made so prominent. David had spoken of His throne being in the heavens; of his "bowing his heavens;" but now, "hear thou in heaven, thy dwelling-place," comes in like a sweet refrain, again and again, reminding us of Him, a thousand years later, who taught us to pray, "Our Father, which art in heaven!" Now, after specifying the devotional uses of this house to Israel, at home or abroad, he says: "Moreover, concerning the stranger (or foreigner) which is not of thy people Israel, but is come from a far country for thy great name's sake, and thy mighty hand, and thy stretched-out arm; if they come, and pray in this house, then hear thou from the heavens, even from thy dwelling-place, and do according to all that the stranger calleth to thee for, that all nations of the earth may know thy name, and fear thee, as doth thy people Israel."

Here, then, we have vividly enunciated the divine idea of a spiritual primacy among the nations, for their good. Israel, an educational nation, a pioneer in religious and civil liberty; a nation formed to individual health of body, health and purity of family, health, intelligence, virtue, and wealth socially, health of mind and

* 2 Chron. vi. 18.

heart, developed by pure worship and vital communion with the Living God, and Him only.

Now, at the close of the prayer, when Solomon said, "'Arise, O Lord God, into thy resting-place, thou and the ark of thy strength,' the fire came down from heaven, and consumed the burnt-offering and the sacrifices; and the glory of the Lord filled the house. And the priests could not enter into the house of the Lord, because the glory of the Lord filled the Lord's house."

Thus the Lord was at home again among his people; on a somewhat modified plan; He the invisible Sovereign, the king his visible representative. His own conception of it He thus expressed to Solomon soon after in a dream. "For now have I chosen and sanctified this house, that my name may be there forever, and mine eyes and my heart shall be there perpetually; . . . . but if ye turn away and shall go and serve other gods, then will I pluck you up by the roots, and this house, which I have sanctified for my name, will I cast out of my sight, and will make it a proverb and a by-word among all nations. And this house, which is high, shall be an astonishment to every one that passeth by it, so that he shall say, Why hath the Lord done this unto this land and unto this people? and it shall be answered, Because they forsook the Lord God of their fathers which brought them out of Egypt, and laid hold on other gods, therefore hath he brought all this evil upon them."

It is a favorite idea with many that sin begins in immaturity. It pertains to a low and undeveloped stage of being, they think, whether in this visible or in the invisible sphere. The idea that sin could commence in the highest celestial spheres, among the very wisest, brightest, most glorious principalities, seems incredible. But have they ever reflected on the possibility of the selfishness of benevolence, the pride of humility, the deceitfulness of sincerity, and the folly of great wisdom? Have they reflected on that truly deepest and most awful of problems of Omniscience, the discrimination of good and evil?—the good use of badness, the bad use of goodness,—and the almost impossibility of finite minds drawing the line? May not a really benevolent mind be so absorbed in carrying out a benevolent plan, as unawares to violate mercy, humility, and even sincerity? Have they duly considered the nature of pride of intellect? The wiser a mind is, and more profound, is he not more liable to think truth his, and that some incense is due him for thinking God's thoughts after him? And have not even the most humble and contrite sometimes detected a self-complacent pride in humility?

If Solomon, with all his wisdom and benevolent public spirit, and devotion, and humility,—for these breathe unmistakably through his earlier utterances and acts,—and in the very focus of such environments designed to produce and preserve benevolence, could apostatize, why not a wiser than he? Surely one cannot call Solomon's mind low and undeveloped. One must see that sin may be the product of the very highest powers and richest endowments in the most sacred environments.

Solomon was public-spirited, and established commercial relations with remote nations, enriching his people and his court, and forming acquaintance with the men and manners of other nations. He had a mind capacious enough to take in much of their raw material of thought. Moreover, as his prayer shows, he knew that Israel was to influence the devotions of all nations. It would naturally occur to him that if those nations were to be benefited by Jewish influences, he "must begin by recognizing and accepting the truth they already possessed. He must be willing to learn of them in order to teach them." It might not occur to him, that in so doing he ran great risk; that he might ere he was aware withdraw his soul from exclusive dependence on the Living God, and subject it to teachings from a lower sphere, violating the delicate chastity of a spirit espoused to God.

Moreover, in the furtherance of this catholic purpose, he might be led to still further multiply his nuptial alliances with other courts, thus subjecting himself, towards the close of a long and splendid reign, to a formidable accumulation of influences. These wives brought other charms and enchantments than those of sense. In their retinue came hierophants, mystics, seers, and devotees of every degree. Among them Solomon found those who had the traditions of the primitive religion. He could converse with them. He could experiment with them in all their curious arts. Universal Oriental tradition ascribes to him the highest proficiency in the magic art.

It is stated: "And God gave Solomon wisdom and understanding exceeding much, and largeness of heart, even as the sand that is on the sea-shore." * This must mean many-sidedness, and liberality of thought. It is a singular comparison, often used to denote great numbers, but here only to denote wideness and expansiveness of comprehension. "And Solomon's wisdom excelled the wisdom of all the children of the east country, and all the wisdom of Egypt." He knew the esoteric mysteries — as we do not and cannot. He knew all that we know of Egypt, and a great deal more. He knew all that Egyptian priests, and librarians, and hierophants, and magicians knew; and more than they; for while they had been progressing in selfishness, deception, and the gradual obscuration of the original Eden Revelation, Solomon had it as reformed by Moses, and increased by

* 1 Kings iv. 29.

direct manifestation of Him who dwelt between the cherubim. Hence the sages of the Nile (to whom Pythagoras, and Herodotus, and Plato, and other Greek philosophers, came as pupils centuries later) found in Solomon no pupil but a preceptor, one who knew more than they did, unless it be of teachings of their oracles, and familiar spirits, prohibited by the Law. "For he was wiser than all men, wiser than Ethan the Ezrahite, and Chalcol, and Darda, the sons of Mahol: and his fame was in all nations round about." "For he spake of trees, from the cedar-tree that is in Lebanon, even unto the hyssop that springeth out of the wall: he spake also of beasts, and of fowl, and of creeping things, and of fishes." In modern phrase, he was a student of natural history. He composed treatises on these subjects. He pursued the inductive method. He observed. He catalogued. He recorded his observations on botany, pomology, dendrology, zoölogy.

"And he spake three thousand proverbs, and his songs were a thousand and five." Literature, theology, belles-lettres, music, art, architecture. His mind was many-sided, copious, comprehensive, "even as the sand that is on the sea-shore." "And there came of all people to hear the wisdom of Solomon, from all kings of the earth that had heard of his wisdom."

In Ecclesiastes we have the late results of the experiments of a lifetime of a mind like the sand of the sea-shore in its thirst for knowledge; a composition alike wonderful for what it is not, and for what it is, — for what it does not say, and for what it says. It does not systematize. It does not philosophize. It does not analyze. It does not synthesize. It does not praise any nation, or scheme, or system, nor denounce any. It breathes the profoundest yet gentlest feeling of melancholy. It is infinitely sad. It is almost too sad to be remorseful. The writer indeed tells his own experience, including his own follies, his own desolate and desperate speculations; but it is not so much himself he is thinking of, as of the whole creation groaning and travailing in pain together. "One generation passeth away, and another generation cometh: but the earth abideth forever. The sun also ariseth, and the sun goeth down, and hasteth to his place where he arose. The wind goeth toward the south, and turneth about unto the north; it whirleth about continually, and the wind returneth again according to his circuits. All the rivers run into the sea; yet the sea is not full: unto the place from whence the rivers come, thither they return again. All things are full of labor, man cannot utter it. The eye is not satisfied with seeing, nor the ear filled with hearing. The thing which hath been is that which shall be; and that which is done is that which shall be done: and there is no new thing under the sun."

These are the quiet yet remorseful musings of a mind genial, benevolent, magnanimous, full; a mind that has beat against the bars of its limitations till it is utterly exhausted. It has been wise and foolish; sane and insane; holy and unholy; — it has known all there was to know, and found the great problem of the universe an insoluble enigma. It has tried all sensual delights; orgies; magic; diabolism even; intoxication; until the capability of pleasurable excitement is gone. It has tried all normal pleasures; thrift, industry; art, science, literature, public spirit, commerce, war, religion; — but to what end? Old age is upon him; when "the grasshopper shall be a burden, and desire shall fail, because man goeth to his long home." His plans have all apparently succeeded; his work has all been, in human estimation, well done; he has enjoyed it in the time of it; but what does it amount to in a world like this? What will become of it the moment he is gone, — and that Rehoboam, or some other imbecile, takes the helm? His people are already complaining of his yoke as heavy. There is that Jeroboam too, with his plots. "Therefore I hated all my labor which I had taken under the sun, because I should leave it unto the man that shall be after me; and who knoweth whether he shall be a wise man or a fool?" He had a shrewd suspicion that he would be a fool, — and so he was; and it was an acute and piercing misery.

Solomon had done well; in many respects he had reformed the Eden-Levitical tabernacle, and intrenched it on Moriah's top for another thousand years; but he had been too complaisant. He says not a word about the Temple, or the Law, or the Covenant, or about his having burned incense at rival shrines, — claiming to be the only true primitive Eden-worship. But he does say: "I find more bitter than death the woman whose heart is snares and nets, and her hands as bands; whoso pleaseth God shall escape from her, but the sinner shall be taken by her." Those compliances with the ancient ritual were not probably intended to be a precedent, or an example; they did not displace nor interrupt the regular temple-service; it was a transient error, — but it was done, and could not be undone; nor could its consequences be averted, namely, the disruption of that very empire he had sought to consolidate. He enters into no details. He merely breathes out the profoundest emotions of sorrow. The only lesson his life teaches is, "Fear God and keep his commandments; for this is the whole duty of man." He had had a splendid opportunity, he had made a splendid use of it; but somehow he had missed the mark. He had been benevolent, but too complaisant. He had not strictly kept God's commandments. He had in fact yielded to the subtle assault of the invisible powers impelling him to reign in a self-glorifying spirit, as distinguished from a disinterested or self-sacrificing benevolence. He meant to reign wisely and well, both for Israel and for mankind; but did not realize that that could not be done without severe self-denial; as he says, — and it is the rock on which he struck, — "And whatsoever mine eyes desired I kept not from them; I withheld not my heart from any joy."

In short, the theory of government Solomon attempted to carry out was a benevolent and wise administration of a perfect system, without painful self-denial. Hence the matchless melancholy of his confessions. That method will not work well in this world, nor in any other world, even were it in the seventh heaven, least of all in a world composed of selfish spirits incarnated for the express purpose of being taught the rudiments of self-denial.

CHAPTER XXIV.

THE PROPHETS.

WE are struck with one fact in reading the prophets, and that is, the severity of their denunciations of the developments in Jerusalem; not merely in the neglect of rites, and forms, and the technics of religion; not merely in idolatry and all its crimes; but in the violation of the golden rule, of common honesty, of chastity, and of benevolence in all the relations of life.

The prophets distinctly charge a worse state of morals in Israel than in surrounding nations. Jerusalem has done worse than Egypt, Nineveh, Babylon. She has done as evil things as she could. Not only that, she is not ashamed; she has lost the sense of shame; she cannot even blush. There is no spectacle in human history more instructive than that of individual prophets dealing with a corrupt, covenant-breaking nation. The nation is a harlot. So freely is language based on this analogy used, that modern sentimentalism is offended. The blows of prophetic reproof are like the strokes of an iron rod, or mace, or battle-axe. God is said to hew them by his prophets. The body politic is so beaten and bruised in the process that there is no place left to strike. Nor is it words alone: all the penalties of their Law (which was restricted to temporal sanctions only) are fulfilled, all the threats of Moses executed, until, "from the crown of the head to the sole of the foot," the whole body politic "is full of wounds, bruises, and putrefying sores." These utterances, and others of like character, which constitute the staple of the prophecies from Isaiah to Malachi, cannot be regarded as an outgrowth of Hebrew or Semitic genius. Analogies of natural growth do not seem appropriate. Analogies of conflict, of opposing systems or parties, seem more in place.

The prophet seems to be the organ of a manifestation from higher spheres; and this manifestation is ever in favor of good morals, fair dealing, the golden rule. Ritual observances, without these, are often declared to be worse than useless. This is the most marked feature of the record from Isaiah to Malachi. The prophets generally were sufferers. "Which of the prophets," said Stephen, "have not your fathers persecuted?" "O Jerusalem, Jerusalem," exclaims Jesus, "thou that killest the prophets, and stonest them that are sent unto thee!"

The Epistle to the Hebrews summarizes the experience of the principal prophets: "And others had trial of cruel mockings and scourgings, yea, moreover of bonds and imprisonment: they were stoned, they were sawn asunder, were tempted, were slain with the sword: they wandered about in sheep-skins and goat-skins; being destitute, afflicted, tormented; (of whom the world was not worthy:) they wandered in deserts, and in mountains, and in dens and caves of the earth."*

Now, that these persecutions of the prophets were a natural evolution, a reaction of the national selfishness against salutary restraint, is easy to conceive; but the question is respecting the prophecies themselves, which caused such reaction. Were they too a growth, a natural product of Hebrew genius?

All spiritualists concede that the prophets were mediums. They also agree in the principle that all com-

* Heb. xi. 36-38.

munications from spirit-sources must be judged by our reason and moral sense; the tree must be known by its fruits. Consistently with these principles, spiritualists must acknowledge that the spectacle presented by the decadence of Israel, from the time of Solomon to the exile, looks like an effort of the divine Spirit, through the prophets, to control that Hebrew disposition, and form it to virtue, truth, and goodness, in spite of its constant waywardness and indocility.

The ten tribes, soon after the death of Solomon, withdraw, and nationalize idolatry, in the form probably of a compromise between the old patriarchal and the Mosaic, or reformed, ritual; they are carried away by Shalmanezer, and disappear from the ken of history; yet there are, no doubt, families left behind of every tribe.

In Judea there are a succession of declensions and reformations, each descent swifter and deeper than the preceding. There are indeed a few here and there, even in darkest times, faithful to covenant; there were seven thousand even in Israel under Ahab. There was a "remnant" in Judea, even though the ruling classes — the court, the priests — were corrupt. It was ever when declension reached its lowest stage that the bursts of prophetic denunciation became most vivid. These, which some have regarded as natural growths of the Semitic genius, are always in inverse ratio to the general health and good morals of the nation. But while the credit of the prophetic unfolding has been given to the Hebrew nature, or Semitic genius, the discredit of the declension has been given to the system. That is the outcome of the system! By the admission of the prophets, the ethnic religions evolved better results; Parseeism bore better fruit. Confucianism and Buddhism were more successful than this; so with Greek and Roman training. Those nations that the Lord left in the care of the cosmocracy did better than the nation which he took special pains to reform. But why not credit the sin to the nation and the system to God? The system failed because it was too good, too exacting. Ethnic systems attempted less, and seemed to succeed better; but the success was temporary. The Mosaic system aimed at simple perfection,—"Do unto others as ye would that they should do unto you." Of course, the recoil of selfishness, guile, and pride was greater from the attempted coercion, but the failure was not so total as it seemed. There was "a remnant" in whom deep spiritual results were attained; and the style of character evolved in these, from the very fact of their being in the minority, called to stand not only against the influence of surrounding nations, with their imposing military, religious, and philosophic systems, but against corrupt majorities at home, was of peculiar value. It developed fortitude, faith, self-denial, patience, and other virtues, in an eminent degree; the gold was refined in a furnace of trial. At the same time, sublime prophecies of the final triumph of truth and love were uttered, growing brighter in proportion as the nation at large grew more corrupt.

Spiritualists cannot look on such prophecies as a natural growth of the national genius; they must regard them as not only emanating from spirits, but from spirits of the highest grade of intelligence and goodness, and as therefore eminently reliable and precious; and wherever there is a direct and palpable antagonism between the philosophy and religion of Israel and that of ethnic systems, so that both cannot be right,—there the spirits energizing through the former were right, and those energizing through the latter were wrong. In short, spiritualists, on their own premises, must admit the existence of two great parties, or kingdoms, in the spirit-world, between whom a great controversy is going on in respect to the principles of good government. Out of this conflict in higher realms all earthly history evolves itself. We watch the game with interest enhanced from the fact that the players are invisible. We strive to comprehend the successive moves on the mighty chess-board, and form some approximate estimate of their play.

CHAPTER XXV.

THE EXILE.

ONE of the most interesting crises in the great game of ages is the seventy years exile in Babylon. To study it aright we need to divest ourselves a little of the associations of our own age, and assume, even though imperfectly, the mental habits of that. We command that buried city on the banks of Euphrates to rise from its sepulchre of ages, and pulsate, as it did then, with the heart-beat of a world's life. And we command ourselves to think as they thought, feel as they felt, believe as they believed, that we mortals are nothing and the immortals all; that we are motes upon the stream, leaves borne upon the breeze, and that the real forces in all the grand drama of existence are from the gods.

We are to see the Golden City as it appeared to that Hebrew Child, fresh from a simple highland home in Judah. What a paradise that rich alluvial plain, through which rolled magnificent Euphrates! No mountains save those mountain-walls with their ponderous brazen gates and lofty towers. It is a magnificent development of the arts, sciences, arms, wealth, literature, and religion of the age. Nebuchadnezzar, who had brought her architectural glory to its zenith, was himself an embodiment or personification of the world-empire, visible and invisible. "Thou, O king, art the HEAD OF GOLD!" In thinking of him and of this "golden city," — this "lady of kingdoms," — we gain an indistinct but impressive image (by analogy) of the invisible cosmocratic prince, whose spirit and policy were here embodied. And in the feelings and principles of that Captive Child we gain a slight conception of the emotions and principles of Israel's invisible Advocate and Friend.

Who could dream that that metropolis, "dwelling upon many waters, abundant in treasures," — that "destroying mountain," from whose gates had rolled the red lava streams of war, could ever pass away? Her monarch had recovered Syria and Palestine, reduced Tyre, and ravaged Egypt, and brought the treasures of the world to enrich his capital! We feel sympathetically, in imagination, the elation, the exhilaration of spirit, in court and camp and market-place. "Is not this Great Babylon that I have builded!" "I am, and none else!" There is no other empire, no other city, no other metropolis, worthy of being named but this! And in this feeling, as all the sculptures show, there is a constant reference to the supernal powers. The monarch says in every public act of worship, In me and in my realm, the intelligences I adore express themselves. We accept the thought. We reproduce the sublime conviction. And in so doing we gain an insight, dim indeed but approximatingly correct, into the realities of the unseen cosmocratic dynasty. We understand something of that cycle of history in the visible and in the invisible world.

Corrupt as the Jewish nation had become, there were families of piety here and there, and individuals, like Daniel and his three friends. And when the iron rod dashed the nation in pieces, these clung with greater tenacity to their sacred writings, and their faith in the Living One. And while they cheerfully obeyed the prophetic command, "Build ye houses, and dwell in them; and plant gardens, and eat the fruit of them; take ye wives, and beget sons and daughters; and take wives for your sons, and give your daughters to husbands, that they may bear sons and daughters; that ye may be increased there, and not diminished. And seek the peace of the city whither I have caused you to be carried away captives, and pray unto the Lord for it: for in the peace thereof shall ye have peace," * they had no thought of abandoning their religion even in its strictest details. The captive child might be taken into favor by the king, but he would never sink into a court parasite, or indulge in the idolatrous feasts of the palace. He would take his own independent course from the very beginning, as holding communion with the living God, and him alone. This was indeed hiding the leaven in three measures of meal. Babylon was, and was to be, the resort of sages from other lands. Here Thales, Pythagoras, perhaps Plato, and other leaders of the world's thought, were to come in quest of knowledge. In anticipation of their quest, providence has brought here a child of singular abilities, resolved from the first to be true to the Lord God of his fathers.

We by no means undervalue the advantages enjoyed by the captive Israelites of acquiring knowledge in Babylon. We are far from undervaluing the more ancient opportunities Moses possessed of rescuing from oblivion whatever was worthy of preservation in the archives of Egypt. He could estimate the Hermetic books correctly, for he had them whole and entire, with living sacerdotal instructors to explain them. So Daniel had access to whatever of primitive revelation had come down in this line of descent. To him the cuneiform tablets were in no need of painful decipherment, conjectural, fragmentary. He had access to royal libraries, with royal librarians at his command. Whatever was really worth preserving he could, and, as we conceive, did pre-

* Jer. xxix. 4, 5.

serve. But he was vastly better qualified to teach Babylon, than Babylon was to teach him. He had in the writings of Moses, and David, and Solomon, condensations of thought and emotion infinitely transcending all Babylon could boast; and he and his three friends were themselves drinking of the water of life at the fountain-head. "God gave them knowledge and skill in all learning and wisdom; and Daniel had understanding in all visions and dreams. Now at the end of the days that the king had said he should bring them in, then the prince of the eunuchs brought them in before Nebuchadnezzar. And the king communed with them; and among them all was found none like Daniel, Hananiah, Mishael, and Azariah: therefore stood they before the king. And in all matters of wisdom and understanding, that the king inquired of them, he found them ten times better than all the magicians and astrologers that were in all his realm." In illustration of this, we have the account, given with all the vividness and simplicity of Oriental story, of the king's forgotten dream, which his wise men can neither reproduce nor expound. Daniel does both, describing the image — symbol of successive world-empires, — gold, silver, brass, iron, and stone; — Babylon, Medo-Persia, Greece, Rome, and a fifth, whose shock the image still standing on feet of iron and clay awaits.

The result of this spiritual manifestation was to place Daniel at the head of the magi and other wise men of Babylon. This is a fact whose profound significance spiritualists can appreciate. Daniel was a medium. The spirits operating through him were of the highest, purest, most benevolent character. The mediumship of Babylon had become sadly corrupt, as the clay tablets recently deciphered abundantly show.* It had been

* Lenormant, *La Magie chez les Chaldéens*, passim.

made the subservient instrument of ambition, worldly policy, and of superstitious terrorism.

Now, however, the college of magicians (if we may so term it) is transformed into a school of the prophets, with a child of the covenant at the head, in whom was indeed "the spirit of the holy gods." Then followed, during a long and useful life, edict after edict from the monarch to the various nationalities of the empire, proclaiming the name of Israel's God. It is a series of state papers of unequalled interest. And if we set a high value on the tantalizing fragments of the clay-tablet records, how much higher on these, preserved to us entire from the archives of the realm? In the exile, therefore, all spiritualists will see a wonderful mingling of mercy with severity, — severity to Israel, mercy to man; for it was overruled to be a grand evangelizing agency, preparing Babylon to be the school of Pythagoras and other Greek philosophers, — a school whose remote effects we are even yet experiencing, while we have no means of accurately traceing them.

CHAPTER XXVI.

THE RETURN.

THREE quarters of a century the captives dwelt in Babylon; for more than two generations they sojourned in a strange land, and called it home. A few old men might "remember Zion," and the far-off hills of "fatherland;" but the majority had never looked upon any other metropolis than Babylon. Even the language of Canaan was partially forgotten.* The child that opened its eyes within Babylon's mountain walls might hear his mother or grandparent tell of Jerusalem, but it seemed like a heavenly vision or dream, — as "Jerusalem above, mother of us all," now seems to us, who have also forgotten the language of our heavenly fatherland.

Many had lost all wish to return. Babylon was enough for them; Jerusalem might seem attractive to those of a visionary and fanatical turn of mind, but Babylon, for practical, matter-of-fact minds, was better. But Daniel's prayer shows that there were those who remembered the Holy City, and fatherland, with deathless affection and longing. These were, in truth, the more spiritual and devotional part of the nation. Thus the wheat was winnowed from the chaff. When their Assyrian neighbors said, "Sing us one of the songs of Zion," — for they were fascinated by the strange wild melody, — the exiles

* Hence the origin of the Chaldee paraphrase after the Return, to be used in the public readings of the sacred books.

replied, as they hung their lyres on the willows, "How shall we sing the Lord's song in a strange land?" Just as we sometimes feel in the great moral Babel of life, when asked to sing the sweet songs of Zion simply as a pastime. To many of the later-born, — ignorant of the story of the past; the sacred scrolls in what was fast becoming a dead language; the traditions and associations of home obliterated as by the waters of Lethe, — the idea of an emigration might seem dreadful and repulsive. But to those who saw in the captivity a chastisement for national unfaithfulness, and in the return a possibility for a higher spiritual life, the case was different. They applied themselves to confession and fervent supplication for forgiveness.

Daniel's prayer is a beautiful instance of this, especially if we regard it as substantially embodying the ideas and emotions of all the more thoughtful and devout. The great idea of a return fills the soul. That backward migration must begin, which shall efface the ties of seventy years like cobwebs, and knit anew the broken threads of national reminiscence and association of ideas on the heights of Moriah, and Carmel, and Hermon, and Lebanon. The seer himself, now old and gray, might be unable to bear the fatigues and risks of the undertaking; but with what fervor he expresses the true national feeling!

"O Lord, righteousness belongeth unto thee, but unto us confusion of faces, as at this day; to the men of Judah, and to the inhabitants of Jerusalem, and unto all Israel, that are near, and that are far off, through all the countries whither thou hast driven them, because of their trespass that they have trespassed against thee. O Lord, to us belongeth confusion of face, to our kings, to our princes, and to our fathers, because we have sinned against thee. To the Lord our God belong mercies and forgiveness, though we have rebelled against him; neither have we obeyed the voice of the Lord our God, to walk in his laws, which he set before us by his servants the prophets. Yea, all Israel have transgressed the law, even by departing, that they might not obey thy voice; therefore the curse is poured upon us, and the oath that is written in the law of Moses the servant of God, because we have sinned against him. And he hath confirmed his words, which he spake against us, and against our judges that judged us, by bringing upon us a great evil: for under the whole heaven hath not been done as hath been done upon Jerusalem. As it is written in the law of Moses, all this evil is come upon us: yet made we not our prayer before the Lord our God, that we might turn from our iniquities, and understand thy truth. Therefore hath the Lord watched upon the evil, and brought it upon us: for the Lord our God is righteous in all his works which he doeth: for we obeyed not his voice. And now, O Lord our God, that hast brought thy people forth out of the land of Egypt with a mighty hand, and hast gotten thee renown, as at this day; we have sinned, we have done wickedly. O Lord, according to all thy righteousness, I beseech thee, let thine anger and thy fury be turned away from thy city Jerusalem, thy holy mountain: because for our sins, and for the iniquities of our fathers, Jerusalem and thy people are become a reproach to all that are about us. Now therefore, O our God, hear the prayer of thy servant, and his supplications, and cause thy face to shine upon thy sanctuary that is desolate, for the Lord's sake. O my God, incline thine ear, and hear; open thine eyes, and behold our desolations, and the city which is called by thy name: for we do not present our supplications before thee for our righteousnesses, but for thy great mercies. O Lord, hear; O Lord, forgive; O Lord, hearken and do; defer not, for thine own sake, O my God: for thy city and thy people are called by thy name."

To this earnest cry, the response was instantaneous, as the prophet himself goes on to inform us. "And while I was speaking, and praying, and confessing my sin, and the sin of my people Israel, and presenting my supplication before the Lord my God for the holy mountain of my God; yea, while I was speaking in prayer, even the man Gabriel, whom I had seen in the vision at the beginning, being caused to fly swiftly, touched me about the time of the evening oblation. And he informed me, and talked with me, and said, O Daniel, I am now come forth to give thee skill and understanding. At the beginning of thy supplications the commandment came forth, and I am come to show thee; for thou art greatly beloved: therefore understand the matter, and consider the vision." *

Just here the veil is partly lifted, and we see controversies going on among the celestial princes. The prophet, finding the years of the captivity drawing to a close, humbles himself with fasting and prayer, and confesses the sins of Israel. Gabriel is immediately sent to communicate that sublime prophecy: "Seventy weeks are determined upon thy people and upon thy holy city, to finish the transgression, and to make an end of sins, and to make reconciliation for iniquity, and to bring in everlasting righteousness, and to seal up the vision and prophecy, and to anoint the Most Holy. Know therefore and understand, that from the going forth of the commandment to restore and to build Jerusalem unto the Messiah the Prince shall be seven weeks, and threescore and two weeks: the street shall be built again, and the wall, even in troublous

* Daniel ix. 7–23.

times. And after threescore and two weeks shall Messiah be cut off, but not for himself; and the people of the prince that shall come shall destroy the city and the sanctuary; and the end thereof shall be with a flood, and unto the end of the war desolations are determined. And he shall confirm the covenant with many for one week: and in the midst of the week he shall cause the sacrifice and the oblation to cease, and for the overspreading of abominations he shall make it desolate, even until the consummation, and that determined shall be poured upon the desolate." *

Again we find the prophet fasting and praying for a period of three weeks. He has a sublime vision, in the course of which the angel says: "Fear not, Daniel: for from the first day that thou didst set thy heart to understand, and to chasten thyself before thy God, thy words were heard, and I am come for thy words. But the prince of the kingdom of Persia withstood me one and twenty days: but, lo, Michael, one of the chief princes, came to help me; and I remained there with the kings of Persia." † Having then strengthened and encouraged him, — for the prophet was overwhelmed by the majesty of the celestial visitant, — he continues: "O man greatly beloved, fear not: peace be unto thee, be strong, yea, be strong. And when he had spoken unto me, I was strengthened, and said, Let my lord speak; for thou hast strengthened me. Then said he, Knowest thou wherefore I come unto thee? and now will I return to fight with the prince of Persia: and when I am gone forth, lo, the prince of Grecia shall come. But I will show thee that which is noted in the scripture of truth: and there is none that holdeth with me in these things, but Michael your prince." ‡

Here, as all spiritualists will not fail to perceive, it is

* Dan. ix. 24–27. † Dan. x. 12, 13. ‡ Dan. x. 19–21.

plain that a division of sentiment existed in the invisible world, and that not merely among spirits of low grade, but among "chief princes." There are two parties, two armies, or two kingdoms, with their respective chiefs. Perhaps the controversy turned for the moment on the question of restoration. Why, it may have been argued, disturb existing arrangements? Why attempt to reorganize that unmanageable nation again in Palestine? Would they not do more good thus distributed among other nations? Would they not be a leaven in all the Oriental civilizations from age to age? especially as the empires of the West were rising fast in importance. It would not be long before a wave of civilization from the Grecian isles would be washing over Syrian plains. Let well enough alone. To put Israel back as an independent nation would only breed strife, and do neither them nor any other people any good. So spiritualists can conceive of the cosmocratic powers reasoning.

A new chapter of prophecy had unrolled before them, containing matters that must excite their latent jealousy. Something is said of Messiah, the Anointed, though couched in ambiguous phrase, something that cannot be ignored. What may be the secret plans of the advocates of the Restoration? Strong must have been the adverse pressure to make Gabriel say, "There is none that holdeth with me in these things but Michael, your prince." Through this adverse influence it may be, in addition to the natural inclination of the exiles themselves, that so small a minority of the dispersion returned. A multitude of families remained, but, in after years, their attachment to Jerusalem, though it had not been practically strong enough to carry them back, became a latent element of romance within them, increasing from year to year, until its power was perhaps greater than if they had returned; so that at great festivals there might be assembled at Jerusalem representatives of wealthy families, — "devout men of every nation under heaven, Parthians, and Medes, and Elamites, and the dwellers in Mesopotamia." Thus studying the history of the exile and return, we deepen our impression of the reality and comprehensiveness of that divine plan, adverted to in a former chapter, which placed Israel in the centre of moral action and reaction for the ages.

CHAPTER XXVII.

MACCABEAN ERA.

THE period between the return and the advent is largely the period of Greek influence; and Greek influence, if not democratic, was decidedly not absolutist, after the measure and manner of preceding empires. In Egypt, Assyria, Babylon, Persia, we find absolutism pure and simple; not a mere human absolutism, but absolutism transcendent. The king not merely pretends to be a god, he fully believes himself such; and more, he actually is the organ and instrument of cosmocratic powers, and breathes the full spirit of their tremendous absolutism.

If, when Persia went down before the shock of the brazen-coated Macedonian phalanx, a new spirit breathed in, spiritualists can understand it was because the cosmocratic powers had themselves progressed; the policy of Restoration had triumphed, as the result of moral action and reaction in upper realms, — the home of ideas, the primeval source of theories, philosophies, theologies, diplomacies, and idealities in general. Israel by the dispersion had become cosmopolitan, yet by the return was centralized. The temple was rebuilt; and the system, less catastrophic, but more philosophic and practical, was there, and could not be dislodged. A change of policy was inevitable. Let the old absolutism go. Here Greece is rising; yonder is Iron Rome, — wolf-suckled. There shall be a new empire of philosophy and art, and Israel shall be made an available element in that.

Alexander enters upon the scene,—descendant of Achilles, son of Philip, pupil of Aristotle, and passionate admirer of Homer. In Homer, contemporary of Elijah, we see a bard of the groves, a *vates*, a prophet of the patriarchal system. From the fascinations of his page we may judge a little the fascination of his living presence, and voice, and lyre (and such as his), upon susceptible minds of Oriental habits, in groves, and high places, and classic fanes, and solemn adyta, with all the accompaniments of sense, and secrecy, and the sanctions of primeval antiquity; and we cease to wonder so much that Israel went after the magnet, and left Elijah alone to pray for death.

Alexander, through all his campaigns and marchings, slept with Homer under his pillow. Homer's martial strains fired his native enthusiasm and shaped his conquering career. The *Iliad* was his Old Testament, the *Odyssey* (that Pilgrim's Progress of antiquity) his New. But it was an age of great men. Demosthenes and Aristotle were contemporary with Plato, Plato with Socrates, Socrates with Herodotus and Ezra, within a space of two centuries after the captivity. Alexander was the Napoleon of the old world, with gigantic plans and large and liberal conceptions. He broke in pieces the slavish despotisms that had preceded him, and sought to equalize and combine the nations in a more liberal empire. Barriers of race and tongue were somewhat broken down; the way was prepared for a larger civilization and higher ideas of life, or what were deemed such. The ideas of the schools became diffused in practical forms, and the Greek language became the almost universal medium of literary, commercial, and official intercourse.

On no nation had all this a more powerful effect than on the Jewish, whether for good or for evil. Offended at their refusal to pay tribute, Alexander, after the capture of Tyre, marched upon Jerusalem, meditating vengeance. Josephus states that he was met by the priests in their robes of office. At first sight, the conqueror rushed forward and knelt to the high-priest with awe and veneration, and on Parmenio inquiring the reason, said that before his Asiatic campaign, at Dio in Macedonia, there appeared to him in a dream this very man in this very dress, and invited him to invade Asia.* The conqueror of the East then entered Jerusalem, offered gifts, and worshipped in the temple; and the prophecies of Daniel were spread before him. From that time the Jews became, as it were, his special *protégés*, as they continued to be of his descendants till the time of Antiochus.

Here, then, was Grecian influence paramount in Palestine. The Jewish system, under the restoration by Ezra, was more ecclesiastical and less political as the oral law or tradition gained prestige. The Jew could be somewhat cosmopolitan without being an idolater. Ritualism interposed a barrier against Greek license. The idea of the unity of God successfully antagonized the subtleties of philosophic pantheism. Of course, sects would arise analogous, as some have remarked, to the typical forms of Greek philosophy.

Thus Alexander was the schoolmaster of nations, and especially of Israel, to teach them Greek and many new ideas. The city he built in Egypt and named after himself, Alexandria, perpetuated his influence, and powerfully affected the thought of subsequent ages. That in all this the cosmocratic powers had a design, all spiritualists will understand; and that in it, to a certain extent, the adverse parties of the upper realms might have

* Josephus, Antiq., Lib. XI. chap. 8.

been agreed, is conceivable. The party favoring restoration, however, we conceive, had deeper designs, inspired by the divine Spirit, than could be then disclosed. Alexander was himself conscious of being the instrument of higher powers ; and when his preceptor Aristotle advised him to treat the Greeks as freemen, but the Orientals as slaves, he replied that it was his divine mission to unite and reconcile the world.

The question then arises, Why should the unseen powers prompt or permit the terrible reversal of this policy by Antiochus, and the attempt to annihilate the Jewish system? Selfishness is divisive, and defeats itself. The prince of the aerial powers did not tempt Alexander to be a drunkard. He was, we may well suppose, ashamed of him. It was mortifying to be obliged to use instruments so liable to go wrong, and, for the sake of temporary gratifications, to wreck great plans. The selfish powers could never calculate the chances of innate development-forces of selfish minds. Alexander died in a drunken debauch, leaving grand designs unexecuted, and his empire fell in pieces. The Seleucidæ continued the same favorable policy towards the Jews, admitting them to equal privileges in the cities, even Antioch, the capital. The consequence was a gradual migration homeward, and they became, both at home and abroad, an element of strength, a bond of union to the empire. For a similar reason the Ptolemies favored them. They were on the frontier between the rival empires, which were induced, as it were, to bid against each other for their favor ; and when Antiochus the Great conquered Palestine from the Ptolemies, although the Jews suffered from the war in their territory, the victor bestowed on them honors and new exemptions. Thus, in an age when no small nation could long hope for independence, there was none so nearly independent as the

Jews. This may have excited the jealousy of the invisible powers. Might this be the stone cut out of the mountains without hands? Might there be here, in this new growth of the covenant nation, some concealed element fatal to cosmocratic supremacy?

Such may have been the motive in worlds unseen for either instigating or at least not trying to prevent a kind of crusade against Judaism, especially as now the grand Empire of the West was drawing nigh, to which the cosmocrats might transfer their ambitious designs, already frustrated by the frailty of older empires. When Epiphanes came to the throne he found an exchequer impoverished by wars and revolts, and tributary to Rome. The Jews had grown rich; vast treasures had accumulated in their temple. They had been fostered and favored. Why should they not fully identify themselves with the empire, in arts, manners, and religion? Thus they would become homogeneous with the Greek population, and render service in proportion to the benefits they had received. The attempt was made to transform them into Greeks. They must relinquish circumcision, give up the Law, and adopt Grecian language, manners, and sacrifices. If the cosmocrats put Antiochus up to this, they blundered. If he did it in spite of them, they doubtless execrated his stupidity, though they may have secretly felt as they did when Haman planned to exterminate the race. By one of those sudden vicissitudes common to Oriental story, the Jews found themselves in a furnace. The armies of Antiochus filled the land with scenes of massacre and blood; the temple was pillaged; swine's flesh offered on the desecrated altars; all copies of the Law were sought to be destroyed. All who had not the true martyr-spirit yielded, and burned incense on Grecian altars. Then rose the gallant Maccabees, and the war of Jewish independence was fought out triumphantly. The army of Israel, animated by religious enthusiasm, like Cromwell's Ironsides, broke in pieces and destroyed hosts much larger than itself, led by accomplished commanders, trained in all the Macedonian arts of war.

Thus, in the empyreal world the princes of Israel prevailed. The cosmocracy, seeing this, accept the result and seek to turn it to their own purposes. They take up the victorious Maccabees and praise them, as if they had always been on their side; and they seek to breathe through them a worldly spirit of nationality quite different from the simple idea embodied in the law of Moses. In that system there was nothing between the soul and God, who dwelt between the cherubim, and whose throne of mercy was the ark containing the Law of Love; and while the nation was for a time isolated, in self-defence, from idolatrous nations, the plan was catholic, and the temple a house of prayer for all nations. But now the Oral Law, or tradition, took precedence of the written law; now the priesthood was usurped by the civil power, in person of Jonathan, youngest son of Mattathias. The national unity, while recoiling to the extreme of exclusiveness towards Gentiles, was now broken by intensity and narrowness of sectarian feeling, as between the Pharisees (or Puritans), the Sadducees (or Conservatives), the Essenes (or Ascetics), and the Zealots (or patriotic Ultraists), and the floating vote, that alternated between contending factions. At the same time, a treaty offensive and defensive was concluded between a Maccabean prince and the Roman Senate.

Thus the tares were sown among the wheat. Thus the cosmocratic powers energized to tie the nation by a four- and five-fold cord. Now let the deliverer come, if come he must. Now let us see the man that shall show us how we ought to administer universal empire.

CHAPTER XXVIII.

THE ANCIENT CITY.

BUT let us look a little more closely at that great city which was then reigning over the kings of the earth; the city, — that is to say the religion, of Rome, — for the Eternal City was, by actual historical evolution, an embodied religion. It was not a civilization which had blossomed into a religion; it was a religion which had embodied itself, spire, stalk, ear, and kernel, in a civilization.

We have traced in a former chapter the probable origin of the ancient polytheism.* De Coulanges, in his interesting work "The Ancient City," attempts to trace the whole system back to the belief that the spirits of the dead inhabited the tomb, and required food in order to be happy. We think his premises too narrow, and have indicated in the chapter referred to what seems to us the more natural causes of the system, namely: 1. The original Eden emblems handed down by tradition and corrupted. 2. The analogies of the material system. 3. Innate national idiosyncrasies. 4. Affectionate commemoration of the departed. 5. The direct agency of spirit communications. All these powerful causes, combined, enable us to account for the wonderful system of ancient polytheism, which is by no means extinct, but still survives under various modified forms and names, exercising a powerful sway over the world's thought and

* Chap. XIII. pp. 113-121.

life. With this modification, we can follow out the argument of De Coulanges with confidence and great profit. The dead were gods, and tombs bore the inscription "to the subterranean gods." Every house had its altar, on which a fire was kept ever burning to the worship, of the departed, who were accounted sacred, and to whom were applied the most reverential epithets. Wicked men, as well as good, became gods, retaining the bad inclinations they had manifested in their earthly life.

The Romans called the departed *Manes*, and their tombs were temples inscribed "*Dis Manibus*," or "θειοῖς χθονίοις." Before each tomb was an altar for sacrifice. If the funeral repasts were neglected, the dead left their tombs; reproached the living for their negligence; became wandering shades; were heard in the silence of night, and gave men no rest till the sacrifices were reestablished. Thus the spirits exerted a powerful agency in the formation of the system. It was forced upon the living. It was not wholly a natural evolution by instinct. Men were really haunted. They had no peace. Powers unseen compelled them to establish the ritual. These deified spirits were called demons, heroes, lares, genii, and other names. On the first of March the perpetual altar-fire, or hearth-fire, was extinguished and relighted, either by friction, or by the rays of the sun concentrated by a lens. This fire they adored as divine, — it was the providence, the defender of the family. Every meal was a religious act, beginning and ending with a religious rite, an oblation, and libation; — thus the divine fire as it were ate with them. This fire was, in their view, not the fire of material nature: it was pure; it was chaste; it was a sort of moral being, endowed with intelligence and conscience, knowing men's duties and enforcing them. Subsequently this fire was named

Vesta (ἑστια, hearth, changed to a proper name); she was regarded as a virgin goddess, a moral order; the universal soul regulating the different movements of worlds, as the human soul keeps in order the human system. In common language they came ultimately to say, indifferently, either "hearth," or "domestic lares," or "penates," or "Vesta."

This religion was essentially private and not public; of many gods and not of one; — though here, as already intimated, we cannot agree with our author in thinking that this was the earliest form. Bunsen states that the names of the supernal gods are found on the oldest monuments; and in Eden, Jehovah manifested himself by his Shekinah-flame. Bearing this in mind, we see that the worship of the mortal ancestor, the nether deities, had practically crowded out that of the One living and true God, even where the knowledge of the fact of his existence and attributes survived. The gods of this domestic religion were as many as the families. The dead ancestor desired no worship save from his descendants. The Greek term for worship was πατριάζειν, (Latin *parentare*,) denoting parent-worship. The family tomb was near the house, not far from the door. The sacred fire of one house had nothing in common with that of another. Every fire protected its own, while it repulsed the stranger. All the rites were kept strictly secret. Each family had its own rites, formulas, hymns. This religion could be propagated only by generation. The father gave to his son his creed, his forms, his worship, the right to continue the sacred fire, offer the funeral meal, and pronounce the formulas of prayer.

This religion was the foundation of the family itself; not generation, not natural affection, not superior strength. Greek and Roman laws make no account of these. The ancient Greek word for family is ἐπίστιον, signifying that which is near a hearth. A family is "circle around a hearth." The word *pater* (father) did not include the idea of generation; *pater* was synonymous, not with *genitor* but with *rex*; the father was the priest and king. The unmarried daughter shares the worship of her father; the wife, that of her husband. She must be dismissed from her father's religion before she can unite with her husband's religion. Marriage is therefore strictly a religious transaction, involving three parts:

1. The act of the father before the family hearth, giving her to the husband, and severing her connection with the household-worship.

2. The πομπη, or carrying her veiled, crowned, dressed in white, preceded by a torch, to her husband's dwelling, with sacred chants, and a refrain ὦ ὑμὴν ὦ ὑμέναιε, and the carrying the bride (after a feigned resistance) across the threshold.

3. The *confarreatio*,—she approaches the hearth; she is sprinkled with lustral water; she touches the sacred fire; prayers are repeated; they share between them a cake or small loaf. She is now in religious communion with her husband, initiated into the worship of the family gods. The old Roman law defines a wife as "a companion in things human and divine." The wife worships no longer her own ancestors, but those of her husband. Marriage is to her a kind of second birth, a regeneration. Divorce was difficult, and could only be effected by a kind of excommunication, a *diffarreatio*, in which they refused to eat the cake together before the fire, and the wife with a strange formula of malediction renounced the worship and gods of her husband. The entrance of polygamy was foreign to such a system, and is an abuse to be accounted for from varied causes of innate development-force and environment.

Here, also, is the origin of the ancient right of primogeniture. The oldest was begotten for the performance of the duties to the ancestors; he was, therefore, the continuator of the worship, the religious chief (or *pater*); he alone should therefore inherit property. The other brothers live under his authority as if they were under that of their father.

Our author makes no attempt to show how rites so beautiful and impressive could originate from the idea that souls lived in the tomb. But to our mind every step in the delineation of these ancient customs deepens our profound feeling that several causes combined in the production of such rites,—the veneration of the dead, and the memory of the Shekinah-flame, the first home of the race, "the presence of the Lord," and the first divinely solemnized marriage. For the marriage relation is, as already shown, in itself a divinely created emblem, or analogic symbol, of the relation between the Lord and his redeemed. Hence Paul, quoting the words of Adam, "For this cause shall a man leave father and mother and cleave unto his wife, and they twain shall be one flesh," says, "This is a great mystery, (that is, a profound analogical symbol,) but I speak of Christ and the Church." * Accordingly when the mighty drama winds up, in the Revelation, it is in Paradise the scene is laid, and there we behold the marriage of the Lamb.

Now all spiritualists can easily see that spirits designing to erect and consolidate a world-empire might take advantage of such traditions and build up a system such as actually existed in Judea, Greece, and Rome; nor will it to their minds look like a mere natural evolution, any more than improved varieties of apples, peaches, and pears look like spontaneous evolutions of seedling

* Ephes. v. 32.

stocks. All improved varieties of fruits demand the intervention of beings of a different species, — by budding, or grafting. So with improved breeds of animals. Improved varieties come indeed, in a sense, by natural law, — but there must be intervention. There must be catastrophism. Grafting is catastrophism. More centuries than lie between us and the pliocene epoch would not improve a cider-apple without a grafting-knife. If the Calavoras skull be genuine, those ages have not much improved the human brain, for you cannot bud brains. The angels attempted an extensive grafting operation, but the results did not encourage a repetition of the experiment. Polytheism was the product of a more discreet policy through the agency of departed spirits, operating through certain psychologic laws by us but partially comprehended.

The object of marriage, according to our author, was to perpetuate the religion of the family. The extinction of a family was the extinction of a religion. It left the household gods unprovided for. They became paupers, tramps, unhappy, revengeful, malignant. The object of marriage was to beget a son who might perform the funeral rites. Celibacy was impious. Sterility was a good ground for divorce. The son must be initiated into the family religion. On the ninth day, the father sacrificed to the fire; the infant was carried several times round the hearth, (thus freeing him from the stain supposed to be contracted by gestation,) and to admit him into this church of the family.

All ancient kinship * depended on this household religion. Kinship between two men lay in the fact that they could worship together the same ancestral gods. Kinship, therefore, ran in the male line only. The foundation of kinship was not birth, but worship. From

* *Agnatio.*

the same source came the right of property. The deceased ancestor, or family deity, took possession of the soil. The altar must not be disturbed. Thus the soil came to be the property of the family.

On the worship of the dead, too, depended the right of succession. The son, not the daughter, inherits, because the son alone can perform the rites of household worship. Thus our author goes on step by step, and traces the genesis of the whole framework of Greek and Roman society to this source. The *gens* (whence comes our patrician idea of gentle blood) was nothing but the family still holding to its primitive organization and unity; the *phratry* was a group of families, with its worship founded on that of the domestic religion; the tribe was a group of *phratries*; the city was a group of tribes. The city (*civitas*) was a religio-political association of tribes and families; the *urbs*, the place of assembly, the dwelling, the sanctuary.

The founding of a city was a religious act. The founder of a city was one who by his prayers and rites called the gods and fixed them in the new sanctuary. *Pater Æneas*, the hero of the *Æneid*, is in reality a religious pilgrim, or "pilgrim father." He is not a freebooter, nor a profane and secular adventurer. He is a holy person, a high-priest, bearing the gods of Troy to their new home. He is the child of destiny; fate guides his every step, and opens a path through all obstacles; he is the instrument of the gods in founding Rome. The city followed the analogy of the family; it had its hearth, its ever-burning fire (the temple of Vesta), its penates, lares, demons, heroes, genii; its prayers and ceremonies, which were kept secret; its daily sacred meals, and its great feasts; in short, the *civitas* and religion were so confounded that it was impossible to distinguish one from the other. The city father was, *ipso facto*, the city priest, and the priest was king. *Pater* meant king. Law was a part of religion, and came from the gods. Law was immutable because divine. Patriotism, love of country, was love of the land of one's ancestors, fatherland, the land of the family altar, fire, tomb. The *plebs*, or plebeians, were foreign to the religious organization of the city and family; they had at first no worship and no family. They had either never instituted the worship of ancestors, or had lost it by neglect, or by crime, or by illegitimate descent. A plebeian was simply a man without a sacred fire. They could not dwell within the city, which was sacred. They dwelt outside, "without hearth or home." They had no father, or religious chief, no hearth, and no marriage,—that which the hearth established being forbidden them; hence the patricians said of the plebeians, *Connubia promiscua habent, more ferarum*, "They have promiscuous intercourse, like beasts." They had no property rights, no law, and no justice. They were a despised and abject class, out of the pale of society; their very touch impure.

The term "people" denoted a very different thing from that indicated by the word *plebs*. *Populus* was an assembly of *curies* or *phratries;* and there were groups of *gentes*. *Populus* then was genteel. The progress of revolution was, first the suppression of political royalty; next, the destruction of primogeniture and dismemberment of the *gens*; next, the enfranchisement of clients; last, the plebeians—gradually acquiring wealth, and a sort of aristocracy and a religion of their own, eagerly adopting Oriental systems, like Buddhism,* when swept that way by floating tides of population—entered into the city, sometimes sword in hand, driving out the

* Do we not see in this an explanation of the wonderful likeness of Romanism and Buddhism?

patricians, sometimes by peaceable means. This, at Rome, was from 700 to 500 B. C. Thus at Rome there were two peoples. The plebeians did not obey the *senatus-consulta*, and the patricians did not obey the *plebiscita*. It was a long and gradual process, by which the antagonism between these two peoples was obliterated, and they were at last formed into one people.

Thus our author shows that the whole framework of Roman society was founded on the worship of the dead. In reality, it was built up by the dead, through their direct, incessant, almost omnipresent influence and control. They were the architects of the elaborate structure. The same religion which had founded society, ... gave man his character. . . . . It showed men gods everywhere, — little gods, gods easily irritated and malevolent. It crushed man with the fear of always having gods against him, and left him no liberty in his acts. His house was for him what a temple is for us. He finds there his worship and his gods. His fire is a god; the walls, the doors, the threshold are gods; the boundary marks which surround his fields are also gods. The tomb is an altar, and his ancestors are divine beings. Each one of his daily actions is a rite; his whole day belongs to his religion. Morning and evening he invokes his fire, his penates, and his ancestors; in leaving his house he addresses a prayer to them. Every meal is a religious act which he shares with his domestic divinities. He leaves his house, and can hardly take a step without meeting some sacred object — either a chapel, or a place formerly struck by lightning, or a tomb. Sometimes he must step back and pronounce a prayer; sometimes he must turn his eyes and cover his face, to avoid the sight of some ill-boding object. Every day he sacrifices in his house; every month in his *curia;* several months in the year with his *gens*, or tribe. Above all these gods he must worship those of the city. There are in Rome more gods than citizens. He offers sacrifices to thank the gods; he offers them, and by far the greater number, to appease their wrath. . . . . He has a multitude of festivals for the dead because he is afraid of them. He never leaves his house without looking to see if any bird of bad augury appears. There are words which he dare not pronounce for his life. . . . . He steps out of his house always with the right foot first. He has his hair cut only during the full moon. He carries amulets upon his person. He covers the walls of his house with magic inscriptions against fire. He knows of formulas for avoiding sickness, and of others for curing it; but he must repeat them twenty-seven times, and spit in a certain fashion at each repetition. . . . . This Roman whom we present here is not the man of the people, the feeble-minded man, whom mysery and ignorance have made superstitious. We are speaking of the patrician, the noble, powerful, and rich man.

Such was the effect of this system, where in an impressive sense "death reigned," with a reign not of love but of fear. Men "were all their lifetime in bondage through fear of death," that is, of the dead.

Gods, heroes, dead men, claimed a material worship from man, and he paid them the debt to keep them friendly, and, still more, not to make enemies of them. Man counted but little on their friendship. They were envious, irritable gods, without attachment or friendship for man, and willingly at war with him. Neither did the gods love man, nor did man love his gods. He believed in their existence, but would have wished that they did not exist. He feared even his domestic and national gods, and was continually in fear of being betrayed by them. His great inquietude was lest he might incur their displeasure. He was occupied all his life in appeasing them.

An impression exists with many minds, that the Bible, especially the Old Testament, is gloomy and despotic. It is therefore proper to give prominence to this picture of ancient classic civilization, as so impartially depicted by De Coulanges, who cannot be suspected of writing with a theological bias.

In fact, Israel was the only nation in which the sanctions of their religious and civil law were expressly temporal only, and in which it was possible to have "*hope* toward God that there should be a resurrection both of the just and of the unjust." In Israel, at last, the worship of the dead had been successfully barred out. Everywhere else on earth there was despotism in this life, and a formidable terrorism respecting the future. There is much in the classic civilization that is beautiful; much that is strong, politic, worldly-wise; especially if we include the systems of philosophy, the mysteries, science, art, literature, jurisprudence. The Empire was despotic, but it was preferable to anarchy or to barbarism. But spiritualists will all admit that the great cosmocratic architects had not succeeded in making men happy. Far from it. The world was very unhappy. And a tone of something near akin to despair breathes through the poetry and the music, and the art and science, yes, the philosophy and religion of the world. The fullness of times had come for the deliverer to appear. And both on earth and in higher realms there was a state of suspense, an expectation of some great event.

CHAPTER XXIX.

THE INCARNATION.

TO those spiritualists who admit that the soul is older than the body, the idea of the Incarnation ceases to present any insuperable obstacles. The question whether it is miraculous or not, is rather a question about words. All spiritualists believe in miracles, provided a miracle be defined to be an event occurring by spiritual agency through some law of nature by us not understood. In this sense all spiritualists may unite with Mr. Home in saying, "The account of Jesus' birth is the chief marvel in all history." *

Nor is the question dependent on the prior question of the divinity or humanity of Jesus. All Christians believe in the proper humanity of Jesus; and although spiritualists generally go no further than that, they may believe that he was of celestial origin, or, in other words, that his birth was the result of a true and proper incarnation. In truth, are not spiritualists, on their own conceded principles, logically conducted to this result? They concede not only that Jesus was a medium, but that he was the most powerful medium that has yet lived on earth. They admit the purity of his life, the sincerity of his testimony, and the devotion and disinterested benevolence of his deeds. On their own principles, therefore, he would be in sympathy with the highest order of spirits, and any communications from the un-

* Lights and Shadows of Spiritualism, p. 84.

seen, through him, would be reliable; it would be safe to accept them, unless clearly repugnant to our highest intuitions of reason and conscience. If, then, Jesus, viewed simply as a man, as indicated in his very common title Son of Man, testifies to his own former celestial existence, that testimony will be, with all consistent spiritualists, conclusive, unless they can show it repugnant to reason and conscience.

Now, it is to be borne in mind that the belief in a celestial pre-existence was very ancient and wide-spread, and was entertained by some if not most of Christ's hearers, particularly among the Pharisees. Can there be any doubt what meaning such hearers, and in fact all his hearers, would attach to a declaration like this, for example, "I came down from heaven, not to do mine own will, but the will of him that sent me"? It may be replied here, that some of his hearers murmured, saying, "Is not this Jesus, the son of Joseph, whose mother and father we know; how is it then that he saith, 'I came down from heaven'?"

This however, our spiritualist reader will please take notice, would only show that some of Christ's hearers did not believe in the soul's pre-existence, — not that they did not understand him as asserting his belief of it. It is well known that the Sadducees (and perhaps others) did not believe in this or any other spiritual tenet.

The very fact that they murmured shows that Jesus did affirm his own heavenly origin. Hence, instead of retracting the statement, or qualifying it as if they had misunderstood him, he proceeds to repeat it four times over, in slightly different forms. "This is the bread that cometh down from heaven." "I am the living bread that came down from heaven." And when some still murmured, he said, "Doth this offend you? And what if ye shall see the Son of Man ascend up where he was before?" Surely, if there is any meaning in language, spiritualists cannot doubt what impression he meant to convey. And as if to prevent the possibility of misconstruction, he presently adds: "I proceeded forth and came from God; neither came I of myself, but he sent me." There are many intimations of this kind which we are obliged to pass without mention. But in the seventeenth chapter of John we have that most beautiful prayer, in which the deepest emotions of his heart, in prospect of immediate suffering, find utterance: "And now, O Father, glorify thou me with thine own self with the glory which I had with thee before the world was. . . . Father, I will that they also whom thou hast given me be with me where I am: that they may behold my glory, which thou hast given me: for thou lovedst me before the foundation of the world."

Consider now the accumulation of evidence as to the credibility of this testimony on the universally admitted principles of spiritualism. Jesus was a good man, of pure and elevated spirit and life; he was the most distinguished medium known to history; he was speaking in the very act of prayer, in the so near prospect of martyrdom, that it is almost like his dying hour. Must not his utterance be accepted as true, unless we can show very strong intrinsic reasons for discrediting it?

And what is it after all? It is a simple question of fact. It is not a question of miracle, in the obnoxious sense of the violation of all laws of nature. It is simply and solely a question of fact: Did Jesus enjoy a glorious celestial existence in the heavenly fatherland; and had he been sent on a mission of love; and was he about to return? That he asserted this is clear. Could he be deceived?—for that he would deceive, no true spiritualist will for a moment imagine possible. Could he be deceived? That would imply that the spirits communicating through him were low and deceptive; and that would imply that he himself was low, and in sympathy with such; for this is a cardinal principle of spiritualism. But it is conceded he was good and pure, and in sympathy with the highest range of spiritual existences, and was also in the highest exercise of devotional and self-sacrificing emotions. It follows that only elevated and truthful spirits would be attracted to him. He could not, then, be deceived on a simple question of fact. Is there, then, anything repugnant to our reason or highest moral sense, in the idea that a celestial being should be sent on a mission of love into this world? Is there anything wrong in that? Is there anything immoral, unjust, cruel, or in any way revolting? If not, then there is no conceivable intrinsic reason for rejecting his testimony, at least on spiritualistic grounds. We will suppose it conceded. We will suppose all spiritualists in this particular to agree with the school of M. Kardec: that the birth of Christ was a true and proper incarnation. He came on a mission of love. Such a birth, even on humanitarian grounds, was a grand event.

A unit was subtracted from the sum of celestial being, and added to that of terrestrial. A star of first magnitude in that upper firmament descended below their horizon. A "glory" suddenly ceased to shine in the bright galaxies of the empyrean. One who had stood high, one who had exercised a great influence, one through whom the sympathies, thoughts, wishes of the Father had found expression, was suddenly absent. He had quaffed a more potent cup than that of the fabled Lethe. He had emptied himself of that native plenitude, impoverished himself of that exuberant wealth, humbled himself from that antecedent exaltation. He could not do this unobserved. He could not wisely do it without preparation. The fullness of times must be reached in heaven as well as on earth. All the principalities and powers of all those wide realms must see the misery of man, and his need of help.

In truth, such was the aspect of earthly affairs, and such the effect of the measures culminating in this embassy, that the public sentiment, so to speak, of the upper realms was flowing strongly in one direction, so that when the great transformation was achieved, the humiliation effected before their eyes, — when they saw such a glorious form sown in relative dishonor, such power sown in weakness, such undecaying vitality sown in decay, such a spiritual corporeity sown in animal organism; in short, when they beheld one of the most illustrious of their order lying a helpless infant, of humble parentage, in a stable, they were filled with wonder and enthusiasm. And when the glory of the Lord shone round about on the shepherds, and the angel of the Lord said, "Fear not; for, behold, I bring you good tidings of great joy, which shall be to all the people; for unto you is born this day, in the city of David, a Savior, which is Christ the Lord; and this shall be a sign unto you: ye shall find the babe wrapped in swaddling-bands and lying in a manger;" — then immediately there was with the "angel a multitude of the heavenly host, praising God, and saying, Glory to God in the highest, and on earth peace, good will toward men." The expression, "multitude of the heavenly host," — πλῆθος στρατιᾶς οὐρανίου, — is very impressive and very beautiful. And it is especially worthy of thought, that in all this transcendent scene there is no element of menace.

In elevated conceptions of this general kind, all true spiritualists can sympathize; and they furnish high possible or probable reasons why the testimony of Jesus should be accepted, in the absence of all reasons to the contrary. And there is also another conceivable general reason, namely, to afford to the race a fresh demonstration of its own celestial origin and immortality. That ancient and ennobling conception was growing dim, and with it the sublime faith of a future immortality. See, then, how that faith is reinforced by the fact testified to by this faithful witness. In speaking for himself, he speaks for his race. He is the second Adam. His favorite title for himself, in later years, was "Son of Man." He was not only a man, but the man, the ideal of humanity. Humanity is not a thing merely of birth. The soul is older than the body. The race is older than its environment. It was because anterior to birth he was in truth one, and the purest and noblest one of the celestial human race, that he is rightly termed Son of Man, — the child of the race, the perfect embodiment of its original celestial character. In natural science, whatever is ascertained, structurally, of an individual of a species, is ascertained of the species. A single pliocene fossil human skull implies the existence of the human species in the pliocene epoch. If that single skull be of average dimensions, it would indicate that the race at that epoch was of average intelligence. A single well-ascertained case of ape-evolution — supposing such a thing possible — would be accepted by all evolutionists as conclusive of the derivation of the species. So the resurrection of Jesus has been universally conceded to carry with it the resurrection of the race.

On the same principle, the celestial pre-existence of Jesus, considered as a man, involves the celestial pre-existence of the species. And whatever weight we attach to his testimony to his own origin as Son of Man, we should attach to it, by implication, as to our own origin.

CHAPTER XXX.

THE ORDEAL.

WHEN you see the distant dome of snow from the environs of Geneva, you think you have seen Mont Blanc; but when you reach the hotel at Chamounix, and gazo upward, you feel as though you had never before beheld this "monarch of mountains." He is never quite the same in any two successive hours of the day — in the cold pallor preceding dawn, in the sheen of noon, or in the fading rose-tints and mysterious spectral beauties of twilight. From every new quarter of the compass — north, east, south, west — you obtain a new revelation, till you feel at last that you can never, at any one time or place, see more than one side, one aspect, of the grand old summit. So it is with Him of whose great white throne of judgment we might almost think Mont Blanc the fittest emblem. We can never see but one side, one aspect, of his character; and however beautiful or majestic it may be, we know that there are many directions from which we may approach Him, many distances nearer or more remote, many times of day as it were, — morning or noon or evening, — from each of which we have a new revelation of his glory. In this chapter we have only one such view, — a view, as it were, before the dawn, through the spectral mists of twilight, brightening into day.

That Jesus was a medium, all spiritualists admit; that as such he was liable to the assaults of tempting spirits, they also concede. Dr. Crowell, quoting Mark's statement, "the spirit driveth him into the wilderness," says, "This is a clear case, if not of possession, at least of obsession." * In this, however, he errs, for Luke says that, "being full of the Holy Spirit, he returned from Jordan, and was led by the Spirit into the wilderness." He concedes, however, in the fullest manner, that there was a real attack made upon him by "dark spirits." "This experience of Jesus is a conspicuous lesson, teaching us the necessity of resisting evil influences with all the determination and persistence of our nature; it is also a conspicuous example of victory obtained over these influences through the exercise of a determined will." In the same connection he cites that most important passage (Ephesians vi. 12) where Paul speaks of the cosmocratic powers of wickedness. There is every reason to believe that Dr. Crowell's sentiments on this point would not be objected to by any class or school of spiritualists; and this is certainly a fact of great importance, for in the passage cited Paul expressly says that those wicked spirits are in heaven, and the terms used, "principalities and powers," indicate beings of high official rank and dignity, like those Daniel calls "chief princes." † Now Paul was a medium, and had had visions, and says expressly that, lest he should be exalted above measure by the abundance of the revelations, "an angel of Satan" was permitted to buffet him.

Spiritualists admit the existence of ranks and grades in the spirit-world. There is "a heavenly hierarchy," they tell us, "to whom are submitted the vast interests and plans for guidance of the myriads of millions embraced within their realm of supervision. . . . The wis-

* Primitive Christianity and Modern Spiritualism, Vol. I. p. 323.

† Πρὸς τὰς ἀρχάς, πρὸς τὰς ἐξουσίας, πρὸς τοὺς κοσμοκράτορας τοῦ σκότους τούτου, πρὸς τὰ πνευματικὰ τῆς πονηρίας ἐν τοῖς ἐπουρανίοις.

dom of the archangelic sphere guides the less progressed unfoldings of the angelic, which is the first below it; and thus down and through all departments."* But how can spiritualists be sure, consistently with their own principles, that all division of opinion and controversy is confined to the lower grades? Is it on the testimony of spirits through modern mediums? But why should modern mediums be infallible? They are not; it is a first principle. And why are they more reliable than ancient mediums, like Daniel and Paul? Daniel shows that controversy existed among the chief princes or archangels. Paul, a powerful medium, speaks of the prince of the power (or army) of the air, and calls him the God of this world. Jesus, admitted by all spiritualists to be the most perfect medium that ever lived, calls him "the prince of this world."

How can spiritualists, consistently with their own principles, set aside this testimony through ancient mediums by that of modern mediums, when they admit that the latter are often deceived? "More than half their communications are impositions," says Dr. Crowell. The Theosophic spiritualists hold that "the laws of polarity do not permit a pure disembodied spirit to manifest itself through a medium of evil life, or in the society of impure investigators. To such magnets, impure influences only are attracted; and we firmly believe that the whole series of physical phenomena, from the rappings to the materializations, is simply a manifestation of the power of the souls of the mediums themselves, or of disembodied souls destined to annihilation."

Pages might be filled with quotations from eminent spiritualists bearing on this vital point. Let any candid spiritualist weigh well the testimony of Mr. and Mrs. S. C. Hall, Mr. William Howitt, Mrs. M. S. Cooper, Hudson

* American Spiritual Magazine, Vol. I. pp. 362–365.

Tuttle, D. Home, and others, and say whether it is safe and consistent to make modern mediums (even were they unanimous) supreme on this point. But consistent spiritualists will remember the teaching of the eminent modern seer, Swedenborg, already cited. "Before the coming of the Lord, hell had grown up, so as to infest the angels of heaven, ... not only confusing the last and lowest, but assaulting the middle heaven, which would have gone to destruction unless the Lord had protected it." If, then, modern mediums are not unanimous, — if they are not more reliable than ancient, — if the spirits communicating through the prophets and apostles, and above all through their Master, are entitled to confidence, — how can spiritualists consistently deny that controversy may have struck through the very highest grades, thrones, dominions, principalities, and powers?

Laying aside the gross monkish and magical notions associated with the word "Satan," which means simply an adversary or antagonist, and with the word "devil," which means simply a slanderer or false accuser, let all candid spiritualists rise to the conception of a great intellectual and moral conflict between Jesus on the one hand, and a lofty spirit of consummate ability on the other, to see whether he would be stanch to the principle of self-denial, truth, and implicit trust in God, or whether he would compromise with the ordinary principles of worldly wisdom and selfish expediency. There is a consistency and congruity in such a conception to a meditative mind. The "fulness of time" had come of which seers had spoken from Eden down. Into these things angels had desired to look. Celestial intellects, from the highest to the lowest rank, had watched each pregnant intimation, from the first great declaration, "Thou shalt bruise his heel, he shall bruise thy head," to the present moment. The designation of the line of Shem; the call of Abraham; the choice of Isaac, of Jacob, of Judah, of David; the splendid outbursts of Isaiah and other seers; the designation of time four hundred and ninety years from Cyrus's decree; the place, Bethlehem Ephrata; the title, Messiah, Christ, Anointed: the sublime outburst over Bethlehem's plains;—all these things, and a thousand others, show that the unrolling of the mighty panorama was not only noticed by powers on high, but studied with the intensest emotion. Now the crisis of the universe is reached. Jesus is physically weak; his antagonist is strong. Jesus is mortal; his opponent one of the immortals. Jesus is a member of an exiled race, in some manner not fully revealed, under ban of the empire; while his assailant is an empyreal prince, leader of the *haute noblesse* of the skies. Jesus was in the wilderness, in circumstances not unlike those of Israel of old when fed with manna, or those of Elijah when sustained by angel viands. The temptations recorded are evidently but a small part of those that occupied forty days and nights,—samples as it were, or specimens.

It could occasion no great surprise to Jesus, long fasting and fainting in the wilderness, that a bright and beautiful form should address him, seemingly a friend, and ask him to perform a miracle akin to the feeding Israel with manna. The precise words recorded in the gospels may have been used, and there may have been other words of similar import, if the temptation was urged repeatedly during the long fast. So, too, it would have excited in Jesus no surprise to find himself caught away (as Ezekiel was, and other prophets) and placed on a pinnacle of the temple, where he could gaze down on the holy place and the assembled worshippers. Should he suddenly descend as with rushing of cherubic wings and Shekinah glory, it would be, full well he knew, the very sign his people were expecting. How strong, then, the impulse to yield to that persuasive voice, "Cast thyself down hence, for it is written, He shall give his angels charge concerning thee, and in their hands they shall bear thee up, lest at any time thou dash thy foot against a stone." These identical words may have been spoken, and others also of similar import. We can easily see the consistency and naturalness of the representation; we can understand that there was a real and formidable temptation; but how is it with respect to the other part of the ordeal. Can we see that that also is in a sense natural, and yet a real test or trial? If we regard the tempter as a state prisoner broke loose from confinement, we can not; but if we regard him as a great political and official antagonist, then we can form a conception of a temptation both natural on a higher plane of thought, and most formidably real.

Nor need we even paraphrase the words of the gospel narrative, but we may suppose many other words spoken in the course of so long a period, for it is explicitly stated that he was under temptation forty days. We are almost compelled to suppose other words were used of which these would be the complement and climax; and though we may not presume to reproduce them, it is not difficult to conjecture ranges of thought which would have been appropriate and natural. That Jesus was shown all the kingdoms of the world and the glory of them, is expressly stated; and it is a very large, a very comprehensive statement, however it was accomplished, whether by clairvoyance, or trance, or vision, or by some means to us unknown.

But to see those kingdoms, and the glory of them, suggests certainly the possibility that something of their history was disclosed to him. As a case in point, recall the visions of Daniel. How wonderfully the chart of future history was unrolled before his mind! A still more wonderful chart of past history may have been unrolled before the mind of Jesus, and that history so represented as to be made to seem glorious, and *to seem glorious to him.* If so, then all the darker and more degrading features of the successive world-empires would be softened or hid, all the brighter brought out prominently. This would, in effect, be a tacit vindication of his own administration by the prince of this world, yet so skilfully managed as not to seem apologetic; it would be simply putting the best construction on the great ethnic governments, and philosophies, and religions, so as to make them seem attractive to such a mind as that of Jesus. There was time enough during the forty days for such a proceeding.

In Daniel's visions world-empires were exhibited as wild beasts; or, if represented in human form, it was with the idea of decadence — gold, silver, brass, iron, clay. To Jesus' mind, naturally, a different impression would be given — the impression of improvement, of progress; decadence, perhaps, in some respects, but improvement in other respects, such as philosophy, science, arts, and laws. Instead of depicting the Roman empire as a nameless monster, terrible and dreadful exceedingly, it would be represented as Agrippa described it in his celebrated speech deprecating revolt, or as comparative theology sometimes describes it now. The prince of this world might say that by the confession of Israel's own prophets the covenant people had been more corrupt than the great world-empires around them; and if the Hebrew system ought not to be held responsible for the corruption of the nation, neither ought the ethnic laws and religions to be held responsible for the corruptions of the world-empires. The fault was in the material, in the masses themselves, — tides of selfish minds continually coming in and lowering the standard. But as to the existing world-empire, we can readily see what representations could have been made to such a mind as that of Jesus.

Suppose for a moment, (if we may venture so far merely for illustration's sake,) a strain of argument somewhat like this, as forming a part of the temptations filling the forty days. Behold the empire of Rome, and compare it with either of the great empires of the past. Its territory extends three thousand miles from the Atlantic to the Caspian, and stretches from the Hebrides on the north to the burning deserts of Africa; yet it is everywhere traversed by paved roads, on which the commerce of the world may move with speed and safety, and all diverse nationalities are thus brought into neighborhood with each other, so that they can be combined in one political system. Roman citizenship, the slow growth of centuries, has extended through the empire its privileges and immunities to individuals, to cities, and to provinces, thus unifying the diverse populations with common political rights; and the policy of the city ever has been, by a wise mingling of clemency and resistless force, to tame the rebellious and protect the submissive. Her policy cruel, barbarous, remorseless? Her cruelties have at least been well applied. The conqueror ought to execute at once whatever cruelties are essential, so as to have no occasion to renew them; otherwise he must be always ready, knife in hand.

Largely considered, imperial civilization breathes a sentiment of regard for law. Compare the oral law of Israel, which has been evolved since the captivity, with Roman jurisprudence evolved in the same period. On the one hand narrowness, unsocial and petty restrictions and absurdities; on the other, sublime conceptions of law as embracing the universe, — a boundless commonwealth and city, common alike to gods and mortals; and as in earthly states particular laws govern particular relationships of kindred tribes, so, it is conceived by Rome's best jurists, in the nature of things, does a universal law far more resplendent regulate the affairs of that universal city where gods and men compose one vast association. It is this noble conception of law as an eternal principle governing the entire universe, wisely commanding what is right and prohibiting what is wrong, which is the proudest characteristic of Roman civilization, and which will be its best legacy to future ages.

Consider, moreover, how this superb empire is further assimilated by the diffusion of the arts and sciences, preserved by secret orders and mysteries through ages of violence, and by the almost universal prevalence among the wealthy and educated classes of two such languages as the Greek and Latin. What could be done for the ultimate literature, art, and science of humanity, with such a language as Hebrew, excellent for the time of Moses, and for the peculiar provincial existence of Israel? What, with such characters as the Egyptian hieroglyphics, or the arrowhead letters and perishable clay tablets of Assyria? And to whom do the Hebrew scriptures owe their widest diffusion? To Alexander and the Ptolemies, and Alexandrian translators! And has not all this been in reality a preparatory work for the great Deliverer so widely expected, — the Star that should rise out of Jacob, — the Anointed One, — him whom Eastern sages came to seek, saying, "Where is he that is born King of the Jews, for we have seen his star in the east, and are come to worship him?"

Yet, great as Rome is, and important as her attainments, there is need of some great intervention to prevent her following the course of former empires. The religions of the world meet in Rome, enfeebled by their very multiplicity, — decaying, — undermined by scepticism. There is a wide-spread unrest, deepening to despair, — an inarticulate yearning for a better system than man has ever known. A yearning for whom? For whom does thy prophetic instinct whisper? For whom but for thee, desire of nations, seed of Abraham, in whom all the nations of the earth shall be blessed!

Great indeed have been and are the corruptions and abuses of religion, and of all social institutions. But it was inevitable. It was the fault of men, not of unseen powers. With all their admitted faults and abuses, the great religions of the world have contained more truth than error, and have been, on the whole, useful to mankind. It is for thee to meet the demand of the suffering, sorrowing nations. It is for thee to seize the auspicious epoch and realize its possibilities. All the indications of the age, all the intimations of prophecy, point to this as the time for some divine intervention. The circumstances of thy birth, and training, and history, to the present moment, designate thee to the responsible undertaking.

There are in Israel reserves of unsuspected power. There are adaptations and qualifications of peculiar value. Above all there is a slumbering volcano of religious enthusiasm of almost infinite momentum. Yet behold how the nation is paralyzed, and its power nullified by intense party-spirit, ambition, and the usual corruptions of society. The Pharisee, Sadducee, Essene, Zealot, Herodian, Samaritan, are incapable of uniting; yet neither can carry the whole body of the nation. They sway back and forth like hosts in battle, with spears and helmets interlocked. How, then, canst thou effect the great and responsible task appointed thee? Is it not clear as the noonday sun that thou must secure the co-operation of the nation, or of some one at least of the great influential parties? Of the Essenes, harmless fanatics, nothing need be said. They are and will be a mere cipher. The Sadducees, amiable voluptuaries, cling closer to the letter of the law, but their conservatism overleaps due bounds, and denies the existence of invisible powers, without a full belief in whom no high enthusiasm, religious, political, or military, is possible. The Pharisees, stanch reformers once, might perhaps be fired with patriotic enthusiasm, if the secret springs of action were touched with skill and tact; and through them, and in connection with them, the great Zealot or ultra-patriotic party might be swayed, on whose enthusiasm all must ultimately depend. Thus one might propitiate the rulers, while cementing upon himself the loyalty of the tribes, leading them on to conquest, not of Canaan, but of the Eternal City.

Think not that the people are unprepared for such a movement. Say not that their spirit is far from pure; that it is proud, ambitious, sensual; that it would but build up another despotic empire, to become corrupt in turn like those that have preceded; and that Israel must first be humbled, purified, brought back to simple faith and obedience. Say not Messiah must reign only by pure truth and goodness, without admixture of guile,—ideas natural to the artless inexperience of youth,—conceptions beautiful in themselves, but impracticable and visionary. If men were good, princes might reign by abstract truth and right; but men are wicked, and princes are not obliged to such strictness, because it would do harm rather than good. All generous enthusiasts begin with such ideal aspirations; but, alas! they find the realities of life are too stern, too inflexible, to yield to poetic fancies. Men must be dealt with as they are. Good and evil are inseparably conjoined in social institutions, — inextricably mingled and blended. Abstract right, absolute benevolence, are in practical life inoperative and void. As well preach humility to behemoth as to yonder self-satisfied Pharisee. What can the easy-living, wealthy, luxurious Sadducee know of disinterestedness? What can the crafty Herodian, the subtle Greek, versed by nature and by practice in all the mazes of diplomacy, know of simple sincerity, which to him must seem like the height of folly? What can the iron-hearted Roman know of pure truth? Abstractions are out of the question. Can there be found one single individual in the nation that knows what disinterestedness is, or would recognize it if he saw it?

What would be the result of appealing only to such motives? It would defeat the very object aimed at. Thou wouldst arouse distrust, suspicion, jealousy, partisan rancor, resentment. All parties would combine; thou wouldst be crushed in a moment, before having time even to begin. Enterprises like this demand time. Great mental and moral changes must be gradual. To give time for gradual change, there must be power. One must be able to command in order to instruct; to coerce in order to convince; and to attain power, one must have at least a place to stand on, and friends, followers, partisans. The fine gold of truth does not become current in ingots. It must be alloyed, hardened. It must be coined. It must bear the stamp of Cæsar. Every consideration of expediency and of duty suggests to deal warily and prudently with the rulers, so as not unnecessarily to excite their fears, rouse their prejudices, or threaten their privileges and emoluments.

Many a promising light has been prematurely quenched by headlong fanaticism. Prudence is not insincerity.

Listen to the counsels of true expediency, — of mature experience. Learn something from one to whom is delegated the care of this world's empires, — a grave responsibility, often thankless, always arduous. Gladly would I shift the burden upon younger shoulders. If in thee I behold my destined successor, gladly would I hail thy coming and smooth thy path to power, saying to thee as Saul said to thine ancestor: "And now I know well that thou shalt surely be king, and that the kingdom of Israel shall be established in thy hand." But till that appointed hour, is it too much to ask that thou wilt yield me that official homage David paid to Saul? All the kingdoms of this world are delivered unto me, and to whomsoever I will I give them. Let me then shed propitious influences around thy path, touch skilfully the springs of action, and guide the current of social thought and feeling. Let me influence not Israel only, but other nations, and guarantee success to thy noblest, most beneficent designs.

Such a line of argument was possible, or one much stronger than this. The defect of this statement is, not that it is more cogent than would be conceivably possible, but that it is probably weak and feeble in the extreme. And the great fact on which its whole cogency depended is, that the adversary made a direct and positive claim to delegated power over the kingdoms of this world, in circumstances such as to make it impossible that claim should be false. The entire reality of the ordeal depends on the fact that he knew, and that Jesus knew, that his claim was true. "All this power will I give thee, for that is *delivered* unto me (παραδέδοται), and to whomsoever I will I give it." * He uses the same word employed by Jesus where he says, "All things are delivered unto me of my father" (παρεδόθη).† This claim

* Luke iv. 6. † Matt. xi. 27.

of delegated power Jesus does not dispute. He tacitly concedes it, as much as he did in a well-known instance in reference to rulers in the visible world, by saying, "Render unto Cæsar the things that are Cæsar's, and unto God the things that are God's."

His reply scarce needs a paraphrase, would not even admit of it, had not the whole scene been so often misconceived. "Get thee behind me, adversary, for it is written, Thou shalt worship the Lord thy God, and him only shalt thou serve." This, in our view, is equivalent to saying, that for him to bend his mind into a receptive attitude; were he to hear, inquire of, seek unto, accept counsel of any angel, or archangel, or other being, than the Living God, even to gain the dominion of the world, it would be idolatry. Thus contemplated, we see that the temptation was very real, very formidable, and of the same general nature that had proved fatal to Solomon and other great men in all ages: that is, to compromise, — to do evil that good may come. He was tempted in that particular as we are, as public men are now, and he met the shock of temptation with the clear foresight of rejection, scorn, contempt, and cruel death. In making that decision, he virtually laid down his life.

CHAPTER XXXI.

REGENERATION.

ONE of the most suggestive passages in the life of Jesus, next to the temptation in the wilderness, is the conversation with Nicodemus. It seems to have occurred at a very early period, before the development of antagonism of the rulers. In fact, this would seem to be the first contact of the Pharisaic mind with him. Nicodemus says not, "Rabbi, I believe that thou art a prophet," but, "Master, we know that thou art a teacher sent from God, for no man can do these miracles which thou doest except God be with him." He has evidently been conversing with his brethren of the Sanhedrim; he evidently speaks in the name of his class or order. If he has come privately, by night, it is not for fear, but from wise diplomacy, and to secure a time when Jesus would be uninterrupted.

It is the first movement on this side the veil corresponding to that on the other side, when the tempter said, "The Pharisees will gladly welcome you as their leader, if you will spare for a time their prejudices." The highest, strongest, most influential, and on the whole most scriptural party here reaches out its hand and feels of Jesus. Nicodemus is friendly; the party is friendly. This young ruler is selected because he is interested personally, and would for his own personal satisfaction enjoy the mission. Jesus understood this; he knew what ideas were stirring in men's minds; he knew what causes were operating, and what effects would follow from any supposable act. This was a move in an opening game of chess. He saw what counter-moves might be made, and what would follow from each.

What conceptions, then, might Nicodemus have had naturally? He had the Old Testament, the Apocrypha, and the Chaldee Paraphrase. He might naturally have read the first book of the Sibylline verses, a Jewish composition then about a century and a half old, foretelling the coming and kingdom of Messiah. He was also probably familiar with the Book of Enoch, of still older date, in part probably as old as the Maccabees, and of such "eloquence and poetic vigor" as to be capable of exerting a marked influence on the imagination of a generation who supposed the scenes described to be impending.

The great question of the age was the coming of Messiah; the end of the world, or age; the resurrection of the dead; the judgment; and the establishment of Messiah's glorious kingdom. Now these are exciting topics at any time. Every question connected with the subject was discussed; and besides minor divisions, the whole nation was divided into two great controversial parties or schools; the Sadducees denying the existence of angel or spirit, and of course denying the resurrection. These great parties had fought it out on every point, and exhausted all their resources, and stood at bay; neither party could convince or conquer the other. Now comes Jesus. The Pharisees look at him. They say, "Here is our man; here is a teacher sent from God. No man could do what he does unless God were with him; we know it. Let HIM speak, then; let him take up our controversy and put our antagonists to silence." Of course they would be ready to back him with all their influence, and stand by him to the last. But there were two points to be considered. "Is he really what we think him to be, judging favorably by his deeds? Is he really with us and of us, so that all the precious interests of our law, handed down to us through so many ages of conflict and suffering, and for which we stand against Sadducean negation and Gentile idolatrous philosophy, will be safe — will not be shipwrecked through our incautious confidence? He may be Messiah; he is, we now feel almost certain. But if he be not fully in accord with the best intelligence and piety of the nation, — if he be not fully identified with us, — then he may be the predicted Antichrist. Let us be cautious; let us feel our way; let us be sure of our ground before committing ourselves."

Then, besides, there were points on which their own minds were not clear; and while approaching him for his party, Nicodemus might anticipate clearing up his own private questionings. What was to be the nature of the heavenly kingdom? What was to be the exact nature of the resurrection? Was it to be a restoration to a celestial mode of existence, as some supposed; or was it to be a return to a terrestrial body of more perfect health and vigor? — and if so, how? Would the righteous be reincarnate by natural birth, or would they appear in angelic corporeities? Such are some of the questions which must of necessity have been rife in every thoughtful mind. But there were points even more difficult. How will it be with the righteous who are alive at the time of the great change? If there is to be a palingenesia, a new heavens and earth, — if there is to be an immortal state, — how will the living righteous make the transition? Will they be translated like Enoch and Elijah, or will they die? If not, — if (as many, perhaps most, supposed) there was to be a beatific change pass upon them, — what was that change, and what sort of a body and state would it produce? Would they, as Isaiah seemed to imply, build houses and inhabit them? Would they plant vineyards, and eat the fruit of them? Would they bear children without painful travail, and have numerous offspring?

If we would realize what must have been the condition of the popular mind then, let us think a moment what it is now, eighteen centuries after Pentecost, and in the midst of the education and science of the age. Let us read the writings of the English Millennarians, and reflect that they represent views very widely prevalent, not merely in the Church of England, but in other communions throughout Christendom, — not merely among the ignorant, but among the most cultivated and scholarly, — the Alfords, Ellicotts, Langes, and Schaffs. Let us then glance at the less educated and scholarly, but equally sincere writings of the different schools of Adventists, who are very numerous, and very much excited for and against the tenet of conditional immortality; then glance at the writings of the New Church, at the writings of Edward Irving and others of what one may call the *new* New Church; then consider the recent wide-spread agitation of the question of future retribution, in almost all denominations; and to all this add the recent literature of spiritualism, and the negative attitude of materialistic science (a kind of modern Sadduceeism); and observe how in all these various classes of minds, embracing, first and last, nearly the whole of Christendom, the great questions at issue are closely connected with the resurrection, and the palingenesia, or regeneration, — and we can see how it might or must have been in Jesus' day. If we cannot help discussing themes of this sort, they could not. If we, with our boasted science, cannot agree, they could not. If many conflicting theories now float in the public mind, — annihilation; sleep; reincarnation; materialization; resurrection at death; resurrection pre-millennial; resurrection post-millennial, — the same theories, or theories of the same sort, were afloat then, held by some loosely, conjecturally, by others tenaciously, polemically, and felt uneasily by all to be oppressive by their very mystery.

Notice the signs of this mental tension, — the visit of the eastern Magi to Jerusalem, and their inquiry, "Where is he that is born king of the Jews? for we have seen his star in the east, and are come to worship him." Call to mind the agitation these words created in the court of Herod and in Jerusalem, and Herod's inquiry of chief priests and scribes where Messiah was to be born, and their ready answer, "In Bethlehem," and their citation of Micah v. 2 in proof. Consider the agitation caused by the proclamation of John the Baptist, "The kingdom of heaven is at hand," and his citation of Isaiah xl. 3. We see at every step a habit of studying the prophecies exactly like that of our adventists and millennarians to-day; and we see all Jerusalem and all Judea streaming to the Jordan; and promptly an embassy from the Sanhedrim waits on John, (not a correspondent of the Jerusalem Tribune, but a committee of the Hebrew Senate,) saying:

"Who art thou?"

His answer shows what was uppermost in everybody's mind.

"I am not the Christ."

"Art thou Elias?"

"I am not."

They do not need to quote Malachi iv. 5; for it was as instinctive as breathing to think Elias "must first come and restore all things."

"Art thou that prophet?"

"No."

They do not need for a similar reason to quote Deuteronomy xviii. 15.

"Who art thou? That we may give some answer to those that sent us, what sayest thou of thyself?"

We see the whole nation, rulers and all, on the *qui vive.* It will not do to have any one creating such an excitement around here and we not notice it. Who aré you? What are you?

He answers by quoting Isaiah xl. 3. So we see the Bible was their daily bread. Prophecy was in the very air. Notice that little incident at the great camp-meeting on the Jordan, where John sees Jesus walking by, and says:

"Behold the Lamb of God!"

There is a whole quarto in the five words. Next we see two rather rough-looking men meet each other in the crowd. They are fishermen from up the country. One says to the other:

"We have found the Messiah!" and he drags him off to see him.

The next day, another encounter between two up-country people, or Galileans. One says:

"We have found him of whom Moses in the law and the prophets did write — Jesus of Nazareth, Ben Iosef."

Says the other: "Can any good come out of Nazareth?"

Says the first: "Come and see." And he drags him off.

All through Christ's life this state of mind reveals itself — this intentness, this absorption, this premonition of impending events of unknown grandeur. Does Jesus perform some striking act, like cleansing the temple (which, if we reflect, was a prodigious thing for a layman to do)? The first question is, "What sign showest thou unto us?" They were thinking of the Shekinah glory — THE SIGN *par excellence*, of which the national imagination was full.

Did he perform some unusually striking work of healing? "All men mused in their hearts if this be the Christ."

Some said, "This is he."

Some said, "Nay, he deceiveth the people."

Herod hears of his deeds. "It is John, whom I have beheaded. He is risen from the dead." A specimen of one class of ideas of the resurrection.

So when Jesus asks of his disciples, "Whom do men say that I am?" the reply is:

"Some say Elias; others Jeremias, or one of the old prophets risen from the dead." That is, a reincarnation, a resurrection by natural birth. That was one of the notions afloat.

And when Jesus has shown them the glory on the mount, as they come down they ask, "Why say the scribes Elias must first come?" And further on, "What shall be the sign of thy coming, and of the end of the world?" It is the logical outcome of the entire ratiocination of the period. This glorification (which now they doubted not was presently to burst forth on all) was the very thing. Everybody was looking for it. But how then about Elias, and the restitution? And how about the living? How were they to get through? And how with all the other things prophesied? Now all these ideas were not only naturally in Nicodemus's mind when he said, "Master, we know thou art a teacher come from God," but nothing short of a miracle could have prevented him from thinking about them. It was to ask questions about just such subjects he had come.

Now Jesus knew just what he was thinking about,

and just what he wanted to say. It did not need any particular prophetic inspiration to know that. Any profound mind thoroughly posted on the ideas of his own day would have known. Without paying any attention apparently to what his visitor says, without noticing his complimentary words, without waiting for him to propound his curious inquiries, Jesus strikes directly at the point, — "Except a man be born again, he cannot see the kingdom of God."

This gives his visitor an opening to ask the very thing he wanted to ask. "How can a man be born again when he is old? Can he enter the second time into his mother's womb, and be born?"

This, as all spiritualists will see at a glance, is equivalent to the inquiry whether the doctrine of reincarnation then believed by many was really true; and, if true, how it could be effected.

"Verily, verily, I say unto thee, Except a man be born of water, and of the Spirit, he cannot enter the kingdom of God. That which is born of the flesh is flesh; and that which is born of the Spirit is spirit. Marvel not that I said unto thee, Ye must be born again. The wind bloweth where it listeth, and thou hearest the sound thereof, but canst not tell whence it cometh, and whither it goeth: so is every one that is born of the Spirit."

"How can these things be?"

"Art thou a master of Israel, and knowest not these things? Verily, verily, I say unto thee, We speak that we do know, and testify that we have seen; and ye receive not our witness. If I have told you earthly things, and ye believe not, how shall ye believe if I tell you of heavenly things?"

Now, to a hearer in such a state of mind as Nicodemus

was, this reply would suggest much. To enter that kingdom of heaven of which he was thinking, one must be born again in the widest sense of the figure. He must be restored to original purity, washed (born of water), and as it were reintroduced into that circle of love, meekness, and truth in which he was originally born by creation in heaven; but he must also of necessity be regenerated bodily (born of the Spirit) by resurrection, or a return into the original conditions of the celestial body. A mere reincarnation would not of itself be sufficient. It might be a means to the end, by placing him once more under remedial influences; but only a means, — he would be no more in the celestial world than he is now. To enter that, he must have not only a pure heart, but a spiritual body. Every one that is born of the Spirit is invisible, like the wind, which is cognizable to sense chiefly by its effects. Nicodemus naturally desired to understand all the secrets of that mode of existence. He wished Christ to rend the veil; to take down the barriers; to answer all his minutest inquiries; to settle all disputes, and make celestial things as familiar to him as terrestrial. This would be to abandon the principle of isolation. Even if he should do this, men would not believe. No amount of miracles would convince them. They did not believe, as it was, the simplest truths relating to their present welfare, which Jesus was telling them every day. Although he performed miracles, — although they knew that he was a teacher sent from God, — they did not believe what he taught respecting their every-day habits enough to amend them. They continued to tell lies, and break the golden rule in a thousand ways, and thought Messiah could make them happy, or that the kingdom of heaven would be happy to them. But if they would not believe these simple practical matters, much less would they those of a more subtile and celestial kind.

Nicodemus thought, perhaps, that it would be easier to be holy if this material environment were abolished. He was entirely mistaken. He must learn the rudiments of holiness here, in and by means of this material environment, or he never could even see that immortal condition of glorious life. He perhaps thought that sin originates with the body, and that to get rid of sin one must get out of the body and go to heaven. He ought to know that sin originated in heaven, and that to get rid of sin men had to get out of heaven and come into the body; and here men must be washed and cleansed through the mildly humbling duties of the body, the family, the state, — by repentance, by faith, by good works, — or they can never enter heaven, nor be happy there if they could.

That reply of Jesus was a decisive rejection of the overture of the Pharisaic or dominant party. He declined to work by party spirit, or to kindle a wild fanaticism without penitence and inward purification. Instead, he immediately commenced a very different plan of action upon the national thought, emotion, and will. He commenced at once healing diseases and casting out evil spirits (one prolific cause of disease); he sent out the twelve and the seventy to do the same. This was a direct movement to produce a healthy physique (which was also contemplated in the Mosaic law); to rescue the material system, the incarnation system, from abuse, and bring it into a normal and vigorous state. This was the design of his mighty works, even more than to give proof of his mission, though this latter object has sometimes been regarded as almost his exclusive ground of miracles. Yet this element of catastrophism had reference to the introduction of a higher era of social and national development; and had it continued for ten, twenty, or fifty years, continually expanding, its effects upon the public health and longevity would have been immense. Sickness and death would have rapidly receded, if not entirely disappeared from the presence of the prince of life ; and with disease and death would have disappeared some of the main causes of poverty and distress ; for it is to be noticed that, as the complement of this work of healing, Jesus commenced a corresponding work of toning up the public mind to a condition of moral health, of which that of the body is, as shown in a former chapter, the analogic emblem. He condensed the whole Mosaic system in the golden rule. This is the law and the prophets. He fell to work instantly, and worked incessantly, all over Judea and Galilee, — teaching in plain language the principles on which alone society can be happy, on earth or in heaven.

The beatitudes are (to use an illustration borrowed from our times) the political platform of his campaign ; or, to use monarchical analogies, they are the conditions of citizenship in his kingdom. He exerted immense power on the common people, to tone up common-sense and conscience and affection to sincerity, meekness, humility, purity, forgiveness, obedience, and faith. These were favorable to good health, and good health was favorable to these. He commenced acting with immense force on both parts of man's nature ; not through schools, or cliques, or sects, or parties, — not, as one might say, at arm's length, — but directly in his own person, and through disciples chosen from the common people, a kind of multiplication of himself. He came right to the patient ; he felt of the pulse of the suffering nation ; he began a direct and glorious battle against disease in its very seat — physical, mental, moral.

Now suppose he had not been violently arrested, — suppose this had gone on with accumulating momentum fifty years, instead of two and a half, — would he not have more than realized all that Moses glowingly depicted? Would he not have brought in a state of society somewhat like that described by the prophets: "There shall be no more thence an infant of days, nor an old man that hath not filled his days: for the child shall die a hundred years old: but the sinner being a hundred years old shall be accursed. And they shall build houses, and inhabit them; and they shall plant vineyards, and eat the fruit of them. They shall not build, and another inhabit; they shall not plant, and another eat; for as the days of a tree are the days of my people, and mine elect shall long enjoy the work of their hands."* And had this continued uninterrupted from century to century, must not such a state of things have extended itself beyond the bounds of Palestine, until the whole world would have been similarly affected, and "all nations been blessed in the seed of Abraham"?

This plan, however, was violently interrupted, and history has developed differently. We submit, however, that its execution was simply postponed, and that the day is at hand when it will be resumed and carried out, without further interruption, to perfect success; resumed, of course, under modified conditions, and from a vastly higher starting-point, but resumed in its main elements of direct personal supervision in the healing of the body and the toning up of mind and heart.

* Isaiah lxv. 17–25.

CHAPTER XXXII.

TRANSFIGURATION.

IT is morning on the heights of Hermon. The snow lies deep and of a velvet softness on those sacred summits, while fields far below are blossoming under the zephyrs of May. There are the lion's den, in those wild jungles, and the leopard's lair, undisturbed by human foot. Those solemn heights, ice-crowned regents of the north, wait some august scene predestined to transpire in their lonely solitudes. Towards those mountains' calm repose, how does some ceaseless attraction sway the wanderer, sighing forth within him the echo of an ancient lyre:

> "Then thou spakest in vision to thy Holy One:
> I have laid help upon one that is mighty;
> I have exalted one chosen out of the people."

Wistfully he gazes towards those cool, refreshing pines, and longs to escape from man into their whispering aisles, and rest with his beloved upon those "heights of Hermon where the Lord commanded his blessing, even life for evermore!" And even as he looks, the voice within him sighs again:

> "I will make Him my first-born,
> Higher than the kings of the earth."

He scales the cliffs of Hermon, where all ancient legends say angels descended when the world was young.

He leaves the multitude afar. He reaches the highest verge of vegetable life. Above, towers a dazzling pyramid of snow, like a throne of judgment white and spotless, bathed in clouds, and refulgent with dawn. Below spreads the wide panorama of hill and vale, lake, river and ocean. Cities and villages are there almost numberless. The whole land teems with life. Yonder they descry their native lake, sparkling in its tiny basin. Yonder, the Jordan winding through the deep valley towards the Sea of Sodom. Yonder lies Tabor, far below, and the wide Esdraelon prairie, and the Mediterranean's blue line along the horizon. All the mighty labors of the past come thronging on the memory as they gaze abroad. They almost seem to catch the stir and hum of men as the seventy heralds go from point to point like fire-flies in the summer's night. A while they converse on all they have endured. Soon they relapse into silence. While He agonizes in prayer, they pass from reverie to dreamless sleep.

Soon an undefined awe steals through their slumbers. Half roused, they seem to hear voices, but the accents blend in the dreamy changes of their drowsy brain. Nearer those voices come, and more distinct; the sleepers sigh, they stir, they wake. Is it the sun's effulgence that overpowers sight? Is it the sheeny reflection of the avalanche above? Are these intolerable splendors that threaten to devour them, the emanations of any created corruptible luminary? And where is he, that man they called but a moment since their master and friend? Can this be the same upon whose face they cannot steadily gaze? Is that His mild, sorrow-fraught countenance now shining as the sun in his strength? And where are those humble garments he wore? And whence comes the whiteness of these royal robes, whose very substance seems woven of sunbeams, glistening with a brilliance no art can imitate, each slenderest fibre and filament trembling as if in the centre of a consuming fire. Ah, it is that sacred form itself whose irrepressible intensity of lustre shoots through all covering, transfiguring opaque matter to transparent brightness.

And who are those who stand conversing by his side? What deep-buried power of reminiscence suddenly wakes from the slumber of their incarnation, to tell them who yon flaming figures be? Their earthly eye has never seen them; no voice has introduced them; yet their exalted intuitions recognize a Moses, an Elias. And what the theme of this celestial colloquy? What word arrests their attention, familiarly breathed by those lips of fire? They hear Moses speaking of an exodus, *his* exodus, which he must accomplish in Jerusalem. And what is that? Is it Death? Do such shining immortals talk of death? Can such an all-glorious Living King as He go down to die? And out of Death's dark womb, out of bondage to the grave, out of that Egypt in the heart of the earth, the Egypt of the dead, must his exodus be accomplished, as first-begotten from the dead? But the sight of Moses, and the sound of the familiar word exodus, causes a train of familiar associations to rush through the minds of the amazed disciples, calling up the tabernacle of old, with all its sublime pageantry of fire and cloud, the glory of the Lord. "Lord, cries Simon, let us make here three tabernacles; one for thee, one for Moses, one for Elias." Yet, as he spoke, an unexpected fulfilment of his words took place. That same ancient pillar of cloud and fire, of which they had read, for which they had yearned, and which they considered the SIGN of the Messiah's coming, lo! here it rolls its volumed folds gleaming with an inward brightness down around them. That sense of awe, and fear, which prophets always described as occasioned by the near approach of God, overpowered them. And while they trembled, a voice seemed to come out of the bright centre of the cloud, "This is my beloved son, in whom I am well pleased: HEAR YE HIM." At this, as prophets always were wont, they seemed to faint, and fall prostrate. But the next moment a hand touches them, a familiar voice addresses them, saying, "Rise, fear not!" They obey. They gaze round. The pageant is gone. There is Jesus alone. And all nature appears just as it did before. "Tell the vision to no man till the Son of Man be risen from the dead," is the charge they receive as they descend from the mountain.

Years roll by: years of toil, tribulation, persecution, change. The nation is scattered; the temple destroyed; the churches smitten sore with persecution. All the fond anticipations of youth, how changed! An old man, just ready to put off his tabernacle, just ready for his exodus (expressive word!), is thinking of the labors of a lifetime. How does it seem to him? Has his life been wasted? Is it all a mistake, a delusion? Is death the end? Is it a plunge into dark oblivion? He looks back to this beautiful scene. He says: "We have not followed cunningly devised fables, when we made known unto you the power and coming of our Lord Jesus Christ, but were eye-witnesses of his majesty. For he received from God the Father honor and glory, when there came such a voice to him from the excellent glory, This is my beloved Son, in whom I am well pleased. And this voice which came from heaven we heard, when we were with him in the holy mount. We have, therefore, the prophetic word confirmed, to which ye do well to take heed in your hearts, as to a light shining in a dark place, until the day dawn and the day-star arise." *

* *ἕως ὂυ ἡμέρα διαυγάσῃ, καὶ φωσφόρος ἀνατείλῃ.* (2 Pet. i. 16–19.)

CHAPTER XXXIII.

THE VEIL RENT.

THE Jewish nation was in a very critical condition; in fact, as the sequel proved, on the verge of destruction. The intensity of popular hatred to the Roman yoke we at this day can with difficulty realize. Fanatic leaders arose from time to time inciting to revolt. The people at one time sought to take Jesus by force and make him a king. And, although he refrained from stirring up such feelings, the rulers, seeing the effect of his words and works, were alarmed. "If we let this man alone, the Romans will come, and take away our place and our nation." *

Jesus saw the impending dangers, and how they could be averted by repentance and faith in God. The covenant was still in force, and the Lord was solemnly pledged to protect them, if faithful to their obligations. In the Sermon on the Mount, and in his other teachings, Jesus explained the principles of the kingdom. He embodied those principles in what we call the Lord's Prayer. But neither of the great parties could see that in these simple principles was their only salvation. They might have laid aside party differences, and united on a leader so powerful in word and deed, if he would have drawn the sword, and employed the usual arts of diplomacy. But to have done this would have been to be false to those principles of good government he came to

* John xi. 48.

establish. The kingdom of God, the kingdom of heaven, was the subject of many of his parables and other teachings; the question being how to rule ignorant and selfish masses so as to do them the most good. In the beatitudes, as they are called, he gives the principles of citizenship, namely, poverty of spirit, meekness, sorrow, hunger and thirst for righteousness, peace-making, purity of heart, patience under wrongs, a forgiving spirit.* So the Lord's Prayer: reverence, submission, faith in God for temporal support as well as spiritual, and for deliverance from temptation.† Jesus saw that these were really the only sound principles of political economy in any age or nation, so far as citizens or subjects are concerned.

So likewise in regard to the character of the prince, or ruler. To rule over ignorant and erring multitudes, he must not resort to deception, to flattery, and appeals to selfish and vindictive passion, nor to any of the arts of diplomatist or demagogue. He must speak pure truth, and appeal only to right motives, and must himself act in accordance with his professions. All rulers, ancient and modern, have either claimed divine honors outright, or a divine sanction, and paternal intention; and under representative forms all government is professedly for the public good; and all parties proclaim in their platforms some of the principles of disinterested benevolence. In practice, however, the aggrandizement of the prince or party has been first, and the good of the people secondary. With Jesus there must be perfect practice as well as profession.

"The kings of the Gentiles exercise lordship over them, ... but it shall not be so with you; . . . . he that will be greatest among you, let him be as he that doth serve."‡ It can be confidently affirmed that his

* Matt. v. 3-11. † Matt. vi. 9, &c. ‡ Luke xxii. 26.

whole life was a faithful exemplification of these principles. He sometimes illustrated them by emblematic actions of a very striking kind, as, for example, when he washed his disciples' feet. "Know ye what I have done unto you? If I your Lord and Master have washed your feet, ye ought also to wash one another's feet."* This was his idea of presiding over ignorant and selfish minds so as really to do them any good. We have studied the temptation in the wilderness, and have seen how it turns on this principle. We may study also with profit the closing scenes of his life.

The trial and execution of Jesus may be contemplated in several different aspects, but in none more worthy of attention than the political. A recent writer, after an able discussion of the subject, sums up as follows: "It was a double trial, and both parts of it were conducted with a certain regard to the forms of the two most famous jurisprudences in the world. In both, the judges were unjust, and the trial was unfair; yet in both the right issue was substantially raised. And in both the issue was the same. Jesus Christ was truly condemned on a double charge of treason. He died because in the ecclesiastical council he claimed to be the Son of God and the Messiah of Israel, and because before the world-wide tribunal he claimed to be Christ, a king." †

The peculiarity of the ordeal was, that he could have easily extricated himself by a little chicanery even at that fatal crisis. If, instead of saying to the Sanhedrim, "Hereafter ye shall see the Son of Man coming on the right hand of power," he had given them the Shekinah sign they demanded, intimating by a syllable his readiness to throw off the Roman yoke, the whole scene would

* John xiii. 5–14.

† Alexander Taylor Innes, "The Trial of Christ." *Contemporary Review.*

have changed in a moment. Let him have intimated his willingness to head a sedition like Judas of Gamala, or Barabbas,* he would have been welcomed with enthusiasm. On the other hand, nothing would have been easier than for him to temporize with Pilate. "Art thou a king?" said the Roman governor. "Thou sayest," was the answer, "I am a king." But he gave Pilate to understand that his kingdom was different from other kingdoms. "My kingdom is not of this world. If my kingdom were of this world, then would my servants fight." †

Jesus was evidently conscious at that moment, as at every preceding moment in his career, that the offer made him in the wilderness was still open to his acceptance. He knew that by what the world would call a justifiable falsehood, and an appeal to what the world would call patriotism, he could open the path to boundless dominion. But "to this end was I born, and for this cause came I into this world, that I might bear witness to the truth. Every one that is of the truth heareth my voice." ‡ He would not lie, either to save his life, or to attain dominion, or to carry out any great scheme of apparent benevolence. It was the vicious principle of doing evil that good may come that lay at the foundation of the corruption of all earthly kingdoms; and Jesus saw it, and knew that that vicious element must be expelled. Thus when certain Greeks desired to see him, expecting, perhaps, to see some hero like those of the Olympian games, he began to speak figuratively about dying, and exclaimed: "Now is the crisis of this world, now shall the prince of this world be cast out!" §

And it was the pressure of this vicious principle upon him in seductive forms, forms of expediency, friendship,

* Barabbas was a robber; he may also have been a Zealot.

† John xviii. 33–38. ‡ John xviii. 37. § John xx. 21–32.

duty, that made the trial peculiarly painful. Thus on a certain occasion, when he had foretold his approaching death, Simon began to expostulate with him, breathing the spirit of sincere but mistaken affection, Ἵλεώς σοι κύριε, — "Pity thyself, Lord," or, as we say, "For pity's sake, Lord, this shall not be unto thee." * This revealed to Jesus so vividly how, in a worldly point of view, the course he was taking might be deemed visionary, absurd, and even wrong, that it occasioned acute suffering. "Get thee behind me, adversary; thou art an offence unto me; thou savorest not the things that be of God, but the things that be of men."

Did not Jesus then see that an invisible agency was making use of Simon's affection to influence him? Simon was not aware of it; and how often had Jesus to admonish his disciples that they knew not what manner of spirit they were of. Now this pressure of temptation under forms ostensibly friendly continued to the last. At the passover, we read: "The devil entered into Judas, and put it into his heart to betray him." † Hence, when Judas had gone out, and his return with temple myrmidons was momentarily expected, he says, "The prince of this world cometh, and hath nothing in me." ‡ But Judas expressed no conscious enmity. Quite the contrary: he took special pains to show that what he did was done through no ill-will to Jesus; but, in fact, from love. "He said, 'Hail Master,' and kissed him." § Possibly Judas thought that at the last moment Jesus would throw off disguise, flash out on his foes, and reign. Possibly he meant to compel him to do it without further delay. If so, he was in fact a perfect image and embodiment of the presiding spirit of the world.

* Matt. xvi. 21-23. † John xiii. 2, 27.
‡ John xiv. 30. § Matt. xxvi. 40.

That Christ could have done what he was so strongly impelled to do, he shows: "Thinkest thou I cannot now pray to my Father, and he shall presently give me here more than twelve legions of angels?" * That the pressure of motive was peculiarly specious and so contrived as to make it seem right, and even a duty, to do what was wanted of him, is apparent from his words, "This is your hour and the power of darkness." † The power of darkness is the power of making a fallacy, an untruth, seem exceedingly bright, and true, and irresistible, and to make the real truth appear absurd and ridiculous. To the worldly mind of that age, Christ's course was mere sentimentalism; and the adversary was able to pour a flood of influence upon Jesus, to make him think so also. At times that influence was all but irresistible, so that Jesus was thrown into an agony, resisting unto blood. But now he is calm; and to the "Hail Master," and the kiss, responds, "Friend, wherefore art thou come?" Jesus could say this to Judas alone with apt significance, or to a mightier spirit whose character and principles Judas unconsciously expressed. Hence when the Roman governor says, "Knowest thou not I have power to crucify thee, and have power to release thee?" he replies: "Thou couldst have no power at all against me, except it were given thee from above; therefore he that delivered me unto thee hath the greater sin." ‡ In this inference the poor tool, Judas, is almost lost sight of, and the master-spirit seems to be present to his thought. Thy power, O Roman, is delegated. The powers that be (visible or invisible) are ordained of God. He to whom was delegated the power of all the kingdoms of this world, hath delivered me to thee; in so doing he has abused that delegated power in the highest degree; so much the greater his guilt.

* Matt. xxvi. 53. † Luke xxii. 53. ‡ John xix. 11.

Thus Jesus throughout that terrible trial was patiently subject to constituted authorities, however they might abuse their power; and asserted his own anointed rights, while steadfastly refusing, by their premature or dishonest exercise, to abridge by one hair's-breadth the term of office of the reigning princes of this world. Now, if the Prince of this world really felt no personal enmity to Jesus; if he used the customary arts and appliances of worldly diplomacy to accomplish a purpose he believed expedient and in a sense justifiable; if he really believed Jesus would yield, and that he would then open to him an illustrious career, at the same time vindicating the substantial correctness of his own policy, — then we see, that, as Saul fell on his own sword, and as Judas went and hanged himself, so the Prince of this world, in permitting that trial to go through to execution of sentence, virtually committed suicide. The two princes were in reality confronted before the tribunal of the moral sense of the ages; both were on trial; and the one, in condemning the other, condemned himself. In vain the "Hail Master," and the kiss; in vain the washing of hands, and the "I am innocent of the blood of this just person," — and the too ready response, "His blood be on us and on our children,"— the full responsibility was on them, and on him who energized behind those poor frail forms of flesh and blood, contending for the supremacy of the universe.

And thus it came to pass that on his cross, above his head, the inscription was placed:

"THIS IS THE KING OF THE JEWS!"

That was the appropriate climax of his career. This is what it costs to be a king of ignorant, selfish, sinful people, with any hope of doing them good! One must be willing to come to this. One must have the heart to say, while thus treated, "Father, forgive them; they know not what they do." Never in the whole of his career, though he saw how ignorant and foolish the people were, and how easily he could have practised on their patriotic sympathies,—how he could have deceived them to believe anything, however absurd, —never did he sneer at them, or scoff at them; never did one word of scorn or contempt breathe from his lips. And when they in their disappointment and delirium cried out, "He saved others, himself he cannot save!" he was saying, "It is finished. Father, into thy hands I commend my spirit." That foolish, deceived, ungrateful people were saved; the dark and cruel deceiver who had held them captive was defeated, and man's final coronation over the universe made sure.

"AND THE VEIL OF THE TEMPLE WAS RENT FROM THE TOP TO THE BOTTOM."

From the gates of paradise until now that mystic veil, token of man's exclusion from his native skies, had hung, the Holy Spirit thereby signifying that the way into that most holy place, the way of return to the tree of life, was not yet made manifest.* Now the primeval oracle is accomplished, "Thou shalt bruise his heel, he shall bruise thy head." The sublime tableau of ages is ended. The veil is rent. The ban of empire is repealed. The handwriting of attainder is blotted out.† The homeward, heavenward way is made manifest; and of all spiritual MANIFESTATIONS this, to the contrite heart, is sweetest, dearest, most attractive.

* Heb. ix. 8.

† Col. ii. 14.

CHAPTER XXXIV.

APHELION.

HADES was anciently supposed to be located in the interior of the earth. At a very early period the Assyrians conceived of it as consisting of seven circles, with gates guarded by formidable figures, in which all the departed, good and bad, were confined. Yet there was even there a deeply concealed fountain of the water of life — a glimpse of a future resurrection. The Egyptian Hades, before the time of Moses, was much more vivid, and its scenes not only described in language of singular intensity, but pictured to the eye in vivid colors.

The Bible is much more reserved in respect to Hades, so much so as strongly to suggest intentional reticence. That Moses should refrain from *post mortem* terrors and employ temporal sanctions only, at the same time prohibiting all converse with the departed, must have been from design on his part, or on the part of the spirit by whom he was controlled; for that he was a true medium spiritualists concede; and this design is one of the most striking features of the system, a consistent part of that policy of isolation by means of this material system of which we have spoken. This policy Jesus did not during his lifetime abrogate. When accused of having come to destroy the Mosaic law, he pointedly repelled the charge. The nation was still under covenant with the Lord, and if they repented and reformed, he was bound to forgive them and defend them against the world. Hence Jesus reveals little if anything new concerning the place and state of the departed. They are somehow connected with this world. They are conscious. They are social by laws of moral affinity, and in some degree according to affinities of race and family. They are happy or otherwise, according to character; and the conditions of reformation are less favorable there than in this life; — but these are features of the conventional belief, incidentally employed to illustrate particular points in his teaching, yet on the whole sparingly and guardedly.

The main object of the parable of Dives and Lazarus, for instance, was to show that if Israel would not repent and reform by motives furnished by Moses and the prophets, which were temporal mainly, neither would they repent though one rose from the dead to add the motives of future retribution.* History has verified this. Those ages in which purgatorial torments have been most vividly depicted have not been the purest. Spiritualists very generally concede this. Those mediums who have most to do with spirits of the lowest sphere, and who describe the gloom and suffering of that sphere in the most appalling colors, do not thereby elevate themselves and others. On the contrary, there is often a visible tendency to deception and immorality. The substantial truth of this statement all spiritualists will concede.

There is another point in which spiritualists are practically unanimous. It is that, dynamically, the condition of the disembodied is inferior. They are indeed in a sense corporeal, they exert power over matter, but they appear to be both physically and mentally dependent on the organism of a living medium. In this they differ from the celestials proper. In these very general statements

* Luke xvi. 31.

the indications of all mediums, ancient and modern, sacred and profane, substantially coincide.

Now, without further speculation as to the question of locality or mode and manner of existence, and cherishing that reserve which seems so fundamental an element of the present economy, all spiritualists will concede that the same general principles on which Jesus was sent on a mission of love to this world, would also, unless there be objections unknown to us, send him to a still lower sphere. And it is noteworthy that in this all mediums, ancient and modern, sacred and profane, do in some sense agree. The general conception of a descent of a celestial being to the Underworld is found in some if not all the most ancient mythologies. All will concede that if the prediction respecting the seed of the Woman was explained to Adam and Eve, this would account for such a universal tradition in an easy and natural manner; especially when taken in connection with the analogic language of nature, where day and night, summer and winter, are continually speaking of a resurrection; and particularly in view of the Levitical types, some of which were expressly contrived to shadow forth the precise truth expressed by David: "Thou wilt not leave my soul in Hades." All spiritualists concede David's mediumship, and can see that, "being a seer," he might in such an utterance be speaking what was true not merely of him, but of his race, and especially of him who was its chief, the Son of Man.

That Jesus did in fact descend to Hades is so manifestly the teaching of Peter,* and has been so nearly the unanimous belief of Christendom, Roman, Greek, and Protestant, from the earliest ages, that the modern attempts to put a different meaning into the words are not deemed worthy of serious refutation. The only

* 1 Peter iii. 18, 19.

question is, what Christ preached, and why. Now, on this point the apostle says: "For this cause was the gospel preached also to the dead, that they might be judged according to men in the flesh, but live according to God in the spirit." * Now give to κριθῶσι ("might be judged") its most common sense, not of a condemning sentence, but of administration of righteous government, and observe that the aorist subjunctive denotes that the judgment in question must be consequent upon the preaching, and we have a sense that is consistent and probable. Christ simply explained to the waiting race that at a future period, not specified, they should all of them, not even excepting the antediluvians, (the extreme case being taken on purpose,) be reincarnate, and so come under the judgment or righteous rule of Messiah "according to men" in human form, in the ordinary conditions of humanity here, in order that they might thus live unto God in the spirit. If it be asked why Christ should make such a proclamation, let Paul answer: "For to this end Christ both died, and rose, and revived, that he might be Lord both of the dead and living," — ἵνα κυριεύσῃ, — that he might exercise lordship over the dead and the living.† He visited them, as their Lord and Redeemer, to proclaim to them good tidings, and exhibit himself as the head of the race, — a moral victor, and as such "holding the keys of Hades," ‡ as a conqueror holds the keys of a captured fortress.

Such reincarnation would be a resurrection to judgment, in the pleasing sense of that term, namely, the administration of government on gospel principles. Jesus distinctly speaks of this. "The hour is coming when all who are in their graves shall hear the voice of the Son of Man, and shall come forth, they that have done good to the resurrection of life, they that have done evil to

* 1 Pet. iv. 6. † Rom. xiv. 9. ‡ Rev. i. 18.

the resurrection of judgment;"* —those who have in fact been reformed spiritually by the system, to their original celestial and immortal condition; those who have not been reformed, into a mortal condition by natural re-birth, in order to come under remedial influences. The general aspect of the resurrection is therefore cheerful for both classes, and it is to be regretted that our generally excellent version should have given it a sombre coloring by translating "they that have done evil to the resurrection of damnation." The word is *judgment*, the same employed by Peter in describing the object of Christ evangelizing the dead, "that they might be judged after the manner of men in the flesh."

This cheerful view is probably that entertained by that most highly favored seer and apostle, Paul, when he described himself as "having hope toward God, that there shall be a resurrection both of the just *and of the unjust.*" Here the resurrection of the unjust is as hopeful as that of the just, so far as the language is concerned.

Spiritualists of the Kardecian school have contemplated reincarnation from a somewhat different standpoint, viewing it more as pertaining to a general scheme of evolution. They will, however, readily concede the possibility of its application also in special modes, at special times, in a comprehensive remedial economy.

It is impossible in the present work to offer any extended speculations upon this most pregnant topic, to which, should circumstances permit, the author would gladly devote a subsequent volume. That reincarnation may have been a feature of past development cannot be denied; but that it is proven can hardly be affirmed. But even if it have entered as a factor into the extremely complicate web of human affairs, the position now

* John v. 29.

assumed is, that it is yet to have, in the near future, an application far more systematic and comprehensive, and in manifest relation to the mediatorial plan.

But while the resurrection of the entire race, at the second advent, by a natural re-birth, (so far as they are yet unreformed,) is a cheerful subject of contemplation, the resurrection of that portion of the race already reclaimed, by an immortal birth, into their native heavenly state, is a more cheerful, a glorious theme. Of this the most conspicuous, and, as many expressions of ancient seers would indicate, the first and only instance thus far, is that of Jesus, — a sublime movement, commencing on the third day, completed at his ascension through all the heavens, far above thrones, dominions, principalities, and powers. Now, if spiritualists are constrained, consistently with their own principles, (as we have endeavored to show they are,) to admit the existence of controversy in very high, if not the highest celestial spheres, they will readily perceive that such a return could not but have a decisive influence upon all the great issues involved. The effects of Jesus' personal presence and testimony respecting his earthly ordeal, and the treatment he had received from cosmocratic chiefs, must react, by intellectual and moral law, upon them.

An ancient seer, who had himself been rapt in vision to the third heaven, describes the effect comprehensively as a purification of the heavenly place.* It effected, according to another eminent seer, a casting down of the accuser, and a concentration of his forces upon this world as a final battlefield,† — a change not magical, or

* Heb. ix. 23. This, according to the common idea of a Pauline authorship. The same would be true if the epistle were written by Apollos, under Pauline supervision.

† Rev. xii. 7-12.

mechanical, not by thunderbolts, or by arbitrary measures of brute force, but by intellectual and moral processes requiring more or less time. How much time such vast changes in other worlds might require, it would be presumption to say. But when Paul wrote Ephesians vi. 12, it is manifest that the changes were yet incomplete. The process of casting down was proceeding, but the cosmocracy was yet in some sense celestial.

CHAPTER XXXV.

EXORCISM.

WE have shown, in the chapter on the Ancient City, the condition to which superstition and the worship of the dead had reduced humanity, even in the most cultivated nations. Lenormant * shows the power of magic to terrify and enslave the people, as exemplified at a very early stage of history. The Book of the Dead makes a similar revelation in respect to ancient Egypt. The power of fetichism and voodooism, and other forms of magic at the present day, over vast masses of the human race, is well known. The phenomena of possession were not peculiar to the Jewish nation, or to the time of Christ. They were probably less prominent there than elsewhere, as that was the only nation in which the worship of the dead had been successfully resisted, and as it were dyked out. It may have appeared more prominent, by reason of special efforts of unseen powers to penetrate the barrier, as waters jet through the dyke, or dam; and by reason of the excitement produced by the presence of Jesus, and his resistless power to expel the invader.

The term "devils" in the authorized version is incorrect, as there is but one who bears the title "The Devil," and he is a celestial being. *Demons* would be more correct, but carries with it the idea of fiendish malignity which the original δαιμων did not possess. It is difficult

* *La Magie chez les Chaldéens.*

to find a term not preoccupied by use in a false conventional sense. The modern term, "the spirits," would perhaps come as near as any our language possesses, to the true sense of δαιμονια, indicating simply departed spirits. They are sometimes called "unclean spirits" in the sense, of course, familiar to the Jews, that is, unforgiven, impure. This is the character assigned them by all spiritualists. Men on leaving the body are just as selfish as we see them to be in the present life. Those that are low and impure linger about the scenes of their earthly life, and seek to possess the bodies of mediums. They do this, not from positive malice, but because they are restless. Such is the uniform and copious testimony of spiritualists of all schools.

A spirit recently deceased says: "This constant desire for earth and earthly matters keeps me still within the old sphere." Another says: "When death comes, the spirit seeks its affinities, let them be in the dark abode of 'outer darkness,' as the Scriptures term it, or in the spheres of light." Another says: "Such spirits are very sensitive, easily take offence, and are very malicious and revengeful when slighted in the smallest degree; they are all very anxious to learn how to escape from their awful doom, and make unceasing efforts to enter the bodies of men and women on earth."

This view corresponds to the indications of the gospel narrative. Thus Jesus describes an unclean spirit, after being expelled, as "walking through dry places, seeking rest and finding none;" and then as saying, "I will return to my house whence I came out." He is indeed a wicked spirit, as all selfish men are wicked men; but he is impelled to enter by his restless and unsatisfied state. Such spirits, it would seem, invade the bodies of mortals; wherever the ties are not drawn tightly, wherever the door is left ajar or unlatched, they enter, disregarding the effects upon the medium,—catalepsy, somnambulism, clairvoyance, trance, ecstasy; or blindness, deafness, dumbness, paralysis, lunacy, delirium. The manifestation made by the New Testament of the state of departed spirits who have habitually violated the golden rule, is very striking. We see them "swarming" about some living victim. We see "a legion" of them in one wretched organism. Look at the picture of the demoniac of Gadara. "And when he was come out of the ship, immediately there met him out of the tombs a man with an unclean spirit, who had his dwelling among the tombs; and no man could bind him, no, not with chains: because that he had been often bound with fetters and chains, and the chains had been plucked asunder by him, and the fetters broken in pieces: neither could any man tame him. And always night and day, he was in the mountains, and in the tombs, crying, and cutting himself with stones."* These spirits are no more hard-hearted than men walking the earth in flesh and blood, who rob, and murder, and seduce female innocence, tempt reclaimed inebriates, and for gain ruin society. They are only as hard-hearted and unfeeling out of the body as in, with less to restrain and amuse and interest them. Hence they recoil from the pure and benevolent presence of Jesus, saying:

"What have I to do with thee, Jesus, thou Son of the Most High God? I adjure thee by God, that thou torment me not." .... "Let us alone! Art thou come hither to torment us before the time?"

And they beg permission even to enter the organism of swine, rather than to be sent into the abyss, as they call it, the lowest sphere of existence.

It is most interesting, then, to study Christ's bearing towards the spirits; especially as all spiritualists agree

* Mark v. 2–5.

that he was a medium of the highest purity, and of course eminently qualified to testify in relation to the spirit-world. It is also conceded by many, if not all the most eminent spiritualist writers, that the Levitical prohibition of magic, and necromancy, in all its forms, was wise and necessary at that time. It is thought, however, that the prohibition fell with the Levitical system ; that the same reasons for it no longer existed ; and that the injunction to "try the spirits" and other indications imply that intercourse with "the spirits" was recognized under the new dispensation.

This is a plausible statement. It is supported with no little ingenuity and copious references to the New Testament. We welcome all such investigations, and cheerfully take our stand by the side of such Bible students upon their own chosen principles of interpretation, to which we trust they will faithfully adhere. There is, however, need of caution, as there are several fallacies by which the inquirer, however sincere, may be led astray. One such fallacy is the confounding of the human race with the angelic.

Spiritualists seem to have taken up the idea without much thought, that all orders and grades in the spirit-world — angels and archangels, thrones, dominions, principalities, and powers — were once men, and commenced their existence here on this earth, or (as Swedenborg teaches) on some other of the innumerable earths of the material universe. The Kardecian and the Theosophic schools may be exceptions to this remark. But how do spiritualists convince themselves of this? Is it not improbable, if the spirit universe be as vast as the material, that the boundless ocean of being should have flowed out from this single planet? There is an immense volume of water that bursts up from unknown depths, at Wakulla Spring, in Florida, forming a broad river; but would it seem to warrant the statement that the whole Atlantic Ocean flowed out of Wakulla Spring? As to other planets, what conclusive evidence have we that they are inhabited by human beings? Have not spiritualists incautiously allowed an element of materialistic evolutionism to slip into their system unperceived? Is not a motion to reconsider that theory in order? Especially as ancient seers, to whose oracles spiritualists, as we have seen, appeal, have something to say on this very point. "Unto which of the angels said he at any time, Sit thou on my right hand, till I make thy foes thy foot-stool?" * It was unto a man that this was said, not to an angel. The whole argument of the first chapter of Hebrews is to show that man, in the person of its representative or chief, is not merely distinct from, but exalted far above all angels, so that in contrast the office of the latter is subordinate. "Are they not all ministering spirits, sent forth to minister for them who shall be heirs of salvation?" †

It is one of the curious illustrations of the superficial method in which the Scriptures are too often handled, that this verse should be constantly quoted in proof of the alleged fact that at death good men become angels. In reality it implies the reverse, for he goes on to say: "For unto the angels hath he not put in subjection the world to come, whereof we speak. But one in a certain place testified, saying, What is man, that thou art mindful of him? or the son of man, that thou visitest him? Thou madest him a little lower than the angels: thou crownedst him with glory and honor, and didst set him over the works of thy hands: thou hast put all things in subjection under his feet. For in that he put all in subjection under him, he left nothing that is not put under him. But now we see not yet all things put under him:

* Heb. i. 5. † Heb. i. 14.

but we see Jesus, who was made a little lower than the angels for the suffering of death, crowned with glory and honor; that he by the grace of God should taste death for every man."

A full exposition of this most important passage is beyond our present limits. It is, however, manifest that a contrast is drawn between two races, in respect to their future dominion. The present world is subject to the angels. There is to be a world, or an age, in which the human race will be supreme over the moral universe. We do not, indeed, now see this accomplished in full; but we do see it accomplished in part by the coronation of Jesus. This conception of the future dignity of man had either been handed down as an element of the primitive Eden oracles, or it had been communicated through the apostolic medium; for Paul refers to it as something well known: "Know ye not that the saints shall judge angels?" * that is, shall exercise jurisdiction over them. Compare, also, that sublime promise communicated through the seer of Patmos: "To him that overcometh will I grant to sit with me in my throne, even as I also overcame and am set down with my Father in his throne." †

So great, so transcendent is this future exaltation of man, that language fails to express it. It is "a far more exceeding and eternal weight of glory," and the mind itself faints under the sublimity of the prospect, for which cause the apostle was constant and earnest in prayer, that those to whom he communicated such ideas might be strengthened with might by the spirit of wisdom and revelation, so as to be able to comprehend and endure a truth so wide and deep, and so overwhelmingly glorious.‡ It is in the light of these grand disclosures that we should approach the question, What was

* 1 Cor. vi. 2, 3. † Rev. iii. 21. ‡ Ephes. i. 16–23; iii. 14–19.

the attitude of Christ towards intrusive spirits of the other sphere? What his bearing was towards the cosmocracy we have seen; but what was his course, and that of his apostles, towards "the spirits" of the lower sphere, or Hades?

We have seen that in the ordeal in the desert Jesus refused to place his mind in the attitude of asking or accepting control from the cosmocratic principalities. After the ordeal angels came and ministered to him, possibly supplying food, as they did to Elijah; so in the Garden there appeared an angel strengthening him; and he intimated that he could have asked the Father to send more than twelve legions of angels to his aid, and not have asked in vain, but he did not. In all these cases he sublimely indicated his superiority to angels, their military subordination to him, and his entire and implicit dependence on God only. Christ's life was full of prayer. But all his prayers were addressed directly and only to God; and so he taught his disciples to pray, saying, "Our Father, which art in heaven."

What, then, was Christ's bearing towards spirits of an inferior grade? It was one of majestic supremacy. He rebuked them. He would not suffer them to speak. He declined their suffrages. Their testimony to his mission was untimely and uncalled for; yet it was, one cannot help thinking, a compassionate superiority. There is not one word of scorn, or contempt, or hatred. He ejected them; he empowered his disciples to do so; but he did it because it was one feature of that work of which we have spoken,— of restoring society to perfect health. It was one step in rescuing this material system from abuse, and securing a perfect soundness, especially of the cerebral and nervous systems. In no case did he or his disciples tolerate, much less invite the invasion of spirits upon the organism of the living. And when the seventy disciples (not having been empowered to exorcise) returned with joy, saying, "Lord, even the demons are subject unto us through thy name!" he checked their exultation, and told them to rejoice that their own names were still standing in the old family record in heaven.

The disciples were sinful men in the body, the spirits were sinful men out of the body; they must cast out the latter for sanitary and benevolent reasons, but they need not exult over them. He recognizes the entire lower realm of spirits as antagonistic to his work; but so also with the kingdoms of this world, as selfishly organized. "The gates of Hades," he says, that is, the army issuing from those gates, shall not prevail. His last commission to his apostles does not reverse the policy of centuries, does not take down the barriers, nor sound a parley; it is still, "Cast out the demons."

Accordingly, wherever the apostles went they discountenanced all commerce with the dead. Thus at Philippi: "And it came to pass, as we went to prayer, a certain damsel possessed with a spirit of divination met us, which brought her masters much gain by soothsaying: the same followed Paul and us, and cried, saying, These men are the servants of the most high God, which show unto us the way of salvation. And this did she many days. But Paul, being grieved, turned and said to the spirit, I command thee, in the name of Jesus Christ, to come out of her. And he came out the same hour. And when her masters saw that the hope of their gains was gone, they caught Paul and Silas, and drew them into the market-place unto the rulers." *

Here was a spirit that seemed well-disposed; did the apostles need this indorsement? Did they say to the sceptical Greeks, Here is proof of immortality stronger than the resurrection of Jesus? Yet the apostle was

* Acts xvi. 16–19.

mild and gentle. For many days he apparently took no notice; and when at length he did, it was more in grief than in anger. Candid spiritualists cannot fail to be struck with the infinite superiority of the Christian faith over the ethnic cultus at this point.

So in the case of Simon Magus,* who was probably an adept in the ancient magic, and a really powerful medium. He became a convert under Philip's preaching. But when Peter and John visited Samaria, we read: "And when Simon saw that through laying on of the apostles' hands the Holy Ghost was given, he offered them money, saying, Give me also this power, that on whomsoever I lay hands, he may receive the Holy Ghost." Nothing could more forcibly show the essential difference of moral character between the two forms of spiritualism, ethnic and Christian. Nor will Christian spiritualists think the indignant rejection of his offer by the apostles was too severe.

The same antagonism appears in the case of Elymas the sorcerer, at Paphos.† He is described as a false prophet of Jewish lineage, probably a specimen of the false prophets that play so prominent a part in Old Testament history. He also, it is probable, was, dynamically, a real medium of considerable power; but, unlike Simon Magus, he assumed an anti-Christian attitude, and sought to prevent the deputy Sergius Paulus from becoming a convert. Now Paul was a genuine medium of a high order, and was controlled, not by low spirits, but was "filled with the Holy Spirit." We see then, how one medium addressed another, how a higher medium a lower, a Christian medium an anti-Christian. "O full of all subtilty and all mischief, thou child of the devil, thou enemy of all righteousness, wilt thou not cease to pervert the right ways of the Lord?"

* Acts xviii. 9–24. † Acts xiii. 6.

Does this seem to any uncharitable and severe? Yet it is no more so than the utterances of some mediums in our own day, to others of an opposite moral character, with which our spiritualist readers are doubtless familiar.

Another curious illustration occurs at Ephesus, where Paul had labored for two years, and where in some cases evil spirits were cast out by aprons, or handkerchiefs, brought from the apostles' body. "Then certain of the vagabond Jews, exorcists, took upon them to call over them which had evil spirits, the name of the Lord Jesus, saying, We adjure you by Jesus, whom Paul preacheth. And there were seven sons of one Sceva, a Jew, and chief of the priests, which did so. And the evil spirit answered and said, 'Jesus I know, and Paul I know; but who are ye?' And the man in whom the evil spirit was, leaped on them, and overcame them, and prevailed against them, so that they fled out of that house naked and wounded." * These Jewish operators evidently regarded it as a kind of magical incantation, — using the names "Jesus" and "Paul" as they would any other spell.

As one result of Paul's two years' ministry at Ephesus, we read: "Many of them also which used curious arts brought their books together, and burned them before all men: and they counted the price of them, and found it fifty thousand pieces of silver." † Those books would now be rare curiosities, and would perhaps command ten times that money; but would it not be rash to accept them as contributing to a revival of pure primitive Christianity?

And when the question came up whether the Christian converts were at liberty to attend feasts connected with the ancient ritual, — a question most interesting not only to the spiritualist, but to the student of comparative

* Acts xix. 13–16. † Acts xix. 19.

theology,—how did the Christian mediums decide? "But I say, that the things which the Gentiles sacrifice, they sacrifice to demons and not to God: and I would not that ye should have fellowship with demons. Ye cannot drink the cup of the Lord, and the cup of demons: ye cannot be partakers of the Lord's table, and of the table of demons." * Here was the encounter of the new gospel spiritualism with the old ethnic spiritualism, the worship of the *dis manibus*, the θεοις χθονιοις, the spirits of the dead. Will not all spiritualists concede that this Christian spiritualism was of a very different character, and of an infinitely higher grade, than that which it encountered, and over which it triumphed? And did it not really continue in force the ancient defensive principle of isolation as against all spirits of the lower sphere? And did it not limit itself to the manifestations of one and the self-same spirit, however manifold the gifts? "There are diversities of gifts and diversities of operations," says the great apostolic medium, "but all these worketh that one and the self-same spirit, dividing to every man severally as he will." † Have not spiritualists overlooked or undervalued this wonderful lesson of the true nature of spiritualism,—a lesson which, on their own principles, ought to be fundamental to their whole practice?

The question then occurs, Did these ancient mediums, these primitive Christian spiritualists and seers, foretell a time when the policy of isolation from the spirit-world would be relaxed, or abandoned? This of course brings up the whole subject of eschatology, a theme too extensive to be discussed fully in our present work. A few suggestions only will be offered in the next chapter.

* 1 Cor. x. 20, 21. † 1 Cor. xii. 4–11.

CHAPTER XXXVI.

ESCHATOLOGY.

ALL existing schemes of eschatology have been based upon the hypothesis that the soul originates in and with the body; but it is possible to look at the question from a different standpoint. If man is a celestial race in exile, — if the incarnation of the race is a defensive and a remedial measure, and if it is part of a grand political problem, so to speak, namely, the reorganization of the moral universe, — then, certainly, our conceptions of the winding-up of the present dispensation must be made to correspond.

We can see that such a grand remedial system might for a long period be interfered with, resisted, and corrupted by those cosmocratic principalities it was designed to dislodge and supersede; and that it might be necessary, while eliminating a few among mankind and training them to stand against world-majorities, to effect by centuries of disclosure the prostration of the thwarting powers. Thus the entire mechanism of the system would be rescued ultimately from their interference, and the way would be open to apply to the race *en masse* the full remedial influences of the system. Whenever that point is reached, all spiritualists will readily conceive that the intercourse with celestial orders might naturally be more free than in former ages, the heavens being now purged, and no longer occupied by hostile powers. At the same time, spiritualists can see that there might be a total shutting off of the lower, more deceptive spheres, — those by whom, as they admit, mediums are often deluded and injured. The embargo might be rendered total, and the spirits of that lower sphere introduced into this world only by incarnation, for remedial purposes. Then the risen saints might naturally be expected to appear and disappear from time to time, wherever desired or needed. Thus those already perfected would be invested with political power over the universe by degrees, being initiated into the government of this world preparatory to administering the government of all worlds. Not that they would be subject to the law of gravitation; not that they would live at Jerusalem, or any other terrestrial locality; but that, being restored now to their native celestial mode of existence, they would out of that sphere, from time to time, appear upon the terrestrial scene. Not only is this conceivable, but, as the apostle expresses it, it is so desirable that even the inanimate creation yearns for it. "The earnest expectation of the creature waiteth for the manifestation of the sons of God." *

Such a hypothesis places the whole subject of eschatology on a new and higher plane. It gives us the better elements of the millennarian scheme, while avoiding the grossness of chiliasm. It includes the truths of gradualism, without denying those of catastrophism. It accepts the better elements of spiritualism, without embracing its extravagances. On such a hypothesis it is evident that the period immediately preceding the millennial epoch might naturally be one of intense antagonism; and there might naturally be delusions of very great power; and this fact leading spiritualist writers concede. And it is also obvious that it would be very natural for many very excellent and candid people to be deceived. There are millions of low and deceptive spirits

* Romans viii. 19.

who might take pleasure in making honest people think the millennium actually begun,—on the same principle that, when in the body, they delighted in imposing upon the credulous. There are many such persons now living, who seem to find an exquisite enjoyment in seeing how far they can deceive their fellow-men, either for the accomplishment of their own selfish plans, or merely for amusement. Such persons, as all spiritualists agree, are of the same character out of the body as when in it; and it is admitted that they do in fact utter through certain mediums much that is false and absurd. Add to this, that this tendency on the part of low spirits to break in, either for relief, and rest, and solace, or to gratify a mischievous mirthfulness, might naturally be taken advantage of by the cosmocracy to effect results not dreamed of by "the spirits" themselves, and spiritualists will see how natural it is that good men should be deceived.

Hence, when the claim is put forth that the millennium is begun,—that the resurrection is now actually taking place in the materializations of the day,—spiritualists ought to be on their guard; and since they admit Christ and the apostles to be the strongest, purest, and most reliable mediums that have existed, they should carefully study their predictions respecting this great crisis.

Now the general character of the interval between the gospel era and the final victory of truth on earth is shadowed out in the New Testament in several ways. It was to be an age of conflict. "Think not I am come to send peace on the earth," that is, as an immediate result. The tares and the wheat must grow together. The leaven was to be hid in the meal. And there is not only a leaven of truth, but also of hypocrisy; and if society could be gradually leavened with the former, it could be counter-leavened with the latter. Aside from these incidental allusions, there are no less than six main lines of prophetic indication respecting the interval in question.

1. In predicting the destruction of Jerusalem, Christ gives some elements that stretch on beyond that event through the whole dispensation. The Jews, he says, shall be led away captive into all nations, and Jerusalem shall be trodden underfoot of Gentiles till the times of the Gentiles be fulfilled. The effect of this has been neutralized on many minds by his saying, "This generation shall not pass till all these things be fulfilled." They forget that "generation" is often used for "nation," and that Moses, in the very prophecy our Saviour evidently refers to, says, "They are a froward generation." Evidently the meaning is, that though thus smitten and scattered, the nation should still survive. Now, carrying the view onward to the close of the "times of the Gentiles," Christ intimates that there will be a period of great tribulation and of intense deceptive agency, followed by a sudden and decisive intervention of divine power, — as sudden and vivid as the lightning shining from east to west.

2. It is generally conceded that the apostles and early Christians expected a second coming of Christ, anterior to any supposed epoch of a thousand years. Many have gone so far as to say that they expected it in their own lifetime. Such do not sufficiently consider the apostle's disclaimer of such an expectation. Having in a letter to the Thessalonians spoken very largely of that coming, he learns that he has been misunderstood by some; he therefore writes a second letter, to correct that error. "That ye be not soon shaken in mind, or be troubled, neither by spirit, nor by word, nor by letter as from us, as that the day of Christ is at hand." "Let no man

deceive you," he continues, "for that day shall not come except there come THE APOSTASY first, and that man of sin be revealed, the son of perdition; who opposeth and exalteth himself above all that is called God, or that is worshipped; so that he, as God, sitteth in the temple of God, showing himself that he is God. Remember ye not, that, when I was yet with you, I told you these things? And now ye know what withholdeth that he might be revealed in his time. For the mystery of iniquity doth already work: only he who now letteth will let until he be taken out of the way: and then shall that Wicked be revealed, whom the Lord shall consume with the spirit of his mouth, and shall destroy with the brightness of his coming: even him, whose coming is after the working of Satan, with all power, and signs, and lying wonders, and with all deceivableness of unrighteousness in them that perish; because they received not the love of the truth, that they might be saved."

Now an apostasy is gradual in its origin and development, and requires time. How much time, the apostle does not say, and may not have known; but it is not likely he thought it would certainly be in his lifetime. The point of special importance is that the apostasy is represented as culminating just before the coming of the Lord. The man of sin, the Lawless One, is destroyed by that very coming of the Lord. There is no room for a millennium prior to that coming. The apostasy covers the whole interval. And most important of all, the crisis is one of intense deceptive agency. The Lawless One comes "with all power, and signs, and lying wonders."

Other indications of the nature of the crisis are found in the visions of the Apocalypse. Many object to the Apocalypse as being practically unintelligible; but spiritualists surely cannot consistently take that ground.

John was a powerful medium and seer, and of a loving, heavenly, pure spirit. He was known among the Twelve as the disciple whom Jesus loved, and he was a great sufferer for the truth. He was an exile at this very time when he received these revelations. He was in a state to attract the purest and highest spirits, and testifies that he was "in the Spirit," and a blessing is pronounced on those that read and hear the communications made through him. Consistent spiritualists, therefore, are bound to test those utterances with care. They cannot discredit the Apocalypse as a whole without being false to their own principles; nor are these visions difficult to understand, at least in part. We may not be able to interpret every detail, but by applying the principles of analogy we can gain certain general results of great value.

3. Thus no one can read the events described under the opening of the sixth seal, without getting the idea of a very great and grand crisis of catastrophism, which, it would be easy to show, did our limits permit, relates to the close of this and the opening of the millennial era.*

4. Another outline of the same interval is given under the trumpets, and the nations are exhibited as persisting in their idolatries until the seventh trumpet sounds, when there was heard a great shout: "The kingdoms of this world are become the kingdoms of our Lord, and of his Christ; and he shall reign for ever and ever." †

5. Again the same general interval is traversed under the vials, and the seventh vial is poured out upon the air, the region of cosmocratic empire, and "there came a great voice out of the temple of heaven from the throne, saying, 'IT IS DONE!'" ‡ Can there be a more impressive symbolization of the end of the present dis-

* Rev. vi. 12–17. † Rev. xi. 15. ‡ Rev. xvi. 17.

pensation of cosmocratic rule, and the ushering in of a better dispensation?

6. The same interval, or dispensation, is again outlined in the emblems of the dragon, the wild beast, and the woman. We have already suggested that the dragon, or serpent, is throughout Scripture the emblem of selfishly organized empire in the invisible; the wild beast the emblem of the corresponding world-empire in the visible; and the harlot the emblem of corrupt and selfish ecclesiastical organization in all ages. We will not attempt any detailed exposition of these emblems, so as to limit them to any one form of civil and ecclesiastical despotism, but rather regard them as constructed with divine ingenuity, so as to include all. Even the mystic sorceress upon whose forehead was a name written, "MYSTERY, BABYLON THE GREAT, THE MOTHER OF HARLOTS AND ABOMINATIONS OF THE EARTH," we would not limit to one age or church, but interpret as including the false churches of all ages, — viewed as in certain great elements of character one city, however differing in detail.

In this general aspect all spiritualists, one would think, might recognize these life-like emblems; and the question is, What is the fate of the civil and ecclesiastical despotisms thus shadowed out? Are they reformed? Do they make their exit gracefully from the stage? Do they die a peaceful and edifying death? Quite the reverse. The wild beast is vanquished on a world-wide Waterloo, "the battle of the great day of God Almighty." The dragon is for the first time chained and incarcerated as a felon; and as to Babylon, a mighty angel takes up a millstone and casts it into the sea, saying, "Thus with violence shall Babylon be thrown down,"—not by gradualism in any form, but by the highest conceivable style of catastrophism.

Now the union of these six outlines, or aspects, of the present dispensation enhances the impression proper to each of them taken separately. There are many indications that during this entire period true believers will be a minority, alternately assailed by persecution and by corruption, always greatly tried in their higher and more ideal susceptibilities, and sustained only by a patient cross-bearing spirit and faith in God; and at the very last, just before the full "manifestation of the sons of God," it would seem was to be the severest ordeal of faith. "When the Son of Man cometh, shall he find faith upon the earth?"

Now the question for consistent spiritualists to consider is, Has the great crisis come and gone by, or is it only coming and near at hand? If the latter, then the prohibition of all intercourse with spirits of low and deceptive character is in full force. Spiritualists cannot help feeling this. There are certain manifestations which they know not exactly how to account for. There are communications which at first sight seem to be good, and which profess to come from "the heavenly hierarchy" itself, which yet are strange. About them lingers an indefinable something exciting distrust. An inscrutable dubiousness attends them, at which the most implicit and enthusiastic are for the moment startled. Precisely at that point should be brought into use the oft-repeated scriptural precept, "Try the spirits." On this all consistent spiritualists agree. And how shall we test or try the spirits? Just here another admitted principle of the system comes in, namely, that we are to test or try the spirits, not merely by their professions,—no matter how fair, how high-sounding, or from what professedly high grade emanating,—but by their general agreement with our reason and conscience, and with the best experience of former ages, and by their tendency to produce good fruits in us. This principle must be of universal application, extending to the highest spirit of all, as well as to those of lowest grade. It is not safe for any man to take it for granted that he is full of the Holy Spirit.* History presents us with melancholy examples of evil deeds done by fanatics who professed, and perhaps really believed, themselves to be actuated by the Holy Spirit.

There are tests which will readily occur to every meditative reader. For example, if spirits present themselves in the name of departed mediums whose lives were pure, truthful, self-denying, — men who stood against the corruptions of their age, and contended for those great principles on which the battle of the ages has turned, — if they come declaring in the name of those men that they have discovered that their former holy and self-denying life was all a mistake, thus repudiating the great principles for which those men lived and died, — all consistent spiritualists should at once distrust those spirits. How do we know but that we ourselves, if faithful even to martyrdom for our convictions, may not after our departure be represented as recanting all the most sacred beliefs of our souls? Especially should this be the case when such great and good mediums as all spiritualists confess John, and Paul, and Isaiah, and Moses — nay, even Jesus himself — to have been, are thus introduced as undervaluing, or even contradicting, the testimony which they sealed with their blood. There ought to be in the very fact such a *primâ facie* evidence of fraud as should throw every consistent spiritualist upon his guard.

And the more magniloquent the phraseology, the more suspicious the message. Inflated diction, grandiloquence,

* Gal. v. 22: "The fruit of the Spirit is love, joy, peace, long-suffering, gentleness, goodness, faith, meekness, temperance."

bombast, are tests by which to try spirits, both in the body and out. The teachings of Jesus are remarkable for their simplicity of style. The same is true of all the sacred writings. The Bible has had a healthful influence upon the English language and literature. It has been remarked that Luther's translation of the Bible created the German language. Simplicity and perspicuity of style are not to be despised, among other tests of spiritual communications. The tried and tested communications of former ages — those that were tested as by fire, those that have been tested anew by the ordeal of ages — are not lightly to be thrown aside at every inflated utterance of mediums of to-day. That would be like mariners throwing overboard charts and tables of logarithms, and working out all the problems of navigation anew. Spiritualists, by such a course, weaken the very foundations of their own faith. Spirits must conform to the simple, well-established, central truths of the kingdom of God, on which personal purity and social well-being have depended in all ages and must depend in all worlds.

And it is around about those principles (self-evident though they may seem) that Jesus foretold the last great Waterloo battle would be fought. Hence, when spirits come, saying virtually, "I am Christ," or bringing any other message flattering to pride or self-conceit, we should know that it is not in any such way Christ prophesied he would come. On the contrary, it does resemble things he said would precede his coming, — things that would be adopted by the cosmocratic powers to deceive incautious and too confiding good men. "Believe them not," he said. "For as the lightning cometh out of the east, and shineth even unto the west, so shall also the coming of the Son of Man be."

If the good spiritualist is deceived it is because he has

not been true to his own avowed principles; because he has undervalued the best responses of the most reliable mediums of long-tried worth; because he has ignored their statements as to the cosmocratic intelligences and their methods, and has not been on his guard against them. He ought to reconsider the whole subject, and ask whether now, at this very moment, there is not more danger of being deluded than at any former period. Not only is not the cosmocracy not yet incarcerated, but, as any one may see who can read the signs of the times, they are making, by a combination of various forms of error and corruption, a more concentrated and formidable attack on good society, in its fundamental elements, than ever before. "Blessed is he that watcheth, and keepeth his garments, lest he walk naked and men see his shame," is Christ's warning for this very day and hour.

The simple question for all who desire to be known as Christian spiritualists, is, whether they can really control the movement as a whole, or whether it is swayed by occult forces and tendencies antagonistic to the instincts of a Christian heart. Can they lead the army, or will they be led in chains by it, their protests disregarded, their talents, piety, and reputation used to give prestige and power to a movement they cannot approve?

CHAPTER XXXVII.

PERIHELION.

THERE are those who think the globe must be purified by fire as preparatory to a new heavens and earth of righteousness. But are ashes, and scoriæ, and lava holier than common loam and fertile soil? Is the crater of an extinct volcano more pure or sacred than any other spot on earth? The earth is holy enough now, and does not need to be purged by fire. All consistent spiritualists feel that it is only the cosmos of human thought, and feeling, and society that needs to be purified, and that by spiritual fires.

But this being granted, there are many who ask, What need can there be of the glorious epiphany, or visible appearing of the Lord? Is it not a return to absolutism and to coercion? Is it not virtually a confession of defeat on the part of truth and motives and the dispensation of the Spirit? And if Jesus said, under the old dispensation, "If they hear not Moses and the prophets, neither will they be persuaded though one rose from the dead," how much more may the like be said under the new? To this spiritualists, if consistent with their own principles, ought to reply, that such an epiphany would not be like the rising of one from the dead to coerce by terror, but the descent rather of the Prince of Life from heaven, not to terrify the evil, but to convince and unite the good. It would be a "manifestation" about which there could be no cavil, or doubt, or denial among the wisest and best of men, those most desirous of knowing the truth, those most interested in human welfare. Such an event would not supersede argument, motives, and the persuasive inward influences of the divine Spirit; it would rather be (like all catastrophic elements of past dispensations) a foundation for new developments of these. As the cloven tongues of Pentecost, the rushing mighty wind, the gift of tongues, the gifts of healing, and other catastrophic phenomena, did not hinder but helped argument and persuasion then, so more glorious manifestations might do again. As the incarnation and resurrection of Jesus and all his mighty works, and those of his apostles, did not abruptly break the lines of progress already established, but all worked in easily, and in a certain sense naturally, with the regular course of development, so a still more glorious "manifestation of the sons of God" might do again. As things now are, progress is perpetually checked, thwarted, impeded, corrupted, antagonized in a thousand ways by unsuspected cosmocratic intermeddling. Such a "manifestation" might be so controlled and proportioned as to strike away all the hindrances and quicken and strengthen all the helps of progress. Instead of being an abrupt ending of progress, it might be as it were a gracious and graceful beginning of a style and rate and breadth of progress so new as to cause all former progress to seem scarce worthy the name.

Of Messiah's first coming, ancient seers had said, "He shall come down like rain upon new-mown fields, as showers that water the earth." "He will not break the bruised reed, nor quench the smoking flax." "He shall gather the lambs in his arms, and carry them in his bosom, and gently lead those that are with young." All these images, denoting extreme gentleness and delicacy, were fulfilled, while at the same time there was a prodigious expenditure, first and last, of what we have ventured to call catastrophic force. Even so it may be again. The epiphany, or "manifestation of the sons of God," may be more glorious than our most exalted imagination has dared to dream, and yet it may work in so smoothly as not to disturb the beat of pendulum in the observatories of the world, or arrest the blooming of the most delicate floweret on the verge of Alpine glaciers.

As the mighty works of Jesus, by himself, by the twelve, and by the seventy, — those reduplications of himself all over Galilee and Judea during his brief earthly career, while going about incognito, as it were, — did not hinder his teaching the people, and developing spiritual truth and motive, but rather helped, so the same may be true should he resume that work, which was interrupted by his death, not incognito and in mortal form, but in unveiled celestial beauty and immortal vitality.

Many have felt an insuperable repugnance to the idea of the local residence of Christ at Jerusalem, and the reinstitution of sacrifices and other features of the millennarian scheme as supposed to be held by some. But spiritualists can consistently dispense with the idea of any such localization, or return to "beggarly elements," while still retaining the conception of free intercourse of mortals with immortals at all times and in all places, according to laws not now fully understood, but then to be fully revealed.

It is indeed a captivating dream that truth and motive should gradually win the day, without any new elements of catastrophism. Each mind, or class of minds, that has thought out a system of truth and of orderly practice, is fascinated with the idea of seeing that system gradually prevail and displace all others, and be the bond and benediction of a benighted world. All will probably admit the possibility of such a result given unlimited time in the future. But ancient seers and modern seers seem to unite in the prognostication of something more satisfying to the benevolent heart than such an indefinitely protracted struggle. The omens are of a crisis, the end of a dispensation, — call it from one point of view the Christian, or call it from another point of view the anti-Christian dispensation, — the omens, by ancient mediums and by modern, are of a crisis.

If indeed the best men were united in religion, science, art, reform, and sociology generally, we might be content to wait, without the heart-sickness of hope deferred; but the difficulty is that the very best men the world over do not and can not agree, either in politics, science, or religion, and the conceded progress of the age does but increase their divergence. Comparative theology finds good men and wise men in every land, under all the great ethnic religions. There are very good and learned Jews. There are sincere Christians of eminent learning in the Roman, Greek, and Oriental communions. There are equally sincere and learned Christians in all the different Protestant communions. There are many benevolent and cultivated minds in that large portion of the community that declines to call itself Christian, or even decidedly theistic. If all these could be gathered together, — a congress of mutual help, — one can see how their power over the masses might be redoubled. If they could agree on any fundamental of religion or politics, faith or works, the result would be sublime. The Divine Spirit might use them, thus harmonious, with grand effect. One might chase a thousand, and two put ten thousand to flight. But suppose on every proposition possible in religion, finance, science, or reform, they stand equally divided, in point-blank opposition to each other, the Spirit of God himself cannot use them for progress. Mr. Finney said, when he tried to have revivals in Boston, "The churches here have put the Holy Ghost into a strait-jacket." It is a rude way of saying what Jesus said to the leaders of antagonistic sects in Israel, "Ye shut up the kingdom of heaven against men." * Not that they intended so to do, but that such was the effect of their divisions.

The affecting and afflicting thought is, that none of these great and good men want to obstruct or hinder; they are all earnestly desirous of a perfect state of society on earth; but what a waste of power! what a waste of intellect! what a waste of time and emotion! Let us estimate the mere waste of production, of life, of time, of brain-power, and of wealth, by war, and the result is appalling. Yet the wars of modern times, as M. Cousin remarks, are only the expression of the collision of ideas. Christendom is on the verge of general bankruptcy by reason of Alps on Andes of war-debts, incurred because good men cannot agree on the simplest problems of faith and good works.

The great ecclesiastical, philosophical, and political systems of Christendom (to say nothing of ethnic systems) hold each other at bay like hosts at push of pike, — a kind of perpetual drawn battle. Meanwhile, deprived of their natural leaders, the lower and more ignorant masses send up hoarse murmurs, and heave with a deep groundswell under the breath of cosmocratic influences, and the horizon grows dark with portents of coming tempest. Jesus saw just a little way ahead all the horrors of that siege in which a nation, by the fury of party and the madness of zealots, committed suicide. It requires but a moderate degree of natural forecast to see before Christendom an infinitely worse fate for precisely the same reason. Good men are divided and their influence neutralized, and there is no reconciler. The breach

* Matt. xxiii. 13.

grows wider, and the enemy thunders at the gates of liberty and faith, and the torch will soon be thrown into the holy of holies.

Now, all spiritualists, if consistent, can comprehend that the complete shutting off of deceptive spirits, high and low, would simplify the problem, since it would leave only the innate development-forces of humanity itself to be dealt with. And they can also comprehend the effect upon good men of an actual, indisputable "manifestation," in glorious form, of the Lord Jesus. Conceive, for example, the effect, the logical and necessary effect, on the mind of the Jews all over the world, if they should see substantially what Saul of Tarsus saw on the road to Damascus. They would say what he said. The conviction would be set home to their understandings, "Then we have been under a mistake all this while." Then there would be a chance for the still small voice to say, "Come and let us reason together." And suppose they should "look on him whom they pierced, and mourn," and be forgiven, cannot all spiritualists see what an effect that would logically produce on all nations? Can we consistently resist the argument of the ancient medium, Paul, "If the casting them away was the reconciling of the world, what shall the receiving them be but life from the dead?"

Spiritualists, if consistent with their own principles, must see that in this way, without terror, without recourse to mere brute force, by simple conviction of the reason through natural laws then first fully unfolded and exemplified, there might be produced a true harmony and co-operation of all good men. That harmony will never come by making war on churches, and creeds, and sects, — a process which only increases the discord, and waste of brain-power and heart-power. Harmony will never come by destructive criticism tearing the Bible to pieces.

Nor will harmony ever come, either, by endeavoring to force the peculiarities of any one sect upon all others; least of all will it come by an uninspired compromise between Christianity and ethnic religions, giving us only one more theology, and that not superlative. But all spiritualists will, if consistent, see that such a harmony as is needed would be logically attainable by such a glorious "manifestation of the sons of God," considered simply as a ground or foundation for the full outpouring of the Holy Spirit. Once shut out and bar out all deceiving spirits, cosmocratic or others, whose influence is the more potent in proportion as it is unsuspected, and who have abused and thwarted and perverted everything; sequester them, purge the air, seal them up to deceive good men no more, fill their places by a class trained to meekness, self-denial, and sympathy with Christ; let Christ appear from time to time wherever needed, — how soon would all good men agree? How easy then to sway the masses, — for the masses love to be swayed; hero-worship is natural, especially where heroes are heroic — as in the case supposed they would be. How easy, then, to rescue this material system from misconception and abuse!

Suppose for a moment science were privileged to ask Jesus in person a few questions — would any distinguished scholar still be likely to say there might be a world in which two and two make five? And would any eminent academician continue to seem to question the axioms of geometry, and undermine the foundations even of mathematical science? And would any great naturalist long continue to say: "In the interests of scientific clearness, I object to say that I have a soul, when I mean all the while that my organism has certain mental functions, which, like the rest, are dependent on its molecular composition and come to an end when I die;

and I object still more to affirm that I look to the future life, when all I mean is that the influence of my doings and sayings will be more or less felt by a number of people after the physical components of that organism are scattered to the four winds"?

Let spiritualists reflect on the actual facts of the case. Let them see the paralyzing effects of the divisions among leading men of first-rate abilities, education, and character. Let them see the waste of enthusiasm, the waste of power, and the painful sense of discouragement resulting. Some good men are dissatisfied with theology; but they are, after all, no better satisfied with science. The conventional belief is abhorrent to them. But neither Atheism nor Pantheism contents them. They are driven towards a state so nearly resembling insanity (for if the denial of the axioms of geometry and arithmetic be not a token of insanity, what is?) as to suggest the inquiry, Are not the cosmocratic powers, in their desperation, really striking at the fundamentals of reason? Are they not aiming to drive the leaders of civilization crazy, in order that they may unchain the wild beasts, and bring on the general overturn and boundless anarchy?

Materialism, indeed, soothes remorse for a while, since the idea of guilt or ill-desert is incompatible with the merely mechanical conception of human volition. But the philanthropist and reformer is not made happy by such a belief. On the contrary, he expresses at times the deepest unhappiness, and asks whether life is worth living. He may be a very sincere reformer, and yet he may say: "I will conclude with a summary of my convictions. There is no benevolence, design, consciousness, and intelligence in what we call Nature. I feel no gratitude for existence, but the contrary. If all the world could have been mine, nothing could have persuaded me, could the choice of existence have been offered me, to accept it. I am of opinion that if there were a God, we should have more to forgive him than he to forgive us. I point to crime, to pain, to tempests, to famines, wars, earthquakes, and so on, forever, to justify my conclusion that we have nothing to hope for — extinction of being is our destiny. The human race will cease to exist, and so best."

All consistent spiritualists can see that such despair would be cheered and cured in a moment, if it saw what Saul of Tarsus saw. And if good men the world over were united, and sat clothed and in their right minds at Jesus' feet, there would be no trouble with the masses. Physical health would soon be perfected, the family reconsecrated, society rightly edified, laws, governments, worship, social institutions throughout idealized, and human society pervaded with sweet heavenly influences. Then into such a world, by the regular and healthful process of reincarnation or natural resurrection, pour in the tide of population, till all that ever claimed the human name since Adam, or before Adam, shall have experienced the benign restorative influences of Messiah's reign. And beyond that, when the work of rescue and renovation is complete, and the exiled race is one with itself and its Lord, then the final reorganization of the entire moral universe, and man invested with supreme dominion, the interrupted work of creation resumed, new intelligent orders summoned into being, and the happy kingdom of God expanding in numbers, and increasing in bliss forever and ever. Such a belief, even if we dignify it by no higher name than a hypothesis, is more cheering than, as we have just seen, the materialistic hypothesis sometimes proves itself. It is indeed more than cheering to those who are able to yield it a cordial assent, and to hold it with a calm and tranquil persuasion of its substantial truth; (that is, in its main features, and allowing for errors of detail;) to such, it fills the mind with joy, and at times with rapture, when faith is clear and the vision unclouded,—when one rises, as it were, and sits with Christ in heavenly places. And at all times it diffuses through the soul a sense of certainty and of peace, which is, perhaps, more desirable than ecstasy, because it fits one for all the lowly duties of every-day life.

There are times, indeed, in almost every life when divine rapture, like wine, seems almost necessary. Such are crises of agonizing effort; of painful endurance; of martyrdom; of darkness and doubt; of temptation; of sudden anguishful bereavement. Then foretastes of the glory are vouchsafed; and we cry, like Simon, "Lord, it is good to be here; let us make three tabernacles!" We naturally long for these exalted frames. We would intoxicate ourselves forever with the heavenly nepenthe, and this would not be wise, nor comport with the general character of the dispensation under which our lot is cast. The average experience of our pilgrimage must be more equable, more commonplace, more commensurate with the elementary conditions of private, domestic, and social need. And it is in the resolute performance of humble tasks and self-denying duties — the tasks and duties lying just within the natural relationships of home and country, that the best and most certain test is found both of our own spirit, and of any spirit witnessing with ours.

We need not go far to seek for crosses, crosses of artificial structure, imported crosses; we have but to take up the rude, home-made crosses of every-day life. If we are made really humble and contrite, if we are more sincere and truthful, if we are practically more disinterested, then we have reason to think that the spirit that is with us and in us is indeed the Holy Spirit. And if with our utmost strength we address our prayer to Him alone, that he would deliver us from the spiritual unchastity of pride and excessive love of human applause, and from every corrupt feeling and every delusive idea, and impart to us healthy fortitude to endure hardness as good soldiers, we have reason to believe we shall be heard. Our bodies even will become temples for His abode. Whatever may be true as regards the second coming of Christ, this form of spiritual manifestation may be more common than it is; and it may be, all circumstances considered, the purest, highest, most desirable form possible to this dispensation. If communion with a departed saintly spirit, or with an angel or archangel, would be desirable, how much more with the highest spirit of all, whose name (*Paraclete*), untranslatable in our tongue, suggests a monitor voice of love ever at our side, ever calling us, ever comforting, ever stimulating and instructing us? This Presence we need not go far to seek. We need not ascend, nor descend, nor cross continent or ocean, to find him, who is with us here and now, in the every-day concerns of life, — at the forge, in the shop, in the nursery, in the thronged mart, — ever ready to reveal himself as our soul's exceeding joy.

This is health indeed, not merely to cherish ideas concerning God, but to know him by his own self-revealing, self-manifesting power of Love. He that loveth is born of God, and knoweth God, for God is love. It is Love's own absolute self the soul pants for as the hart pants for the water-brooks. It is his very self inbreathed, as it were, into ourself, however effected, with open vision or without, in the body or out of the body, which we yearn for as better than life. We see the infinite beauty everywhere, but it is veiled. We come near the intense effulgence, but it is hid from us. "My soul followeth hard after thee!" we cry. "O Lord, I beseech thee show me thy glory!"

> "O when shall the veil be removed,
> And around me Thy brightness be poured!"

This is the real homesickness of the human race, though, alas, they know it not! Some have found out the truth. Some have heard him say, "I am thy portion and thine exceeding great reward;" and they have lain still like a babe on its mother's breast. They are quieted forever. "They hunger no more, neither thirst any more." You may see them in the most menial stations of life, performing the humblest tasks. But, "The peace of God that passeth understanding keeps their heart and mind." They feel the attraction of the central orb; they know they are moving on the homeward track; they tremble with presentiments of what that beatific vision may be;—but even now they are not orphans, for God is with them. As the balloon struggles against the cords that confine it to earth, so do they sway upward and heavenward. As it was with Jesus, so it is with them, as life wears on and the shadows lengthen, and the time of their departure is at hand. "O Father," they cry, "glorify thou me with the glory which I had with thee before the world was." There is a certain incandescence of soul produced by intense love which powerfully affects the body. Even earthly affection, in its purest forms, illumines and transfigures the countenance. But the Love of Loves, when he reveals himself, produces an inward ardor, permeating the dull tabernacle with cherubic radiance; an ardor which, if carried to its height, must lay the frail form as dead at His feet. And is not this the secret of the glory of the spiritual body, that it will simply coruscate from within, inflamed by His contact? As the star, long circling round its remote orbit, rushes blazing to its perihelion; so the exiled soul, long absent from its God, rushes incandescent to His Presence, to go no more out forever.

Published by

Facsimile Publisher
Ashok Vihar, Delhi-110052 (India)
Website: www.facsimilepublisher.com

Distributed by

Gyan Books Pvt. Ltd.
5, Ansari Road, Daryaganj, New Delhi-110002 (India)
E-mail: books@gyanbooks.com, Website: www.gyanbooks.com

2 222000 014124